KV-050-882

Lexical Variation and Attrition in the Scottish Fishing Communities

Robert McColl Millar, William Barras and Lisa Marie Bonnici

EDINBURGH
University Press

© Robert McColl Millar, William Barras and Lisa Marie Bonnici, 2014

Edinburgh University Press Ltd
The Tun – Holyrood Road
12 (2f) Jackson's Entry
Edinburgh EH8 8PJ
www.euppublishing.com

Typeset in 10.5/12 Janson by
Servis Filmsetting Ltd, Stockport, Cheshire,
and printed and bound in Great Britain by
CPI Group (UK) Ltd, Croydon CR0 4YY

A CIP record for this book is available from the British Library

ISBN 978 0 7486 9177 7 (hardback)
ISBN 978 0 7486 9178 4 (webready PDF)

Contents

Acknowledgements   iv
Abbreviations   v

1 Language attrition and lexical variation and change   1
2 The history and culture of the Scottish fishing communities   16
3 Methodology   34
4 Analysis of the data   65
5 Conclusions   164

Notes   174
References   182
Index   190

Acknowledgements

The research upon which this book is based was made possible through funding from the Arts and Humanities Research Council ('Fisher Speak: variation and change in the lexis of the Scottish Fishing Communities'; Grant no. RGA 1129). All three authors would like to make plain their gratitude to Michael Hornsby for his ground-breaking work on this project in 2008–9.

We would like to thank all the citizens of Anstruther, Eyemouth, Lossiemouth, Peterhead and Wick for their help and patience while this research was carried out. As well as those who generously filled in the questionnaires and discussed their responses, special thanks must be given to the staff of the Arbuthnot Museum, the Rev. Graham Crawford, Alan Dearling, Linda Fitzpatrick, Mary Glass, the staff of Ladywell House, Stephen Leitch, the staff of the Lossiemouth Fisheries and Community Museum, Jim Miller, the Norris family, the staff of Saltgreens Residential Home, the staff of The Scottish Fisheries Museum, Shane Strachan, Iain Sutherland, Jenny Szyfelbain, Sheila Taylor, Ian and Fay Waddell and the Wick Heritage Society.

Finally, this work would have been impossible without our families: Elspeth, Mairi, Oliver, Richard and Sandra. This book is dedicated to all of them.

Abbreviations

The following are abbreviations for reference works frequently used in the study.

BC	*Buchan Claik* (Buchan and Toulmin 1989)
CD	*Caithness Dictionary* (Sutherland 1992)
CSD	*Concise Scots Dictionary* (Robinson 1999)
CW	*Caithness Wordbook* (Miller 2001)
DD	*Doric Dictionary* (Kynoch 2004)
DOST	*Dictionary of the Older Scottish Tongue*
DSL	*Dictionary of the Scots Language*
ENV	*In My Ain Words* (Murray 1982)
Glossary	*A Glossary of Scottish Dialect Fish and Trade Names* (Watt 1989)
LG	*Lossie Glossie*
LSS	*Linguistic Survey of Scotland*
SND	*Scottish National Dictionary*
ST	*Scots Thesaurus* (McLeod et al. 1990)

1 Language attrition and lexical variation and change

1.1 Introduction

In late September 2012, Mr Bobby Hogg, the last survivor of the final generation who spoke the traditional dialect of the fishing population of Cromarty, a small Scots-speaking enclave to the north-east of Inverness, died at the age of 92. The story appeared to resonate with people around the world. It was picked up by the international media and discussed as far from Scotland as Fiji. The Scots dialects with which this book is concerned are also almost all in danger of being 'swamped' by larger-scale linguistic units. While, in contrast to Cromarty, it is unlikely we will ever be able to talk about a 'last speaker' for most of these communities (population levels are too high), the dialects' autonomous status appears rapidly to be being broken down. In the following pages we will be focusing on mapping and analysing these changes. In this initial chapter the theoretical bases for the research will be introduced and critiqued.

This book is centred in observing and evaluating two discrete but inevitably connected subjects: the study of lexical variation and change, and the study of lexical attrition. The first could be described as concentrating on the changes in use, meaning and form natural to all living language varieties. Words change meaning and use, new words are introduced, people from different backgrounds use different lexis on occasion, but the dialect itself continues its passage through time. The study of lexical attrition, however, concerns itself in the main with those occasions where, with some personification, we can say that a dialect is being 'stripped' of the lexis which helps define it as a discrete unit; which may, indeed, be its primary distinguishing feature. In the most extreme situations, inhabitants of a particular place cease to maintain the local dialect in its full lexical form. Bugge (2007) may actually represent evidence for both processes at work on Shetland dialect. This chapter will concern itself with the theoretical and, to a degree, methodological concepts necessary to provide a grounding to the study as a whole, although methodological discussion related to the creation of the research instruments employed in the study will be presented in greater detail in Chapter 3.

1.2 Lexical variation and change

Since practically the beginning of the modern study of dialects (itself integral to the early breakthroughs associated with historical linguistics), interest has been taken in the ways in which lexical use varies and changes within communities, across space and time, particularly since this is the feature of linguistic change of which laypeople are very aware. From the very beginning of scholarly work on these issues it became the norm to employ a questionnaire (or a cognate device) in order to record lexical knowledge and use, rather than more 'natural' elicitation techniques. We will discuss these issues in greater depth in Chapter 3. Here, however, it is necessary to enumerate the issues and problems involved, since these are vital to our understanding of why these studies have generally been downplayed in sociolinguistic investigations.

Any dialect of any language has a highly finite set of sounds, for instance. It is (and was) straightforward to record and analyse these sounds (even before mechanical or electronic recording became possible) with a comparatively brief sample (although it might take longer to record distribution of sounds according to use). Morphological use is also generally straightforward to observe, since even in languages such as Finnish, with a relatively large inventory of inflectional morphemes as well as agglutinative tendencies, word formation processes are circumscribed. Syntactic use is more difficult to collect and analyse through direct observation, because some – particularly complex – structures may not be terribly common, but nonetheless form a central part of the language's nature. Nevertheless, in comparison with lexical use, there are easily definable boundaries around what structures any language can produce.[1]

It is also true, of course, that the lexis of a language has limits. There is considerable dissent over how many words (or, underlying them, free and bound morphemes) a native speaker of a language knows (for a discussion of how problematical this is even for one language – English – see Anderson and Freebody 1981), but there can be little doubt that the number of words over which he or she has command, while numbered in the thousands (and probably in the tens of thousands), is also finite. Unlike any of the other linguistic levels, however, *which* tokens any given native speaker knows are likely to be different in relation to the knowledge base of any other native speaker. If their backgrounds, life trajectories and ages are similar, there is a good chance that their vocabularies will also be similar; even then, they will never be exactly the same. When social, economic and cultural differences between speakers are greater – as they often are – the lexical tokens known may, beyond words to do with elementary human existence and function words, naturally, differ considerably. Linguists, of course, have a considerable knowledge of the vocabulary – indeed, often the jargon – of linguistics and actively produce the same when discussing their specialist fields. Their knowledge of the equivalent 'craft' terminology in nuclear physics is, inevitably, circumscribed; it is also likely that the physics vocabulary linguists employ may not be used correctly in relation to the norms of that field. Because of these vagaries and because of the fact that lexis is much more context-dependent than any other level of language, it is fair to say that even common words may not occur frequently in certain conversations. You would be unlikely to use any kind of automobile manufacture-specific lexis when discussing early Scottish history, for instance (unless through a probably rather contrived analogy). But the problems that attempting to observe lexical use can produce go further than this. Finding out which words a person knows, but rarely if ever uses, is, of course, very difficult to elicit 'naturally' (indeed the very term *naturally* is problematical).

A further feature which is inevitably problematical is that many literate speakers have native speaker competence in the vocabulary of the written standard language of their polity and that of at least one other dialect. Naturally, closely related dialects often use the same words in the same way. Sometimes, however, they do not. In Standard English, for instance, *starvation* refers, in origin, to death by hunger, later being bleached to reference towards a feeling of great hunger (and, eventually, to a very mild sense of want); in Scots, the same word refers to extreme cold. Speakers of a somewhat divergent dialect may carry around and largely keep separate two (or more) meanings derived from standard and dialect (the fact that near-synonyms are also possible within one dialect is also noteworthy). They may also confuse or even blend their meanings, however. Some speakers may be highly aware of what constitutes one dialect or the other; others may not. Personal experience may mean that particular semantic fields are better represented than others in one variety than in another. Someone from a Scots-speaking background who has never studied zoology or botany is more likely to know the names of birds and wild flowers in Scots than in Standard English, for instance, since he or she was introduced to them in the former variety and has no reason to know their 'Sunday' names.

For all of these reasons (and probably for a number more), recording and analysing lexical use is fraught with problems; studying lexical variation and change is even more problematical, primarily because, like all essentially sociolinguistic projects, it does not truly anticipate a 'system within which everything holds', or at least not a circumscribed, relatively limited, one.[2] Rather, a three-dimensional set of usage patterns, partly different for each speaker, is traced. More of these methodological issues will be discussed in Chapter 3. What needs to be pointed out in this chapter is that the study of lexical variation and change, while possible and highly rewarding, is highly problematised. As the next section will demonstrate, the study of lexical attrition, which underlies this book, is particularly so, since recording ongoing change involving loss of lexis with no apparent compensation from within that variety's word formation processes is confused, confusing and inherently incomplete.

1.3 Language attrition

1.3.1 First language attrition

In recent years a major research agenda has grown out of the scholarly analysis of second language acquisition: the study of first language attrition. As Schmid (2011) has ably demonstrated, a considerable scholarly literature bears witness to a striking truth: with some individuals at least, the taking on of a new language (often due to migration) as the primary – often the only – language of everyday use has a deleterious effect on that person's command of her or his first language. This can be termed *language attrition*. Structures may no longer be adhered to – German speakers living in an English-speaking environment, for instance, may, when speaking their first language, not always observe the *Satzklammer*, the 'sentence brace' construction (*ich habe das getan*, literally 'I **have** that **done**'), preferring instead to reproduce the structural norm in English *(ich habe getan das* 'I **have done** that'); phonological systems may not be entirely water-tight (so that, for instance, a speaker of a language with phonologised nasalised vowels might replace them with vowel plus nasal constructions which echo the phonological system of the dominant language of the place she or he is living, even when speaking her or his native language). Lexical use may represent the apparent (or, indeed, actual) loss of vocabulary items by individuals, their place being taken by words borrowed directly from the dominant language (to use one of

Schmid's most striking examples (2011: 2 and elsewhere), Gertrud U., a German Jewish refugee to – and long-term resident of – the United States, uses *refrigerator*, rather than *Kühlschrank*, in her German).

In a very real sense, therefore, the phenomena associated with first language attrition mirror those connected to second language acquisition, with the difference that the clines of development run in opposite directions for the two phenomena – increasing loss of competence rather than increasing competence, to simplify somewhat. In this school of thought language attrition is normally portrayed as an essentially individual phenomenon (although obviously a mass of people in the same situation are likely to present similar – as a broad brush – features). People from similar backgrounds who have gone through similar experiences (which include the change in dominant language in their everyday lives) will probably all demonstrate similar phenomena in their use of their first language. But the extent to which attrition takes place is inevitably different from person to person. It can at the very least be surmised that factors such as treatment from speakers of their first language when emigrants lived in their original environment (whether, for instance, your experience of Germany, Germans and the German Nazi regime was only a matter of a few unpleasant but not life-threatening months before emigration or involved years of increasing persecution culminating in *Reichskristallnacht*, the government-instigated pogrom of November 1938), length of stay in the new environment and your attitudes towards your new country and its language, whether you settled down with a speaker of that language and had children, and so on, should all in some way or another affect your use of the new language and your old one. Moreover, your general linguistic ability must affect both your retention of your old language and acquisition of the new. It must be accepted, we believe, that this apparently individualistic, perhaps even atomistic, vision of attrition can probably be generalised in such a way as to portray how whole populations may face these changes.[3]

Beyond this, we need to recognise that the form of *attrition* which concerns Schmid and others is primarily related to the language of emigrants from the mother tongue area, a point which further emphasises the individual results and reactions mentioned above. This particular research trend has – at least at first glance – rather less to say about attrition in the 'home' environment. Where a dominant language affects the use of an autochthonous language, the sense that what is being described is largely individual rather than collective in nature must also be borne in mind. In order to overcome these issues we need to turn to a discussion of the linguistic effects of *language death* (otherwise, *language shift*).

1.3.2 Theories of language death (language shift) and their value in the study of linguistic attrition

Since practically the very earliest times in which our ancestors had the ability to use language, there has probably never been a period when speakers of some languages have not dominated the speakers of others to the extent that the latter groups have switched across to the former language. Indeed, as Dixon (1997) points out, if there had not been a steady attrition of native languages over the centuries, the number of languages now spoken would run into at least the millions. The 6,000 or so discrete languages now spoken stand as living testimony to ongoing language shift. On a grand scale, Dixon suggests that occasionally – but regularly – one language (or set of languages) will become associated with a group, event or idea of considerable historical, economic and social force. Languages without these associations rapidly contract, often eventually disappearing altogether. This 'new force' could be a major change in agricultural methods – the Scottish Highland Clearances, for instance, where Gaelic retreated in response to the spread of English, was essentially a matter of change in land ownership conceptualisation and land use patterns – or a natural disaster (including famine), as with, for instance, the effects on the vitality of the Irish language in the aftermath of the Potato Famine of the late 1840s. But language shift is also innately associated with political or religious change, as with the collapse of spoken Hebrew as a result of the destruction of the kingdoms of first Israel and then Judah and the 'Babylonian captivity' which followed, with the acquisition by the exiles of Aramaic, the regional lingua franca, or the replacement of all the native languages of continental Western Europe (with the exception of Basque) by Latin, in response to the spread of Roman power. How this all happened at ground level to individuals and groups of speakers (whether, for instance, the change was perceived as cataclysmic or was barely noticed) is not central to Dixon's model, naturally.

Underlying, however, and acting in a complementary manner, is a research thread with its basis in an ethnographic, indeed anthropological, survey of language use, the most striking early example of which being Dorian (1981), dealing with the 'death' of Scottish Gaelic in eastern Sutherland, based on fieldwork she carried out there in the 1960s and 1970s. Leading on from what was said above, the decline and loss of Gaelic in many areas of the northern Scottish mainland in the nineteenth and early twentieth centuries was due to a large extent to the economic and social effects caused by the spread of a new agricultural norm – large-scale capitalist exploitation of sheepherding rather than the pre-existent subsistence level blend of cow-rearing and cultivation of a limited number of crops, all carried out by kinship groups – in the wake of the suppression of the Rebellion of 1745–6, leading to major population movements, of which Sutherland formed a centre. But in the coastal settlements of eastern Sutherland, the changes involved were rather more nuanced. Prior to the influx of people 'cleared' from central Sutherland, the inhabitants of the towns were generally speakers of Scots (but writers of English), as was the case in most of Scotland at the time, while the local peasantry spoke the local Gaelic dialects; some bilingualism would naturally have been the norm. With the advent of the new, largely indigent, population, instructed by the Sutherland estate to become fishing communities in order to exploit the potential wealth of the herring fishery during the Napoleonic wars, a new 'pecking order' developed. Over the course of the nineteenth century the native peasantry moved from Gaelic to English (perhaps to demonstrate their 'nativeness'). People native to the coast also developed prejudices against the new fishing population. These prejudices lessened the amount of contact between communities; it practically prohibited intermarriage. Gaelic therefore became a marker of the fishing communities, a separateness enforced by the outside and willed from the inside. When the fishing contracted in the wake of the Great War, the language itself gradually lost speakers: its status (and purpose) as an identity marker had gone. By the time Dorian was carrying out her fieldwork, knowledge of Gaelic was confined to older people. Most interestingly from our point of view, the kind of Gaelic Dorian's informants produced was of a very variable type: some forms were close to native speakers' models; others made 'mistakes' which could almost be interpreted as 'non-native'.

Dorian developed the concept of *semi-speaker* for this type of language use. Semi-speakers were normally able to understand spoken Gaelic without any real difficulty. When they were asked to produce Gaelic, however, they demonstrated avoidance – or lack of knowledge – of some of the features which mark off Gaelic from English, in particular elements of the case system expressed through initial consonant mutations but also Gaelic's dominant VSO element order. These semi-speakers did not all behave in exactly the same way, naturally. Rather, a continuum existed between speakers who made occasional 'errors' in their Gaelic and others who may have had a relatively broad lexical knowledge (although this need not necessarily follow) but found it difficult to put together even quite simple utterances. What is striking about all of these speakers is that they are not second language learners of Gaelic. Instead they could be seen as first language users of the language, at least to begin with. What can be suggested therefore is that life experience has led many of these speakers to cease using the language in certain (or indeed all) linguistic domains for an extended period, thus 'stunting' their ability in their native language. It should be noted, however, that speakers of rather different abilities often lived side by side with each other, quite probably largely using English in communication with each other.

This continuum is not fully theorised by Dorian; it is considered at that level by Sasse (1992), however. Sasse presents (in a two-dimensional medium) a three-dimensional view of language shift, including both sociolinguistic and linguistic features (and the features which bind them to each other). Essentially, he suggests, loss of social prestige as much as loss of native speakers can lead to language shift. Socially aspirational members of the A community (those who speak the language which will eventually be abandoned) will tend themselves to begin avoiding using their native language, particularly around their children, who may grow up using T (the target language) as their main use language. At the same time education policy and general literacy norms may mean that A is, as it were, 'beheaded'. It may be very difficult, if not impossible, to speak about abstract concepts, have discussions of politics, and so on, in any other language than T because A's lexical richness has been curtailed in semantic fields related to prestigious and/or abstract concepts in particular. This will further erode its social cachet. The fact that the middle classes of the A community are moving towards T means that it becomes a primarily working-class code, with even less status in a middle-class dominated society. Eventually these forces will produce an outcome where no native speakers remain. Sasse suggests, however, that languages can often have an 'afterlife', with words, phrases and rhymes being retained in memory and often used as expression of identity. Sometimes this is semi-jocular; at other times it represents a serious attempt to express central features of a person's and a group's view of its discrete nature.

In tandem with this sociolinguistic discussion Sasse interweaves a linguistic analysis. As A lowers in prestige, it is likely to lose a great many lexical items, often in highly prestigious fields, meaning, as we have already seen, that speakers nearly always use T vocabulary – and, quite often, T structures – in these contexts. This phenomenon has been termed *stylistic shrinkage* (Campbell and Muntzel 1989: 195). The decision by aspirational parents *not* to use A with their children is unlikely to mean that these children will not actually learn A. It does mean, however, that they are likely to learn the language mainly from their peers rather than directly from their parents. Inevitably this means that these speakers will learn A rather later than T and may never gain full control of A's structure (something seen in the major 'simplification' of the grammatical gender system of Dyirbal, an Australian language, in the course of the twentieth century;[4] despite evidence of this type, Myers-Scotton (2002) denies that phenomena along these lines exist). This 'simplified' variety may actually be taken up by their peers as a marker of identity. To elders, this new variety may appear 'corrupt'; this will mean that A's prestige will drop a great deal. When we accept that these processes are unlikely to happen once but are much more likely to happen repeatedly, a vicious circle can be said to have been created.[5] Naturally, many of the features mentioned here are similar if not identical to those put forward by Schmid and others for linguistic attrition in the language use of immigrants, although the sense of linguistic community is central to its analysis.

1.3.3 Dialect attrition

The loss of originally central linguistic features as a process of attrition is not confined to languages; it is also present with dialects of all types and sizes (if a true linguistic distinction can be made between *language* and *dialect*: see Millar 2005: ch. 2). As with languages, dialect shift or loss has probably always been a feature of human life (although its more limited nature means that it is likely to have been commented upon rather less). In ancient Greece, for instance, there were a number of quite different varieties of Greek – Attic, Ionian, Doric, Arcado-Cypriot, and a number of others – spoken and to some extent written. Mutual comprehension and tolerance was widespread even during periods of tension and war. With one exception, that of Tsakonian, spoken in the central Peloponnese, which is at least in part of Doric descent, *all* modern Greek dialects are descended from the Attic-Ionian *koine glossa* 'common language', spread in the first instance by the armies of Alexander the Great and his successors and associated with the highly successful and long-lived Hellenistic civilisation which followed. It was the form of Greek which non-Greeks learned. Eventually all other dialects declined in use and prestige until they were wholly replaced, even on their native soil (for a range of references to this phenomenon, see Millar 2010b: ch. 4).

As we might expect, therefore, the fundamental underlying sources for dialect attrition can be found in change triggered by sociolinguistic processes. In the last two hundred years, impressionistically, the process appears to have become more common – particularly in Europe, perhaps – than was previously the case. Urbanisation, agricultural change, cheaper and easier short-, medium- and long-distance transport and mass education appear to be the chief causes for the acceleration of the process. While it would be wrong to say that people did not move around before the advent of modern transport or that social mobility was unknown, most people did stay very close to where they were born and also had normally essentially the same occupations and rank as their forebears. They did not come into contact to the same extent with outsiders and had no abstract sense of a *language*, and therefore no sense of 'incorrect usage', which the prescriptive learning of a national standard brings. Since the nineteenth century at least there has been an ongoing complaint literature about the imminent threat of the death of traditional dialects (often compared favourably with the new, 'corrupt', urban dialects).[6] While their demise has been somewhat exaggerated, there can be no doubt that much that was highly localised in people's speech patterns is passing, or has passed, away.

In recent years discussion of these matters has become quite widespread, in particular in Europe, as summations such as Britain (2009), Goeman and Jongenburger (2009), Røyneland (2009) and Vandekerckhove (2009), all derived from a special issue of the *International Journal of the Sociology of Language*, demonstrate.[7] While there are contraindications at work and two processes, apparently contradictory, may combine to encourage the same outcome, certain features appear to be present in many cases. In the first instance – as seen in the dialects of central Italy (Ferrari-Bridgers 2010), the Maastricht area of the southern Netherlands (Hinskens 1996) and the north-east of England (Watt 2002), new regional varieties (termed in Dutch *tussentaal* 'between language') have developed, often falling somewhere between the standard and the local dialect, but with local phonological features in particular maintained and even spread across prior boundaries. On the other hand, studies such as Wolfram and Schilling-Estes (1995) and Soukup (2007) demonstrate how previously geographically and to a degree culturally discrete varieties can gradually (or not so gradually) merge with larger-scale varieties.[8]

What is striking about many of these studies is that phonological and structural patterns are often given precedence over lexical analysis. Indeed, in the excellent Britain (2009) lexical erosion is only briefly discussed (pp. 124–5); Wolfram and Schilling-Estes (1995: 702) also touch upon this phenomenon. While a number of reasons could be put forward for this lack – many of them the methodological explanations which will be returned to in the following section and, in particular, Chapter 3, it needs to be recognised that the apparently daunting nature of the process has not put off researchers in Scotland, perhaps because it is lexical erosion which has been the most generally marked feature in change to the dialects of Scots in relation to (Scottish) Standard English.[9] What is it about the historical linguistic ecology of Scotland which encourages this interest?

1.4 Lexical change and attrition in Scots

1.4.1 The historical background

This concentration on lexical change away from traditional usage derives from a series of historical events and tendencies which, while not peculiar to Scotland, are certainly unusual within the English-speaking world.[10] As is well known, Scots, the Germanic vernacular of Scotland, was the only dialect of 'English' which maintained its literary and literate status into the age of print, producing, in the course of the fifteenth and sixteenth centuries, a literature as impressive as any written in Europe at the time. It is quite possible to imagine an alternative history where a standard Scots would have been given the same status internationally as modern Norwegian has today. That this did not happen can be attributed to, among other things, the use of the English Bible in Scotland during the Protestant Reformation and the Union of the Crowns of 1603, which led to the movement of the royal family and elements within the upper nobility south to England. These events removed the patronage so necessary to writers using Scots at that time, particularly due to the unavoidable truth that, for writers, the economic and other rewards associated with the use of English were considerably greater than was the case for Scots, especially since Scotland had to wait until well into the sixteenth century before a permanent printing press was established in the country.

That is not to say, of course, that many literate Scots speakers changed their written (never mind spoken) language to Standard English overnight. On the contrary, as scholars such as Meurman-Solin (1993) have demonstrated, a gradual shift from Scots to English practice in orthography, morphological representation, and so on, lasted something like a century for the whole group (although the usage of individuals can appear considerably more chaotic in relation to any tendency towards Scots or Scottish Standard English norms). It should be borne in mind, however, that while, by the end of the seventeenth century, writing Scots had become a rather solitary and eccentric pastime, most non-Gaelic Scots continued to speak their local dialects as default code, employing, if literate, a rather uncomfortable Standard English when this became necessary.

With the Union of the Parliaments of 1707, only the law and the Scottish Presbyterian Church Settlement remained as specifically Scottish entities. Both often jealously preserved their terminological Scotticisms, such as, in the language of the law, *propone* instead of *propose* (although in both cases – especially with the law – decision making was actually carried out in London, with a Scottish face maintained). In such a climate, the educated professional classes of Edinburgh in particular began to move towards Standard English as the model for not only their writing but also their speech. Since so much that made Scots *Scots* was lexical, 'improvers' of Scottish language use were primarily concerned with sensitising their audience to words and phrases which were considered *Scotticisms* to be avoided (see, for instance, Dossena 2005). It is difficult to tell how effective this type of 'therapy' was either in the short or the long term, but it would be fair to say that the attitudes held by many Scots about the vernacular were solidified around this type of initiative by the end of the eighteenth century. While most middle-class Scots would have continued to use the vernacular as their primary code well into the nineteenth century (and, in 'provincial' towns, well into the twentieth century), control of (Scottish) Standard English was a central feature of their self image.

Contrary tendencies began to be felt in the eighteenth century. As we have seen, writing in Scots had become practically moribund in the seventeenth century; in the next century, however, poetry began to appear in the vernacular, often written in an orthography which gave occasional nods to the Middle Scots conventions but was primarily based on contemporary English models. Many of those who wrote in Scots would have been associated with a range of political beliefs which were definitely in opposition to the prevailing orthodoxies and could be analysed as 'radical' (despite their Jacobite connections). Part of this opposition might be seen as being oriented around a linguistic expression of Scottish identity in the face of unionist hegemony (for a discussion, see Freeman 1981). Considerable irony is present in the fact that writers of the calibre and fame of Robert Burns were celebrated in essentially the same middle-class circles which were also keen on removing Scotticisms from their own speech and writing. As McClure (1985) points out, there is no reason to expect that admiration for a language in writing implies admiration for the spoken language – the opposite to this is defined by him as the *Pinkerton Syndrome*, after a late eighteenth-century commentator who considered spoken Scots to be corrupt and 'ugly' while at the same time praising the written literary form. But it is certainly evidence for a possibly confused (and definitely complex) set of associations for Scots and, in particular, perhaps, its lexis (for further discussion of these issues, see Dossena 2005 and Millar 2000, 2004 and 2005).

As Aitken (1979 and 1992) pointed out and Dossena (2005) has developed, these connections and apparent inconsistencies have led to a situation where some elements of Scots lexis are used as overt and highly conscious markers of Scottish identity, even among people who naturally speak a variety much closer to the Scottish Standard English end of the continuum and would never use a variety which could be classified as an example of a discrete Scots (a set of usages described by Aitken as *overt Scotticisms*). At the same time, many Scottish people may use a considerable number of words and turns of phrase which they consider to be English, but which are in fact purely or almost completely Scottish (termed *covert Scotticisms* by Aitken), albeit on occasion with an Anglicisation of forms. Many middle-class Scots also appear to have a considerable command of Scots lexis, but seem only capable of using it when impersonating someone – often elderly or working-class (Macaulay 1991: 185–6). For whatever reason, therefore, knowledge of specifically Scots lexis is rather more widespread than might otherwise have been expected, possibly acting as an identity marker (albeit of a complicated and contradictory type: Millar 2010a).

1.4.2 Lexical attrition in the Scots dialects

Yet evidence suggests that the Scots dialects, while retaining many of their phonological and structural features, are gradually losing their specific lexis, with its replacement on occasion by colloquial English and 'slang' terms (indeed many younger speakers in particular often do not make a distinction between local dialect usage and 'slang', the ephemeral use of language in an eccentric way, involving the use of neologisms and unpredictable semantic uses). In the first instance, unusually for studies of linguistic change in the English-speaking world, there can be little doubt that interest in, and concern about, apparent lexical attrition have been and are promoted formally and informally by native speakers rather than researchers, perhaps because, as we saw earlier in this chapter and will return to on a number of occasions in this book, methodological concerns and issues with a quantitative treatment of the material involved in lexical variation and change have encouraged fewer scholars from embarking on major research in this field than is true for the study of phonological and even morphosyntactic variation in Scotland. Nevertheless some work – often of a high standard – has been carried out in the last fifty years for that country, in particular, perhaps, Macafee (1994; a Scotland-wide discussion can be found in

Macafee 1997). These studies include research on lexical change in urban areas (Macafee 1994; Pollner 1985; Agutter and Cowan 1981) and rural (Lawrie 1991; Middleton 2001); knowledge of what were once central Scots words has become gradually at best patchy and often non-existent, largely along a continuum based upon age, with Hendry (1997) and Richard (2003) concentrating on the vocabulary knowledge of children.

Particularly interesting for this book are those studies dealing with lexical knowledge and change in coastal communities. McGarrity (1998) presents similar findings of primary attrition for the (former) fishing settlement of Torry in Aberdeen in relation to weather vocabulary, while Schlötterer (1996) investigated the knowledge of shipbuilding, maintenance and fishing technology terms among older members of communities stretching from the East Neuk of Fife to the present border with England. Downie (1983) also covered lexical knowledge and use within communities along the southern coast of the Moray Firth, taking a much more semantically general approach to what could be termed local vocabulary than either McGarrity or Schlötterer.[11] Of course situations such as these do not necessarily illustrate total collapse for local lexis. As studies such as Downie (1983) and Richard (2003) demonstrate, some local lexis does survive, particularly when it marks local identity. The methodologies these studies employed will be discussed in Chapter 3.

The research described in this book takes the debate on lexical attrition in Scotland rather further than was previously the case by locating the research in communities which were previously quite separate from the surrounding areas and which had, through the common experience of a common occupation and heritage, a generally acknowledged dialect with considerable lexical difference from mainstream local dialects. Moreover, the study attempts to compare usage along a wide swath of the Scottish coast, including both smaller and larger communities, the inhabitants of some of which remain actively involved in fishing, while in others the fishing trade has become essentially moribund. While many of these words and phrases were connected directly with fishing and its ancillary trades, words for the local environment and for traditions were also central, as we will see in the discussion of our corpus in Chapters 3 and 4. Given that most of the Scottish fishing communities have become separated from this work heritage, a fundamental question needs to be asked: to what extent can we say that these local vocabulary traditions – so closely connected, it can be assumed, to local identity – have survived? For the first time, a survey of this type will be informed by all of the theoretical positions discussed above, whether they relate to *language* or *dialect*.

1.5 Concluding thoughts

Linguistic attrition appears to be at the heart of much lexical change in traditional (and, indeed, non-traditional) dialects in the industrialised and post-industrial worlds. Given the speed with which a discrete language with a limited speaker base can cease to be 'living' in any meaningful sense, it is not surprising that attrition of the central natures of traditional dialects can be equally brutal and rapid. This has been generally well established in relation to the structure and phonology of these dialects. As we have seen, however, the same amount of analysis cannot be said to have taken place for lexical attrition; this book is intended to right this problem, at least in part. In the next chapter we will turn to a discussion of the history and culture of the Scottish fishing industry, paying particular attention to the communities considered in the research. The question of methodology will be reconsidered in Chapter 3.

2 The history and culture of the Scottish fishing communities

The relatively cold and plankton-rich waters of the North Sea and the Norwegian Sea have historically been fertile in both flora and fauna; the east coast of Scotland lies at the heart of this wealth. From a plenitude of different edible shellfish to the prevalence of deep-sea fish such as cod relatively close to land, this life has long been visible to the humans who live round the seas in ways not always possible on other coasts. Moreover, certain fish species – most notably herring – often came in close to land in vast numbers, regularly following seasonally predictable migration patterns (Coull 1993: 15–17). This description cannot hope to give more than a taste of the fecundity of the seas in this area, and ignores its mammal life – seals, dolphins and porpoises and, in particular, whales – and fish such as salmon, eels and trout which move from salt to fresh water during their life cycles.

2.1 General history

Given this fruitfulness, it is not surprising that fishing has been a major part of food production practically since humans arrived in north-west Europe. But as Coull (1996) points out, the development of a specialist fishing population, rather than a population which included fishing among its range of food-gathering activities, is relatively recent, with most fishing communities dating from no earlier than the fifteenth or sixteenth centuries and many from the seventeenth or eighteenth. This period has nevertheless been long enough for these communities to develop a strong sense of difference – cultural, certainly, but also often linguistic – from their landward neighbours.

Archaeological finds have demonstrated that skills in fishing had developed from an early period; in particular, in the use of shellfish as bait and of increasingly complex hooks, often employed on long lines with many other hooks. Until the medieval period, however, available boat technology meant that deep-sea fishing was not possible for many people who dwelt beside the coast, although more capital-intensive shipbuilding technologies which would allow long periods of fishing in distant waters along with improved preservation techniques in salting, drying and smoking, largely imported from the Mediterranean, Scandinavia[1] and the Baltic, began to be introduced to the larger ports as the Middle Ages progressed.

Indeed, there is some evidence that specialisation as fishing communities was imposed from outside as part of the growing feudalisation of political and economic power in the later medieval period (in areas where this power was not fully established, such as the Northern Isles, a tradition of combining subsistence farming with fishing continued well into living memory). In our communities, however, groups of individuals and families appear to have been instructed to become specialist fishers and given the technological means to make this change. The population was rarely free, however, and a portion of the haul was owned by the feudal overlord. This relationship can still be seen in the names of fishing communities whose foundation we can actually date, such as Fraserburgh and Gardenstown, where the settlement is named for the founder family (although it is noteworthy that the latter is generally known as *Gamrie*, for the district of which it forms the centre, and the former is normally merely *The Broch*).

Possibly due to the lowering of average annual temperatures in the late Middle Ages – the 'mini Ice Age' – the North Sea became particularly rich in sea life. During the same period, improved shipbuilding technologies led to the possibility of long-term sojourns at sea at a considerable distance from the home port. Indeed, fishing fleets from the British Isles were soon exploiting the resources of the cold waters around Iceland, Greenland and, eventually, Newfoundland. The ideology of the Protestant Reformation – largely successful in Britain – led to the downplaying, if not rejection, of Friday and Lenten fasts, with its concentration on a fish-based diet, over a large part of northern Europe. Economic forces then led southern, largely Catholic, Europe to rely on the dried fish – in particular, cod – produced by northern Europeans. Although not immediately connected with the large-scale ramifications of these changes, the Scottish fishing communities were stimulated – sometimes even brought to life – by them. Economic specialisation became a possibility.

The new monocultural fishing communities were not, of course, all established in exactly the same way. Some communities – Aberdeen being a particularly striking example – were already settlements of some size, largely concerned with long-distance trade and shipbuilding, where fishing played a part in the general economy; others, including settlements later of some size and significance such as Peterhead, were, prior to this, at most seasonal fishing havens used by a peasantry largely engaged in agriculture.

The fishing trade has always been capital-intensive. The construction, outfitting and maintenance of boats, the housing of crews and families, and the acquisition of bait for the long lines so necessary for, for instance, cod fishing imply considerable outlay before the returns – which are seasonally unpredictable – are perceptible. Lockart (1997: 37–8) reports that

> It is said that over 100,000 tons of mussels were lifted from the Clyde estuary last [nineteenth] century. Eyemouth fishermen were known to have used over 900 tons in one year.

Beyond this, means by which fish could be cured and carried to the large markets to the south of Scotland had always to be calculated in. Thus, from the very beginning, the Scottish fishing industry involved tension between the 'owner', the person or concern who funded the industry, and the crews, who risked their lives to make a profit for the owner, often for very limited returns to themselves.

Until the end of the eighteenth century, finance for the new enterprise generally came from local landowners. Service in the fishing trade was often seen as being, in part, a form of feudal obligation. Indeed, in some parts of Scotland – most notably Angus – the fishers were among the last serfs (although they were not described in this way: Nadel-Klein 2003: 29). By the nineteenth century, however, economic liberalisation meant that a number of richer fishers were able to buy boats and employ other fishers as their crew. Yet even the richest skippers could not run a port: more capital was needed than was available through fishing alone. In the nineteenth century in particular this position was taken by the fish curers and merchants in many harbours. In several – Montrose being a particularly good example – the merchants also often controlled the best and most available mussel beds, so vital for bait, although, as we saw in the quotation above, some of the wealthier and more populous communities were eventually able to buy bait from considerable distances as a unit when this was necessary. The curers may even have attempted to enforce the use of their beds, adding to the revenue they received from the fishing community. Naturally, relationships of this sort soured very quickly.

The fishing communities perceived themselves, and were perceived, as a race apart from the farming and merchant communities which surrounded them. It was a common saying in the North-East of Scotland – used by members of the fishing community and others – that 'the corn and the cod dinna mix' (Thompson 1983: 15).[2] Indeed, there was considerable prejudice against the fishers, in particular where a fisher town was connected to another town, often at the top of a set of cliffs (or at least a steep incline). The distinction between the two communities was often illustrated architecturally, with the *fishertoun* being crowded with houses, each often idiosyncratic in their design (Miller 1999: 2, and elsewhere). Non-fishers often accused the fishing community of having poor hygiene (possibly because of the connection between fish and a less than pleasant odour); the reality was that on practically all occasions the houses of members of the fishing community were almost obsessively clean (Miller 1999: 2). The danger of infection before the development of antibiotics – particularly acute in the gutting process, but present in almost all activities associated with fishing – instilled this tradition of hygiene in almost all aspects of the fishing communities' lives; the never-ending cleaning and repair of nets falls within the same drive.

It was common for both the fishing and landward populations to perceive the former as having come from elsewhere. Thompson (1983: 15) suggests that the 'first true fishing communities represented social disturbance rather than tradition, a response of the disinherited driven to the margins, and still far from secure'. Separation was emphasised by the fact that in most fishing communities a rather limited number of surnames predominated, surnames which were not necessarily common in the surrounding area (Miller 1999: 4). Indeed, due to this relatively limited naming tradition, many people were known by nicknames (also known as *by-names* and *tee-names*) to distinguish between individuals with the same or similar names (Miller 1999: 4–6; Smylie 2004: 154). Some of these clarified descent (by both the male and female line), but many related to the character of the person involved or stories connected to him (Anderson 2007: 45; Nadel-Klein 2003: 67, 100–1). Even early twenty-first century commentators (for instance, Anderson 2007: 3) suggest a continuing tradition of fishing as a vocation in some families.

Although there is considerable evidence that a large part of the fishing communities in most areas was made up of the descendants of people who lived nearby along the shores of the North Sea before fishing became a discrete trade, it is also clear that movement – often over a considerable distance for the time – was a central feature of many foundations. Skilled fishing families were often 'poached' from one community by another, arriving at a new location with subtly different traditions and language. In later times, many temporary crewmen (often termed *haufdalesmen*) on east coast fishing vessels came from the Highlands and Western Isles, leading to an ongoing, although perhaps ephemeral, presence of Gaelic in a range of Scots-speaking communities

(Coull 2008b: 227).[3] These contacts were not always friendly (Taylor 1988: 60), although often a sense of community pervaded relationships (Taylor 1988: 39–40). East coast boats were also often based in Mallaig (Wilson 2009: 62) and other western ports periodically during the annual herring fishery. These contacts also exposed many Gaelic and Highland English speakers to Scots, an introduction demonstrated dramatically by Neil M. Gunn in his novel *The Silver Darlings* (Gunn 1999 [1941]).

Connected to this sense of separation are folk-historical origin stories told by the communities themselves. Anson (1932 and 1950) presents a tradition of Norse origin for the fishing communities of the east coast (see also Miller 1999: 5). At a local level, these reports can become both complex and confused. Miller (1999: 7) comments that

> A number of stories used to circulate on the Black Isle [a promontory to the north of Inverness] to explain why the fisher people of Avoch spoke so differently from their neighbours: these included the coming of 'foreigners' from England in the Middle Ages, the people being descendants of Cromwell's troops stationed in Inverness in the seventeenth century, or of Norse settlers, or of wrecked Breton fishermen. The Avoch form of Scots fits neatly into a spectrum of dialects found from Caithness to Buchan and, although some 'foreign' genes may be present, it is far more likely that the original fishers who settled here as a Scots-speaking enclave in a predominantly Gaelic region, came from somewhere east along the Moray Firth.

The fact that these origin myths exist, however, tells us a great deal about the way fishing communities view(ed) themselves and their neighbours. These wide-ranging origins nevertheless seem to be at odds with the close-knit nature of fishing communities and the fact that, until relatively recently, members of the communities generally remained in close proximity (Rush 2007: 22, 217) or, if they did leave, often moved back in retirement (Nadel-Klein 2003: 101–2, and elsewhere).

In the course of the nineteenth century a new, industrialised form of fishing began to develop. Technologies of fishing and boat building worked hand in hand with the greater need for mass production brought about by the growth of urban populations. In terms of the Scottish fishing fleet, this meant the development of the herring fishery beyond the immediate vicinity to include long-term following of the shoals around the British Isles for a number of months. There had always been some contact between different communities; this was now extended considerably, with boats from different places being brought together in a range of ports throughout the summer. There was, of course, considerable interplay between ports, including intermarriage. This annual migration was not confined to the menfolk of the fishing communities; many young women also moved from port to port acting as gutters and packers. A highly skilful job, gutting and packing provided some financial independence for the *fisher lassies* (or *fisher quines*, in the North-East; for a discussion of the gutting migration, see Bochel 2008).

This female presence at the heart of the fishery might be seen as a continuation of the *fishwife* tradition (Coull 2008d), where female members of fishing communities, often characteristically dressed, travelled around country districts or occupied customary sites in urban areas to sell fish landed by their menfolk. The strength and stamina of these women were proverbial, as was their eloquence. The demands of this and other parts of the trade, along with the skills learned from a young age, probably explain why most wives of fishermen came from fishing backgrounds themselves (Miller 1999: 4; Blair 1987: 5; Nadel-Klein 2003: 51). Naturally, the advent of relatively cheap and rapid forms of transport led to the decline of this particular form of employment.[4] The tradition of direct sale inland mutated into the fish van archetype: in both rural and urban areas fresh fish was, and to a degree is, regularly sold from the back of a (now refrigerated) van. Perhaps significantly, these vans were generally driven by men, possibly because of their (perceived) connection with a 'male technology'.

Female members of fishing communities also contributed to the central employment until well into the twentieth century by helping in the mending and cleaning of nets (although many men were also employed in this when ashore), a continuation, perhaps of their role in mending, assembling and baiting *smaw lines*. *Great lines* (or *gartlins*), associated with the deep sea fishery, were normally baited aboard the fishing boat by fishermen (Fenton 2008b: 90).

By the end of the nineteenth century most fishing communities had felt the impact of steam technology (something of a sense of the changes these technological developments produced can be found in Sutherland no date). Steam-driven vessels had the great advantage, of course, of not being entirely dependent upon wind and tide. The engine could also be used to winch the larger nets which were becoming the norm. Their great disadvantage was that they had to carry their fuel with them, making the vessels heavy and costly to run. Following economies of scale, therefore, fishing boats became larger. With the new technology of trawling, which almost completely replaced the great lines in fishing for cod and haddock, ever greater yields, requiring, again, larger vessels, became the norm.

These changes had two immediate knock-on effects. In the first place, it made it more difficult for average fishers even to part-own a boat. The expense involved grew even greater with new technologies such as radio, sonar and radar, introduced in the course of the twentieth century. While these undoubtedly made fishing safer and to a degree more straightforward, they also made the trade increasingly capital-intensive. This meant that the old share system (see, for instance, Thompson 1983: 151–2) was replaced by a situation where fishermen became wage-earning employees; the social distinction between crew and skipper (sometimes also mate) became considerable (Coull 2008a: 203). Moreover, the new boats needed fair-sized harbours to work from, because of both their size and the processing needed for the weight of their hauls. Smaller fishing villages could not compete (Coull 1993: 95–6) and, by the middle of the twentieth century, many fishermen from small settlements were commuting to nearby larger settlements for work.

The third effect was slower in coming to light, but inexorable. More thorough and scientific fishing methods, coupled with new technology and the industrial pollution which affected the southern North Sea in particular, meant that that sea became rapidly over-fished in the early twentieth century.

Moreover, in the aftermath of the Great War, the collapse of the German economy and the partial withdrawal of the Soviet Union from international markets meant that two of the largest importers of Scottish herring disappeared almost overnight. Even when the fishing was pro-ductive, therefore, it was far less economically viable. Fishing seasons became shorter and harvests often thinner. From an early period central governments became aware of the problem and introduced everything from quota systems to absolute bans on fishing particular areas. How effective these measures were is difficult to gauge, particularly since they were notoriously difficult to police. What can be said is that, while fortunes could and can still be made in fishing, the industry as a whole has generally declined (sometimes dramatically) in size and importance since around the end of the First World War (see, for instance, Coull 2008b).

In the period following the Second World War, these changes became evident throughout Scotland. Only the largest and best main-tained ports could support an industrial level fishery. New technologies, while expensive, meant that fishermen could 'see' what was happening underwater in ways which were previously unthinkable, leading to further lessening in stocks in the North Sea, thus encouraging even greater concentration on northern waters; in particular, around Iceland and the Faeroes, both of which had recently either become independent or autonomous and were therefore particularly attuned to the uphold-ing of their sovereignty and protection of their fish stocks. This led to a standoff lasting almost thirty years in the case of Iceland – the Cod Wars – which almost became live conflict on more than one occasion and which was eventually won by Icelandic and Faeroese interests in the late 1970s, with disastrous consequences for the Scottish deep sea fishery.

During the same period, the United Kingdom acceded to what was then the European Economic Community, one result of which being, eventually, the Common Fishing Policy, which established fishing quotas for each part of the Community's waters. The rights and wrongs of how these quotas were (and are) established and the extent to which their basis is scientific or part of political horse-trading is beyond the remit (thankfully) of this book. What can be said is that the increase in some fish populations in the North Sea during the 1980s because of total bans or limited fishing was often cancelled out by too rapid a return to full-scale fishing. A number of scientists (see, for instance, Roberts 2007) have suggested that industrial-level trawling in particular has had a catastrophic effect upon the ecology of the North Sea which can only be reversed by lengthy and severe controls on fishing.[5] Naturally, such a ban or near-ban would practically finish the Scottish fishing tradition, even if new styles of fishing came into being after the ban's lifting.

Yet even the 1980s and 1990s, so difficult for almost all Scottish fishing communities, proved highly profitable for a small number of large and cutting-edge technologically equipped vessels, based in particular at Peterhead; because of the depletion of many traditionally favoured fish, new species, often including shellfish, were concentrated upon. Whether this success can be continued indefinitely is still under consideration by most observers.

2.2 Fisher culture

By the nineteenth century, therefore, most fishing communities were to some degree set apart from their landward neighbours; at the same time, connections had been formed with other fishing communities, sometimes at a considerable distance. This separation was partly choice; it was also a form of ghettoisation by the non-fishing population. There is no doubt that there were occasions when fisher folk were made to feel like second-class citizens, unwelcome in the larger regions of which their communities formed a part (Nadel-Klein 2003: ch. 2). As we have already seen, this was often expressed through the idea that the fishing trade was itself dirty and that those who took part in it were inevitably affected by this pollution. One chant used by young men from farming backgrounds during fights with their fisher opposite numbers (recorded in Buckie) has it that 'Fishing dowdies bait the line, / Catch a codie give to the swine' (Thompson 1983: 251); interestingly, the pig is a taboo animal on a fishing boat. The distaste for (or at least divorce from) the fisher way of life felt by outsiders was a constant throughout the period when fishing was a common – often dominant – coastal occupation (Anderson 2007: ch. 3). Nevertheless, Thompson (1983: 251) reports that 'on the boats almost the only men recruited from the countryside were the engineers and firemen, and these were regarded as a separate group, wage-earners rather than sharemen, known as the "down below men" or "the black squad"', reminding us that prejudice ran in both directions.

Elements of fisher culture were unique. Given the perils of their occupation – still dangerous today with technological help; far more so even in the recent past – it was inevitable that superstitions would become an integral part of the everyday routines of the community. While some of these traditions were unique to one community or stretch of coast, it was unusual for there not at least to be analogues in other ports. A striking example of this is the *wedding flag* tradition. On the return from the final herring fishery of the year (often that associated with East Anglia), after which weddings traditionally took place, the boat which contained a bridegroom would be decorated for its return to port; this decoration included a flag of sorts which could be seen from far out at sea (Rush 2007: 238).

Some of these traditions are quite natural: the sea boots that fishermen wore when fishing were not acceptable on dry land, for instance, partly because of the desire to keep sea and land separate, but also related to avoiding wear and tear on land for what were often expensive articles. Others were based on long-standing, if difficult to explain, beliefs, such as the idea that women were rarely welcome upon a boat. Along the same lines, Protestant ministers were considered unlucky (Blair 1987: 7), although, strangely, Catholic priests were rarely considered so in Catholic areas. These beliefs had a linguistic dimension. Most fishing communities in Scotland developed a *taboo*-avoidance language. Euphemisms and circumlocutions were regularly used when onboard ship for beings and things which were helpful to fishermen (such as the fish themselves); on other occasions, because the being or thing being referred to is considered unlucky, such as religious ministers or, for reasons which are now unfathomable, pigs and rabbits (Anson 1950: 36–7; 41; Anderson 2007: 44; Nadel-Klein 2003: 48, 141). Rituals also existed for removing bad luck if the taboo object had been accidentally named: in many parts of Scotland, the offending person (and often his crewmen) would shout the local equivalent of *cold iron* and touch that metal, if possible (Anson 1950: 41 and 43; Taylor 1988: 73). We will discuss these phenomena further in Chapter 4.

In a similar vein, many communities developed a taboo of avoiding certain people on the way to fish. These *ill-fittit* people were considered bad luck, even if they said nothing to the fisherman in question; often a day's fishing would be abandoned because of this (Anson 1950: 34; Taylor 1988: 74–5). Nets would on occasion be burned if they were felt to have been contaminated by evil (Taylor 1988: 73).

Another trait often attributed to fishing communities by outsiders is an attachment to evangelical religious traditions (Thompson 1983: 202–24). To a degree this is true, particularly for the fishing communities north of the Tay. While in most of Scotland (with the exception of the former mining communities, another high-risk occupation), the most popular Protestant denomination follows the Presbyterian tradition (whether this be the Church of Scotland or, particularly in the Highlands, the dissenting Free Church or Free Presbyterian Church), a doctrinally mainstream system, alongside some Baptist, Congregationalist and, particularly in northern Scotland, Episcopalian congregations, fishing communities have a much more diverse religious culture. Unusually for Scotland, Methodism is common in these centres; Pentecostalism is not unknown. Traditions such as the Christadelphians, practically non-existent elsewhere in the country nowadays, remain strong in some places. Baptists are much more common than the national average; the same is true for Jehovah's Witnesses and Seventh Day Adventists. The (Plymouth) Brethren are particularly strong in the fishing communities; both closed and open congregations of a variety of hues attract considerable numbers of adherents. Although the slide away from religious observance is tangible in these communities as it is for most of Scotland, adherence nonetheless is still more prevalent than elsewhere (indeed it is worth noting that several of our Wick informants were recruited from Salvation Army meetings). Dickson (2002: 307) suggests that, beyond the *anomie* that living in relatively new settlements encourages, the fundamental egalitarianism of fishing communities provoked an individualistic association with religion: no outside agency was capable of telling fishing people where to worship in the way an agricultural landlord could (for a discussion of the central precepts of evangelicalism and how these relate to artisan individualism, see Hutchinson and Wolffe 2012: ch. 1).[6]

The conversion to Evangelicalism came in the mid- to late-nineteenth centuries, with its final peak in the period immediately after the Great

War (Dickson 2002: 189), connections made much easier, of course, by the peripatetic nature of much fishing business. It was often associated with charismatic members of the communities themselves, who had gone through conversion elsewhere (Dickson 2002: 113). The denominations involved have many features in common which were not emphasised in the mainstream: a concentration on self-help and of family-based endeavour and discipline; an egalitarian tradition of self government. Perhaps most importantly, practically all were strongly temperance: alcohol and other 'sinful' pursuits were to be avoided. Tradition has it that before these changes, fishing communities had had high levels of alcoholism and its attendant ills. A side-effect, certainly, of the conversion was greater prosperity and well-being (although, inevitably, much hypocrisy was also present). Thomson (1983: 5) comments that

> ... the fishermen's religion has its own special, complex relationship with the local economy. A religious revival, for example, may be born of economic desperation, yet in time, with changing circumstances and opportunities, it may itself provide one of the means towards renewed prosperity.

Many of the smaller communities remained 'dry' until quite recently. Thompson (1983: 130–1 and elsewhere) does suggest, however, that trawlermen, particularly from bigger ports like Aberdeen, may not have participated in this culture to any extent, with reports of drunkenness onboard and onshore being widespread.[7]

Naturally, changing work patterns and alterations in social mores inevitably have taken their toll on the traditional cultural paradigm of the Scottish fishing communities, even if there is some evidence in some places that elements of fisher culture remain vibrant. Given that some ports were larger or more successful than others, and that the cultural patterns discussed here are nuanced in different ways in different places, the research upon which this book is based sought out a representative sample of Scottish fishing communities. These are (from north to south): Wick, Lossiemouth, Peterhead, the villages of the East Neuk of Fife (in particular, Anstruther) and Eyemouth. These range from large, active fishing towns (Peterhead), through villages where some fishing continues but where most inhabitants now work in other industries (Lossiemouth and the East Neuk) and may also act as commuter centres for nearby urban areas (particularly true for Eyemouth), to a former major player in the fishing and whaling industries (Wick), where fishing is no longer permitted, by EU fiat. In the following sections, the history and nature of these communities will be briefly illustrated and analysed.

2.3 The individual communities

2.3.1 Wick (population: 6,960; 2001 Census)

Given its status as a good (although not failsafe) harbour (its name, stemming from the Norse word for 'inlet' demonstrates the association) almost at the northernmost point of the Scottish east coast, fishing has always taken place from Wick, although most other settlements on both the north and east coasts of Caithness were also active in the fishing until recently. Wick, however, as Sutherland (2005) demonstrates, had achieved an importance beyond its immediate environs by the Early Modern period. During a large part of the nineteenth century, Wick was something of a boom town, in relation to both the herring fishery and whaling. This made the town rather polyglot. Sutherland (1983: 29–30) comments that

> By 1830 the resident population of the town had risen to nearly 2,300, a number which was augmented during the summer by about six to seven thousand visitors. The languages of at least 10 European countries could be heard on the streets any day. Dialects from all the fishing ports of Scotland lay on the tongues of many of the visitors, and three thousand of the migrants spoke only Gaelic.[8]

When Wick was the chief port of the herring fishery in the late nineteenth century, the British Fisheries Society instigated a great breakwater to protect the vessels in the harbour from easterly gales in particular. Unfortunately, a series of these very storms destroyed the breakwater in the 1870s. Coull (2008a: 191) suggests that this setback encouraged the growth of Peterhead and Fraserburgh as herring fishery ports, while at the same time saddling Wick with debts owed on a project which had failed. Despite these setbacks, however, Wick remained a major player in the fishing and, particularly, whaling industries well into the twentieth century. Like other communities, however, the industries involved gradually contracted over that century. In the case of Wick, moreover, this contraction was further encouraged by the considerable distance between Caithness and major centres of population. When the concentration in the fishing industry on the preservation of fish through the use of smoking and salting was replaced by the foregrounding of fresh fish (often, eventually, frozen soon after being caught), this distance became a hindrance due to shipping costs. Moreover, Wick's position as a 'forward station' for the North Atlantic fisheries was gradually undermined both by the development of larger boats which did not need to take on provisions or land catches as early as possible as well as by the complete decline in northern whaling (Foden 1996). From the Second World War on, decline was ongoing and permanent, reaching its peak in the 1980s, when fishing in Caithness disappeared altogether except from a few boats registered in Scrabster, beside Thurso (Sutherland 2005: 159–60).

2.3.2 Lossiemouth (population: 6,720; General Register for Scotland 2008 estimates)

Lossiemouth developed as a fishing port in the first decades of the nineteenth century, with a herring curing yard being opened in 1819 (Anson 1950: 56). As the first Scottish port to adopt the new Danish technology (Anson 1950: 56–7), Lossiemouth was associated in particular with seine-netting (Coull 2008c: 269).

Although Lossiemouth is not an active fishing port now, a number of members of the fishing community 'commute' to other ports (including Peterhead) to work in the deep sea fisheries (Stewart 1999: 3). Until the 1950s, however, the town, along with a number of other Moray Firth ports (in particular, perhaps, Buckie), maintained a considerable fishing fleet associated with both the herring and line fisheries. Lossiemouth had a name for having a particularly evangelical fishing population. Certainly, their sense of self-awareness was considerable; this was particularly true for those living within the Dog Wall – the *Doggers* – who considered themselves to be the most *fisher* of all the fishing peoples.[9] This tight-knit tradition was at variance with the fact that the town was, for a large part of the nineteenth and twentieth centuries, a holiday resort – often for well-heeled visitors – and, in the mid-twentieth century, became associated with a nearby Royal Air Force base which both provided work away from the fishing and brought with it considerable movement of people from elsewhere (Hughes 1985). The fate of this base was sealed by the Westminster government in 2011.

2.3.3 Peterhead (population: 17,450; General Register for Scotland 2008 estimates)

Along with nearby Fraserburgh, Peterhead remains, unlike most of the communities considered in this study, a major fishing centre. The town has been a fishing port of some importance since the Early Modern period. By the nineteenth century it was involved in line, herring and, eventually, trawl fishing, as well as acting as an outfitter and repairer for boats from other ports. It was also a major whaling port (Buchan 1986). Peterhead was also established as a harbour of refuge through massive construction efforts partly associated with convict labour on a coast with few, if any, naturally safe harbours (Coull 2008a: 204–5). By the end of the century it was among the most successful fishing communities along the coast, attracting workers from smaller or less successful ports: while local names such as *Strachan* or *Buchan* are common, names like *Sutherland* suggest movements across the Moray Firth from the small harbours which Dorian (1981) discussed.

The fishing industry in Peterhead (as elsewhere) declined after the First World War. Nevertheless, the size of Peterhead's harbour in comparison with many others nearby was sufficient to encourage the movement of considerable numbers of active fishers from smaller communities into the town (Miller 1999: 9–11) As we have already seen, some of Peterhead's fishing community were able to weather the later twentieth century and create an at least temporary boom town. To some extent this prosperity was due to the decline of Aberdeen as a fishing harbour, due to labour problems in the 1970s (as discussed, for instance, by Wilson 2009: 58). The trade is often connected technologically with the North Sea oil industry (Bealey and Sewel 1981; Moore 1982), which also uses Peterhead for ancillary provision.

As well as being Scotland's most prosperous fishing port, Peterhead serves as a major centre for the Buchan region. Other local employers include the high-security HM Prison Peterhead and the local power station. In the past, the town was also associated with biscuit manufacture. Many local people now commute to Aberdeen every day, but remain resident in Peterhead. Many people originally from elsewhere also commute from Peterhead, largely because of the price of housing there. The town has a central museum whose primary focus is the fishing trade.

2.3.4 East Neuk of Fife: Anstruther

Given that Fife is a peninsula of considerable length, with two major estuaries running on either side, it is inevitable that its coasts have been associated since the beginning of recorded history with fishing. This is particularly the case on the East Neuk, the promontory extending from the peninsula proper to the south-east, and its towns: Crail, Anstruther and Cellardyke, St Monans and Pittenweem. Here good (if small) natural harbours give access to deep water, water much more of the open sea than is the case further up the Forth (although Buckhaven in central Fife was also a major fishing port in the nineteenth century; as Dobson 1992 and 2008 demonstrate, the East Neuk had a long history of commercial shipping separate from, but eventually replaced by, fishing).

The area's prosperity was founded on the *Lammas Drave*, where great shoals of herring would pass along the southern coast of Fife most years (or at least at regular intervals), although *great line* and *smaw line* fishing for cod and other species also contributed to local prosperity and occasionally maintained communities when the herring were either scarce or low-priced (Smith 1985 provides a useful narrative of the fluctuations and final collapse of herring fishing from these ports). Crail in particular also demonstrates by its architecture a long-standing association in the medieval and Early Modern eras with the Low Countries and northern Germany. According to the General Register for Scotland 2008 estimates, Anstruther (and Cellardyke) had 3,527 inhabitants, Crail had 1,730, Pittenweem had 1,620 and St Monans 1,280.

Following Coull (2000), it can be established that Crail in the medieval period was pre-eminent in the fishing in the East Neuk. Although herring dominated at the time, fishers were also involved in long line fishing, in particular for cod. This led, from an early period, to deep sea fishing far from the coast. Indeed, so fruitful was the herring fishery at Crail that fishers from the North-East came to the town in the eighteenth century.

In that century the other villages of the East Neuk also began to take part in the fishing in an organised way, possibly as a part of the *improvement* programme followed by the local landowners. In the nineteenth century this continued, with new and better harbours being built for all the villages and Anstruther (along with Cellardyke) in particular becoming a major fishing port.

At this time, Fifers were at the heart of the Scottish fishing industry: taking part in the full herring fishery around the British Isles, involved in the deep sea cod fisheries to Shetland and beyond and being in the forefront of new fishing technologies, in particular the *Fifie*, a safer and larger fishing boat designed for longer sea voyages and, in the late nineteenth century, the conversion to steam.

As with so many other smaller fishing ports, the villages of the East Neuk reached their apogee of production and number of vessels before the First World War; nevertheless, fishing has continued, albeit largely concerned with the harvesting of unusual shellfish for the restaurant trade. Some cod fishing has been maintained, however. Rush (2007) presents in a literary autobiography the story of a child living through the last years of the herring fishery at St Monans in the period immediately after the Second World War. At that time at least the fishing in its various forms still dominated the life of his extended family – although the suggestion is that this ceased to be the case in the late 1950s. On the other hand Anstruther plays host to the Scottish Fisheries Museum, meaning that local people have at least a little passive knowledge of the local fishing trade. The museum was for a while unpopular among significant members of the local population, primarily because the way it was developed by the then curators was felt to have taken little interest in what local people considered should be represented about the local fishing trade; this viewpoint now appears to have changed (Nadel-Klein 2003).

2.3.5 Eyemouth

Eyemouth, the southernmost of the fishing centres covered in this study, had a population of 3,410 according to the General Register for Scotland 2008 estimates. Along with the village of Burnmouth (included in these figures), it lies at the land end of an inlet which provides one of the few relatively safe natural harbours on the east coast between Berwick-upon-Tweed and North Berwick.

As Aitchison (2001) recounts in his excellent history of the trade in the town, fishing was largely ancillary to other related trades – particularly smuggling (Wood 1998: 62) and legitimate sea carrying – until the early nineteenth century. Nevertheless, fishing's position as emblematic of a number of resented feudal taxes levied by the established Church gave it considerable importance both as a radicalising force in religion and politics and as a means of establishing a local identity for those who made a living from the sea. Although relations between the propertied classes of the immediate neighbourhood and the fisher community were not always adversarial, there was always sufficient tension on both sides for cooperation to be difficult.

The originally small population of the settlement grew considerably in the late eighteenth and early nineteenth centuries, largely due to the population clearances common throughout the Borders (Aitchison and Cassell 2012). The development of large-scale fishing led to immigration from further afield. Highland names such as Ross are by no means unknown in the town. Locals call themselves *Haimoothers*.

In the early nineteenth century Eyemouth found itself at the very source of the summer herring *drave* at the mouth of the Firth of Forth. Indeed, at its height, ships from all over eastern Britain sought temporary refuge and landed their catches there; its fishers also took part in the winter haddock fishery close to shore. Many of the families in the community owned their own boats; a share-based (*dale*) system was offered to boatless members of the community. In good years, the town could become prosperous through fish; in the lean years, however, the town's inhabitants could come very close to starvation. As the nineteenth century progressed, Eyemouth became embroiled in three problems not really of its making. In the first place, the town had been bypassed by the railway. A number of less well-favoured sites which did connect to the national network were able to sell their wares when they were fresher and also more profitable (Coull 2008a: 187).[10] Secondly, the harbour, at the mouth of the Eye, was not large enough to accommodate the larger boats and fleets that new forms of fishing were producing. Finally, the harbour had a tidal bar, which meant that boats could not enter it safely, no matter the condition of the sea, except when the tide was in. As we have already seen, the development of a safe harbour, which at times seemed within the grasp of the town, was never achieved. Each of these drawbacks meant that the Eyemouth fishers had to be faster to bring in the catch and more willing to brave the elements than any other fishers on the coast. Indeed songs of the time celebrated the ubiquity of the Eyemouth fishers in all places around the British Isles where the herring fishery took place (Wood 1998: 51).

On 14 October 1881 – *Black Friday* – almost all the fishing population of Eyemouth were caught up in a particularly vicious gale. Although a considerable number of fishers survived the disaster, 129 fishermen – the *pickit men* – lost their lives, leaving around 93 widows and 267 children under working age without fathers (Aitchison 2001: 197). The scale of the disaster cannot be exaggerated, of course, or its effects on later developments in the town (Wood 1998: 42).

Certainly, Eyemouth would never again be the leading fishing town it had been before (although it is salutary to note that fishing was resumed less than a fortnight after the disaster: the living still needed to eat, no matter the trauma and the risk). The new fishing techniques associated with steam power – most notably trawling – required a capital outlay greater than most in Eyemouth could afford. Moreover, although the town eventually gained a rail spur and an extended and deepened harbour, this was a case of too little, too late.

Nevertheless, fishing has continued, albeit in ever decreasing numbers, in the town, generally for inshore fish and delicacies like crabs and lobsters. The sense of community in the *fishertoun* appears to have continued. From 1997, the European Union supplied funding to regenerate the harbour area. Largely catering to pleasure craft, the area also includes a boatyard. A small amount of largely 'hobby' fishing continues.

2.3.6 Discussion

It is readily apparent that these communities are similar to, but nonetheless different from, each other, often due to a combination of cultural, economic, historical and geographical forces. At the same time, the issues these communities have faced over the last 200 years (and, indeed, still face) are remarkably similar, despite these distinctions. This is likely, it is to be suggested, to make some of the findings of the research described in this book look, at a general level, very similar, along the coast while, when dealing with specifics, differences between ports may appear considerable. Despite these many differences and similarities, however, there was a time when lexical use was often the feature which marked a community off from its near and distant neighbours. The fishing trade was a central (indeed perhaps *the* central) source for this distinctiveness in our communities. Before we turn to these points, however, the methodologies underlying this study need to be discussed.

3 Methodology

This study involves two central methods necessary to the development of the research: the construction of a corpus of lexical items, and the use of a questionnaire during interviews with participants in the five locations to determine the levels of current knowledge of some of these items.

3.1 The corpus

3.1.1 The necessity of the corpus

An investigation of the historical distribution of lexical items associated with the fishing industry requires the use of a range of resources. Some of these have national coverage, and are reasonably accessible in libraries; many are not widely available, but are held by libraries in several of our communities. In addition, some texts result from local initiatives, and are genuinely *owned* by the communities whose language they document: the project copy of the *Lossie Glossie*, for instance, has pencilled-in additional definitions. With the exception of national resources such as the *Dictionary of the Scots Language* (DSL; http://www.dsl.ac.uk), these sources have not been digitised and are not available online. Clearly, the compilation of a corpus of fishing-related lexis is an important step toward determining how this lexis is subject to attrition over time.

3.1.2 Construction of the corpus

The corpus is structured according to a series of semantic categories and sub-categories. The textual sources for each entry are noted, together with any indications that certain terms have specific space: in some instances, the source text itself implies the specific space of the items; texts with a national coverage often indicate a given item's geographical spread.

3.1.3 Sources

3.1.3.1 National

Within Scotland, the primary national source for contemporary (and recent) Scots lexical use is the *Dictionary of the Scots Language* (DSL), an online resource combining the multi-volume *Dictionary of the Older Scottish Tongue* (DOST) and *Scottish National Dictionary* (SND), along with an ongoing online update. Based partly on the materials put together for the *Oxford English Dictionary* (OED), DOST was concerned primarily with lexical use during the fifteenth and sixteenth centuries and is therefore not particularly applicable to the task at hand; the corpus underlying SND, however, is based upon the use of modern Scots. The literary bias this undoubtedly gives to the SND corpus is partly counteracted by the fieldwork and questionnaire distribution efforts carried out in the 1950s. A word's geographical extent can be arrived at on a variety of occasions; non-literary, as well as literary, examples illustrate gradations of meaning and also bring usage to life. The contemporary nature of these examples is now questionable. With this in mind, from the late 1990s on the online versions of the SND, and now the DSL, have incorporated new materials from print sources of various sorts. Inevitably this has meant that additions have been piecemeal and have tended towards applying nuances to pre-existing categories rather than creating new headwords and major categories.

If using SLD were the only way of constructing the corpus, a trawl for appropriate lexis would be extremely time-consuming, particularly since the disparate elements of the corpus – DOST, SND and updates – are not yet fully integrated. But the team behind the SND has been particularly fruitful in creating dictionaries based upon its corpus, more approachable – and affordable – than the mother product. The best known of these is *The Concise Scots Dictionary* (CSD; Robinson 1999), essentially a one-volume encapsulation of SND, without examples (except when necessary), but retaining both pronunciation guides and etymological information. Its layout represents a considerable improvement in coherence compared to its parent. It would be time-consuming, but nonetheless relatively easy, to extract useful fishing-community specific material from CSD. Thankfully, this is not necessary because of the publication of the *Scots Thesaurus* (ST).

ST follows something like the pattern found in standard thesauri. The introduction (p. xv) does, however, state that

> The main part of the book is divided into groups . . . covering a wide variety of subjects, including the natural world, human life and society, as

well as emotions and character. This arrangement reveals the richness of the Scots language and will help the user to increase knowledge of it and to find words in particular subject areas.

While none of this would be foreign to any thesaurus, it is unusual to see the developmental – even didactic – purposes of the work emphasised. But this is not such an uncommon feature for work intended for a wide readership, including those who might not be as conversant with a language as the original informants.

Although the layout of ST remains largely faithful to that of CSD, there are a number of occasions where its editors have decided, normally with good reason, to depart from the practice of the mother volume. For instance, ST does not give multiple spellings (necessary in CSD because Scots is not standardised), pronunciation or etymological information for headwords. Multiple spellings would confuse the issue at hand – meaning – and also take up a considerable amount of space, given the number of occasions in which common words (normally also those with a range of spellings) recur in the thesaurus. Since the headword employed is normally the first in the CSD entry (and therefore that by which the entry is alphabetised), it is easy to move from thesaurus to dictionary and find alternative – often regional – spellings there. The lack of pronunciation and etymological data is also not problematic. Knowledge of local pronunciations might give guidance over how a native schooled in English spelling conventions might write a particular word, but this connection is not crucial to the pursuit of meaning. Etymological information, while again interesting in itself, does not provide further depth to the meanings dissected for the various words.

ST does, however, give date and provenance information. Both are particularly useful, since they allow the possibility of disregarding material which is not twentieth century or current and also of developing an idea of where particular usages are present. Naturally, neither date nor provenance is infallible: nor are they intended to be. They nonetheless provide a useful pattern later researchers can base their distributions upon. For our purposes the thesaurus style naturally has many advantages over the dictionary. It also presents a number of potential problems, or at least sticking points. The same word – or indeed sub-meaning – can turn up in a number of guises. This produces reduplication for the designer of the corpus. More importantly, however, the categories produced might well encourage the thesaurus makers to over-divide meanings to fit the many categories on offer.

3.1.3.2 Regional

Probably the closest work to a dictionary describing regional Scots lexis within the area covered by this book is Kynoch's *Doric Dictionary* (DD; 2004), originally published in 1996. The work covers North-East Scots usage, largely (although not entirely) of a rural and traditional type. Generally, it appears accurate and consistent, natural, perhaps, for a native speaker with considerable experience in the use of dictionaries.

An unfortunate tendency in the book is its only partial distinction between historical and contemporary usage. DD provides a list of some sources, a number of which date from the nineteenth century and are literary in nature. One, *Eppie Elrick* (Milne 1955), is actually set in the early eighteenth century; its author appears self-consciously to have archaised some of the language further. But DD also employs many more modern sources. These appear to include works in the SND tradition, although this is not explicitly stated; again, the potential for overlap is present. Finally, Kynoch appears to have used both his own recording of the usage of 'expert' speakers along with introspection.

Buchan Claik (Buchan and Toulmin 1989; BC) could be said to be one of the best 'amateur' word-lists produced in Scotland. It demonstrates a deep knowledge of the traditional culture and ways of the Buchan area in particular, and was written by natives who were also dialect writers of some ability. Buchan was born in Peterhead, came from a fishing background and was connected with the trade in one form or another all of his working life. Many entries were produced by only one of the authors; this is credited in the text.

Of course, as this publication is the work of enthusiasts, unusual ordering and structuring (not, of itself, necessarily a bad thing) is commonplace. We are rarely told what word class a word is a member of; thankfully, we are regularly told how and where a word is used, however. It is a great pity that other fishing communities are not so well served.

A good example of such neglect is the dialect of Eyemouth, where no specialist lexical surveys have taken place. Indeed, Kennington's *As Spoken in Berwick* (2006) appears to be the only word-list dealing with the dialects of South-East Scotland. The pamphlet has the peculiarity, however, that the author appears genuinely or wilfully ignorant of the Scottish background to traditional Berwick speech. This means, for instance, that he attributes an immediate Dutch origin for *stot* 'hit, bounce', when it is a very common Scots word. Despite these peculiarities, the pamphlet nevertheless provides a fair, if limited, survey of the local dialect's vocabulary. Unfortunately, despite Berwick's importance to the herring fishery, only the vocabulary of the Tweed salmon fishery is given prominence. Few corpus items were derived from this source.

Small size does not always limit a work's use. This can be seen with the *Lossie Glossie*, a word-list produced by and for the local library and community of Lossiemouth (LG). So integrated into the local community is the word-list, in fact, that the copy given to Millar in 2006 has pencil annotations, containing suggestions when the glossary is vague over a type of fish or article of clothing. It is obviously a work in progress and is all the better for that.

Caithness is blessed with two word-lists: Sutherland's *Caithness Dictionary* (CD) from the 1990s and Miller's *Caithness Wordbook* (CW), published in 2001. Both are obviously the work of people used to handling lexical material to do with their local communities for a variety of purposes. There appear, again, to be connections to the SND tradition, although these are rarely made explicit. One small defect both works have is a tendency to make much of the unique nature of the Caithness dialect when the words in question are more widely distributed.

Mary Murray's *In My Ain Words* (1982; ENV), somewhat less ambitious in scope, is an attempt to produce a vocabulary of the traditional dialects of the East Neuk of Fife by a native speaker. It is particularly useful for our purposes because it is laid out largely in units of meaning (or subject matter) rather than alphabetically. It acts rather like a shorter BC for the East Neuk, providing considerable numbers of examples of use. It is obviously intended as a heritage item, containing a number of historical photographs.

Finally, there is Robert Watt's *A Glossary of Scottish Dialect Fish and Trade Names* (1989; *Glossary*). Intended as a glossary for civil servants connected to the fishing trade, it is as exhaustive a survey it is possible to imagine, particularly in relation to names given to fish. As we will see in Chapter 4, Scots words for a variety of species appear only to be found in the glossary. This glossary appears to have been partly based upon an earlier anonymous glossary (Anonymous 1928).

A number of other sources, generally cultural or historical in nature, were also mined for lexical items. As we will see, a number of authors who did not have lexical use in mind often provide nuanced examples of words which would otherwise be lost.

3.2 Scholarly discussion of the lexis of the fishing communities

A few discussions of vocabulary use among the Scottish fishing communities exist, most notably a range of articles by Mather (1965, 1966, 1969, 1972) and one by Downie (1983). Each represents a considerable resource, although they are largely anecdotal or based upon limited exposure to the areas in question as fluctuating sociolinguistic entities. Neither represents the totality of the areas discussed in this book: Mather concentrates in the main upon southern and central parts of the Scottish east coast, Downie on largely the southern coast of the Moray Firth.

Two dissertations on these topics exist: Schlötterer (1996) and McGarrity (1998). The former is primarily concerned with the survival of terms related to the building and upkeep of fishing boats, which is not a central feature of this book (for reasons which will be discussed in the next chapter); nevertheless, there are aspects of Schlötterer's book which are of considerable service to 'putting flesh on the bones' of the otherwise ill-served south-eastern fishing varieties. His research methodology is unashamedly dialectological, however: his findings are based on the responses of a small number of older males. McGarrity's work has as a central concern the knowledge of weather terms in Torry, one of the fishing villages within Aberdeen. Because her materials relate primarily to a community not covered by this study, her materials have not been used directly in the corpus; a number of her methodological insights have proved useful (albeit with some critical analysis) in the construction of the questionnaire for the main survey of this research, however.

3.3 Archive materials

Scotland is blessed in having the School of Scottish Studies at the University of Edinburgh. Due to various nationwide surveys, such as the *Scottish National Dictionary* and the *Linguistic Survey of Scotland* (LSS), as well as more focused surveys, a considerable archive – written and recorded – exists of Scottish language in the recent past. The archives on this occasion did not prove terribly fruitful as an independent resource, largely because a number of scholars – in particular Mather – have already trawled their resources. Where features are new, however, they have been coded SSSA (School of Scottish Studies Archives).

3.4 The structure of the corpus

From practically its inception, the corpus has been intended as a thematically organised word-list. Although some editorial decisions were made over how a word should be defined, in general the central analysis of meaning in each source is maintained. This means that no attempts have been made to 'correct' meanings given by a particular authority, beyond placing the unexpected meaning in a context where other, more mainstream, meanings are present. Further discussion of how these relationships work will be given in the following.

The corpus lies somewhere between a dictionary and a thesaurus. Unlike the mainstream thesaurus tradition associated with *Roget's Thesaurus* and its intellectual and methodological offspring (see Aitchison and Clarke (2004) for a discussion of these traditions), words and meanings of words are laid out in alphabetical order within each semantic field (or sub-field). This has the disadvantage that words of similar meaning are not necessarily placed beside each other, thus sometimes presenting a rather fragmented sense of collocation and connotation. But since the primary purpose of the corpus is to lay out words rather than meanings, the ready finding through alphabetisation of particular words is very useful indeed.

3.5 Semantic structure of the corpus

The initial plan for the corpus was to follow, as closely as possible, the semantic distinctions worked out for the ST. Over time it became apparent, however, that this would necessarily obscure some of the more obvious connections. ST is concerned with (as near as possible) the complete Scots semantic distribution. Because our Corpus is intended for different, more semantically circumscribed, purposes, a new framework better constructed for our purposes was devised. The decisions involved were not, of course, without their own problems and, inevitably, arbitrary boundaries. Nonetheless, generally the divisions and sub-divisions appear to work well.

The corpus is divided into five essential units, of rather different sizes:

1. Fishing trade
2. The sea itself
3. Weather
4. Flora and fauna
5. The seashore and its environs.

Sub-divisions of these are laid out in the following ways:

1. Fishing trade
    1.1. Fishing
        1.1.1. Fishing: fish
        1.1.2. Nets and related technology
        1.1.3. Lines and related technology
        1.1.4. Creels and other fishing traps

1.2. Maintenance of boats
1.3. Boat types and building
1.4. The fishing business
    1.4.1. Fish processing
        1.4.1.1. Fish dishes
1.5. Clothing
1.6. Times, weather and seasons of the fishery
    1.6.1. Fishing seasons
    1.6.2. Times of day
    1.6.3. Weather phenomena falling at same time annually
    1.6.4. Weather forecasting
1.7. Traditions of the fishing communities
    1.7.1. Old customs and superstitions
    1.7.2. Taboo avoidance language
    1.7.3. Local nicknames
2. The sea itself
    2.1. 'Moods' of the sea, storms, etc.
    2.2. Tides and currents
    2.3. Waves
    2.4. Seaweed
3. Weather
    3.1. Good weather, improving weather
    3.2. Muggy, oppressive, 'close'
    3.3. Dreary
    3.4. Unreliability, change
    3.5. Dry and hot phenomena
    3.6. Inclement, stormy conditions
    3.7. Wind phenomena
    3.8. Mist and fog
    3.9. Thunder and lightning
    3.10. Wet weather, rain
    3.11. Cold weather phenomena
    3.12. Clouds
4. Flora and fauna
    4.1. Fish
    4.2. Shellfish and other marine animals
    4.3. Seabirds
    4.4. Marine mammals
5. The Seashore and its environs
    5.1. Behind the shore
    5.2. Harbour
    5.3. Shingle and sand; grass

A number of editorial decisions were taken. In the first instance, the ST entry is given before all others. This need not be a commentary on accuracy (although it is probable that trained lexicographers will be more likely to give an accurate and to-the-point definition than would informed laypersons); rather, we wished to place at the start of an entry a resource readily available to all readers, given that some of the local collections are not. No further order was imposed after this. In general, references from collections which provided dictionary-like meanings were given prominence. Ease of understanding was foregrounded.

During the construction of the corpus it became apparent that words, meanings and how they were laid out often differed considerably from source to source. Partly this appears to be due to ability and experience in constructing complex analytical patterns of this sort; more often, however, it seems due to differing viewpoints and interests.

There were, for instance, times when ST (or SLD from which it is derived) presents a more useful or accurate definition. Thus the CW provides the following definition:

> palmer scarf guillemot (SLD: in Ork[ney]: 'descriptive term for
>   something big or fine: e.g. "palmer of a duck"'),

scarf being, generally, a cormorant or a shag. It is obvious that the original meaning of *palmer* has either been lost in Caithness or the phrase has been reinterpreted – although the origins of any collocation need not shed any light on what a word means now. There are also occasions where local resources give a more useful interpretation of a word's meaning than the national and scholarly resources. For instance, with

drabble	*of rain* drizzle [*Aberdeen; west Angus*] (ST)
drabbly, drabblichy	showery, drizzly [*Banff; Aberdeen*] (ST)
drably	(of weather) wet, disagreeable (DD)

DD adds the judgemental and emotional sense missing in ST.

The non-scholarly (or at least non-linguistic) resources are often very useful in giving extra colour which is regularly missing due to the detached tone necessary for scholarly work. For instance, in the entry for *scrae* we find

> scrae to dry fish; dried fish (CD; SLD: Sh[etland] Cai[aithness]
>   Ork[ney])
>   The coalfish could be preserved by being hung up in the sun to
>   dry, sometimes without salt, when they were known as 'scrae'.
>   According to a Caithness description, they were cleaned, left in

salt and water for a while and then hung in the roof until they
became as hard as a board. It was common even at the start of
the twentieth century to see 'a string o' scrayed sellags hingin' up
in e' [*sic*] roof'. (Fenton 2008a: 87)

CD and SLD both provide sufficient information to allow understanding of the phrase should the reader ever come across it. But the Fenton
(2008a) definition contains significantly more information on how the
process was actually carried out, along with an example of its use in
Caithness dialect.

The various collections can also provide considerable evidence of
how different viewpoints can be reconciled. For instance, the meaning
of *brae* in a seashore sense can best be done by comparing discussion in
a range of sources:

brae the (steep or sloping) bank of a river or lake or shore of the sea
  (ST)
doon the braes on the sea-shore (BC)
bray 'At Berwick-upon-Tweed, the mayor in the year 1285, one
  Robert Durham, ordered herring, among other fish, to be sold "on
  the bray" alongside the boat that landed them, and the fishermen
  were not allowed to carry the fish ashore after dusk.' (Smylie
  2004)

'The walk "roond the braes" was described as early as the eighteenth
century as "being a tonic to city people".' (Wood 1998: 70)

The almost proverbial senses of this word in these contexts is really
only established by 'triangulating' evidence. Something similar can be
seen with *fry*:

fry parcel of fish taken home by fisherman for his own use (BC)
  'The Aberdeen owners disapproved of such charity [giving away
  fish free to poor families at the end of the trip], and tried to stamp
  it out. In 1922 they were pressing the city council to introduce
  special bye-laws to suppress the giving away of "illegitimate 'fries'"
  at the fish market. The crews were regarded as having a right
  to haddocks for "fries", and the skippers and mates could give
  away more fish. They would do this especially when prices were
  very low: occasionally a skipper-owner would even empty his
  fish boxes on the floor, and invite bystanders to help themselves.
  But generally those outside the crew who received "fries" were
  friends of the skipper. They were usually unemployed fishermen.'
  (Thompson 1983: 129)

or *arles*.

> arles   An earnest given on striking a bargain (DD)
> small sum of money in exchange for verbal promise on part of
> women and girls to work for herring curer (BC)
> 'At the time of hiring, curers advanced a small sum, called *arles*,
> which bound a girl to stay for the entire season. This was never
> more than £1 and usually less.' (Nadel-Klein 2003: 73)
>
> airles   fees paid to herring gutters (CD)
> erles   hiring fee for herrin' lassies (ENV)
> 'you'd to sign a paper, and you got arles . . . Ye were arlesed, ye
> see, ye was fixed. Fen ye took up your arles, ye was fixed. Ye
> couldna ging to another body, ye was ta'en to court.' (Thompson
> 1983: 170)

The human relationships and toil associated with *arles* is best illustrated
not through disinterested discussion, but rather by people intrinsically
connected to it.

On a number of occasions a range of definitions can also give an
idea of the metaphorical extension of a word, as here with *lug*, the most
common Scots word for 'ear':

> lug   the corner of a herring net *now* [*North-East; Angus*] (ST)
> lugs/beckets   large loops on corners of net (ENV)
> lug stane   one of the series of stones attached to the lower corner of a
> herring net to make it hang vertically in the water [*Northern*] (ST)

Single references can also provide interesting instances of this phenomenon. For instance, Scots *sappie* can mean, according to SLD, 'full of sap
or substance', although it can also mean 'waterlogged'. In BC, however,
it is said to mean 'water laden with fish'.

Examples of this could be said to form part of a range of words where
meanings were extended from other occupations. For instance *sook*, historically the same word as *suck*, is interpreted thus by CWB:

> sook   drying power of wind

Although this word is only recorded with this meaning for Caithness,
experience dictates that it is actually quite general (alongside *sooch*) with
this extended meaning across a large part of Scotland. More unusual is
an extension of this meaning, again recorded for Caithness:

> sook   to dry fish (CD)

There are also occasions where different sources appear to disagree
over word meaning. For instance, with

torn bellie   herring which has been split or broken by careless handling
   now [*Shetland; Northern; Fife*] (ST)
torn-bellies   herrings attacked by sea predators (ENV)

The national resource attributes the broken nature of the herrings described by the word as being due to human agency, while the local Fife resource attributes the damage to predators. It is, of course, likely that, since both processes could bring about the same result, that we have here an example of concentration on part, but not all, of the full meaning for the expression.

As a final point, the lexis used by the Scottish fishing communities also has at times a beauty, a poetic turn, which is difficult to quantify. Two examples must suffice. The first

dog afore his maister   the swell of the sea that often precedes a storm
   [*now Banff*] (ST)
high swell, forerunner of approaching storm (BC)

is powerful primarily because of its litotes. The second

evendoon   *esp of very heavy and continuous rain* straight, perpendicular
   (ST)

is evocative primarily because it sees rainfall in terms of its relationship to the perpendicular.

When it came to the collection of present-day data on lexical knowledge in the fishing communities, we used a structured questionnaire to elicit a controlled set of data that would stand comparison with the contents of the *Fisherspeak* corpus, formed from material from dictionaries and other resources as well as material provided by informants in the various focus sites. However, mindful of the potential for the continued existence of evocative and almost poetic lexis, we attempted to allow scope for some open-ended responses in the hope that such examples might still be produced.

3.6 The questionnaire

As discussed in Chapter 1, questionnaires have stood the test of time as an element of dialectological (and to a lesser extent sociolinguistic) practice, with ongoing modifications (a summary of the development of the questionnaire is available in Chambers and Trudgill 1998: section 2.3). Essentially, questionnaires suffer from a degree of formality from which sociolinguistic interviews do not. For literate people – which includes everyone considered in this research – a paper filled with questions is reminiscent of school; possibly also of parts of school experience not remembered fondly. The trick, therefore, is to lessen the formality of the instrument, downplaying concerns about being 'correct'.

In the early days of dialectology, questionnaires were largely the property of the investigator. He or she would ask informants about their lexical use, following a set pattern. Very early on it was discovered that asking 'what do you call a *table*?' was not an effective way of learning about local lexis. Many people found it difficult – even impossible – to state an effective equivalent once the prestige form has been uttered. Very quickly, researchers learned that asking a question along the lines of 'what do you call the piece of furniture you eat your dinner on?' or 'what do you call this?' (pointing to a table) were much more effective (although see Ong 2002).

This tradition of researcher-prompted and often lengthy, 'live' questionnaires continued well into the twentieth century. Indeed the *Survey of English Dialects* (SED) conducted in the 1950s and 1960s is, perhaps, both the final and most nuanced example of such dialectological enquiries. Taking many hours to complete, and administered directly by a researcher with a chosen 'expert' in the local speech, it was both extremely thorough and undeniably flawed in attempting to represent the speech of a community as a whole.[1] Despite its admirably collated findings, surveys of this type have always been methodologically questionable.

From early on in the development of dialectology, attempts to overcome the difficulty of not having a representative survey were sought. In an age before true mass communication, postal questionnaires presented an opportunity to cover a wide area while also randomising the subjects. Postal addresses do, of course, give some idea of social (sometimes ethnic) status. There is no exact correlation between residence and background, however. In that sense, therefore, postal questionnaires had sociolinguistic features denied the mainstream dialectological questionnaire tradition, even if we have to accept that the primary reason the post was employed was monetary. Three major problems have dogged the postal questionnaire tradition, however. In the first place, in particular in the nineteenth century, the levels of literacy necessary for the completion of a questionnaire were not regularly represented. Secondly, the rates of return for postal questionnaires are nearly always low, whether due to lack of understanding, time or interest. The return rate increases a little when return postage is provided, but the results are still unimpressive. Finally, some of the responses on a questionnaire demonstrate that the subject has misunderstood a question or questions. Since there is no comeback normally, data may quickly become dubious. With the growth of the internet, web-based questionnaires of this type have become common. On a major forum like *Linguist List* there can be as many as two or three requests weekly for help in filling out or finding informants who will fill out questionnaires of this type. While it is likely that an online survey may be more attractive than the process of filling out a question-naire manually and then returning it by mail, the geographical and social spread inherent in a postal questionnaire is unlikely to be present (or even replicable) in such a convincing way in an online equivalent.

A number of methodologies have been employed hitherto to collect a selected number of lexical items from various parts of Scotland. These include:

1. Direct questioning/translation, e.g. 'What is your word for *x*?' (LSS), with some researchers being very specific to the local area, e.g. Riach (1971–2, published in 1979, 1980 and 1982): 'What is the Galloway word for *x*?' and Schlötterer's (1996: 13) technique of phrasing the question as, 'What is your *local* word for . . . ?'
2. Indirect questioning, e.g. terms being elicited after giving the inform-ants a definition (Agutter and Cowan 1981).
3. Recognition of dialect words e.g. Macaulay (1977); Nässén (1989) and Lawrie (1991).
4. Questionnaires e.g. Macafee (1994); Schlötterer (1996); McGarrity (1998).
5. Picture/word recognition, e.g. Hendry (1997); Middleton (2001).
6. Word-in-context translation, e.g. Hendry (1997); Middleton (2001).
7. Qualitative interviews (Macafee 1994).

Self-reflective feedback from a number of the above researchers shows that that no one methodology is, in itself, the ideal way of collect-ing data. McGarrity (1998: 62) notes that, when using the translation method, 'many [informants] found it difficult to supply/recall a suitable range of Doric weather expressions.' When asked which dialect words they recognised, only 11 out of 35 informants in Nässén's 1989 study on Shetland Scots knew a significant amount of the lexicon elicited. Lawrie (1991) came across a slightly different, but related problem; whereas most informants in Fife had a passive knowledge of the dialect, the overall majority tended to use Standard English on a daily basis.

Indirect questioning techniques were little more successful. Agutter and Cowan (1981) investigated 33 words in Larbert (Stirlingshire) among 10 adults and 10 children by giving definitions and seeing how often these words occurred; unfortunately, the return rate for the adults was 17.4% and only 11.1% for the children.

Questionnaires have been favoured by some researchers. Macafee (1994) found her own questionnaire in hindsight to be 'too long' (p. 48) and her main technique within the questionnaire to elicit lexical items was the translation method, which, as we saw above, has not proved particularly successful elsewhere. McGarrity's questionnaire (1998: 49) proved more successful but her primary aim was recording attitudes, using a Likert scale.

More relevant for our study, Schlötterer (1996) used a questionnaire based on Wright (1964), and Elmer (1973). In his study of south-east coast Scots, Schlötterer (1996: 11) employed three types of question:

1. Naming: 'What do you call . . .?'
2. Completing: 'To get the mussel out of the shell, you have to . . .?'
3. Talking: 'What types of boats are used here?'

Schlötterer's techniques were broadly similar to other questionnaires in that two of the question formats he used were 'closed': a specific answer was being sought. But he also used a more 'open' form of questioning, where the informant was encouraged to talk at length. Schlötterer (1996: 12) noted that a standardised interview, using a questionnaire, precluded establishing a more relaxed relationship with the informant. Time limits ruled out the use of a non-standardised interview. A compromise was to use a 'talking' question to start off the questionnaire, putting the inform-ant at his ease and to establish a 'master–pupil' relationship – with the researcher as pupil (Schlötterer 1996: 13).

Schlötterer (1996: 13) points to the paradox of posing questions in Standard English but expecting vernacular replies. His solution was, as referred to above, to ask for the 'local' word to be given in reply. His point is valid, since researchers entering the community risk, somehow or other, stifling the range of responses through use of external code. But Schlötterer was largely interested in fishing trade terminology, inevitably involving the participation of primarily older men. Using his techniques within the framework of vocabulary connected with and used by the whole community would be less useful.

Macafee (1994: 1) suggests a solution lies in the use of qualitative research techniques. Walker (1985) lists the advantage of qualitative methods as giving the researcher unanticipated and privileged infor-mation, access to analytical tools which work better when the topic becomes too complicated but also ways of handling data that do not fit a preconceived analytical format (1994: 4). Very importantly, Macafee (1994: 4) states, 'the most productive interaction between [quantitative and qualitative] data turned out to lie in the contradictions between them.' Questionnaire use, designed to elicit information on lexical knowledge or use, is therefore both ubiquitous and highly flawed. The observer's paradox, always present in fieldwork, is inevitably at its strongest when instruments of this type are used.

With this in mind, a number of scholars – in particular Llamas (1999; see also Kerswill, Llamas and Upton 1999) – began to experiment in the mid 1990s with using a more open-ended lexical elicitation method, through the use of mind-maps (otherwise, *spidergrams*). Participants were not asked to give word-for-word correspondences; instead, they were given a series of partly completed diagrams on sheets of paper, with an over-riding title of, for instance, *emotions*, along with sub-headings, such as *anger*. Clear instructions were given that participants were to fill out as many words as they knew, in relation to the topic, underneath the headings. Normally no mention was made of whether the vocabulary elicited was local, colloquial or standard. It was found from an early period that these mind-maps were more fully (and enjoyably) filled out by two people rather than one, since elicitation appeared greater when ideas were bounced from one person to another. The researcher would then go through the mind-maps with the informants.

This methodology empowered the informants, with the researcher in the guise of 'student'. The 'free' nature of the task approximates to the Labovian sociolinguistic interview, but focuses the informants' attention on local language: the mind-map stands as indubitably a genuinely new and thoroughly sociolinguistic way of assessing lexical knowledge and use.

3.7 Construction of the questionnaire

Some of the problems which the project's methodology evinced became apparent in the early stages of fieldwork, carried out by Michael Hornsby in the target communities during 2008 and 2009. Efforts were made to find 'good' speakers who were born after the fieldwork associated with the LSS and the SND. In theory, this should have given a greater sense of currency among the 'best' speakers now.

In practice, however, results were not encouraging. When faced with large gaps on the page where informants were expected to produce a range of vocabulary items (thereby encouraging the production of a larger repertoire), most informants produced only one or two words, even when the fieldworker attempted, in the discussion after the mind-maps were filled in, to elicit more words, phrases and meanings. Groups of between five and ten informants, rather than the intended two or three, produced more material, but its general quality, in terms of range and depth of words elicited, was not great.

Despite this rather disappointing conclusion, it was still felt that a return to the traditional questionnaire format might remove all opportunities for open-ended thinking. Open elements were therefore included within a questionnaire, rather than as a supplementary feature, as originally intended.

A draft questionnaire which incorporated a considerable degree of discussion and open-ended answers was therefore constructed. It was decided that, unlike Schlötterer (1996), specific words for normally outmoded net and, in particular, line, fishing would not be concentrated upon, primarily because these would almost inevitably foreground the old in relation to the young and, quite regularly, men over women (although gender- and age-specific questions were eventually attempted in the final questionnaire). But fishing technology could not be ignored entirely, given that it was once central to the way of life and identity of the communities. The same was true for fish. Coastal animal life was to be given some importance, however, largely because, whether an informant was intimately connected to the fishing trade or not, he or she would come into contact with these animals on a daily basis. Weather lexis was included for the same reasons.

The plan had been to include a small section of questions (perhaps five out of fifty) where the words sought were local to that particular place and where often there was no evidence for a similar word or words being used in any other of the focal communities. For a variety of reasons, this intention was abandoned. In the first instance, while the way in which the questionnaire was to be constructed (and also the material investigated) almost inevitably meant that quantitative analysis could not be applied to the evidence supplied, the 'local section' did nonetheless mean that there would be a section of the questionnaire which could not be compared between places. Since it was very likely that there would be considerable local variation in relation to the other, non-local, questions (particularly, perhaps, the open-ended ones), the questionnaire came to be identical wherever it was applied.

The pilot questionnaire was finalised by the beginning of July 2010, and was tested by Lisa Bonnici in Peterhead that summer. It was intended to be as varied an experience for informants as possible, moving from topic to topic throughout the document and each informant's potential experience (although often one question would have a follow-up question on the same or similar topic). Practically all of the topics were related to the informants' experience as coastal inhabitants whose heritage at least was connected to fishing; this final point was intended to encourage the elicitation of material not shared by their landward neighbours. The one partial exception to this mix was the open-ended questions which began and completed the survey. These were designed both to attract the informant's notice towards lexical use and meaning and also to present a fairly unstressful first couple of questions (since nearly everyone would have views on how language has changed over a brief period) and to help him or her relax at the end.

The questions did not require the same completion tasks, in an attempt to avoid monotony. Some questions were open-ended (**O**), seeking a range of words about a particular topic. These were the descendants of the planned mind-maps. A number of these open-ended question sets used a photograph in the elicitation process (**OP**). Other questions were closer to traditional dialectological methodology, with a local word being given and a translation or explanation (normally the latter) being sought (**T**). Some of these, while only giving one word, were looking for a range of answers (**TO**). There was also one which was based upon the discussion of the differences between separate beings or things (**D**). The pilot questionnaire was structured as shown in Table 3.1.

Certain semantic fields seemed unexpectedly to lend themselves to particular elicitation formats. This was particularly true for fishing trade words, where word-for-word translations appeared easiest in assessing knowledge of specific lexical items and semantic fields. Apart from the oldest fishing technology, which goes back centuries if not millennia, most trade items have been introduced in the last two centuries. Once technological advance has become embedded, it is very unlikely that much lexical or terminological variation will be felt necessary until the next set of technological innovations produces it. Although terms for a particular appliance or design inevitably vary along the coast, the English word rarely does, so that, for almost all words and phrases of this type, a word-for-word equivalence is possible. Despite this, however,

Table 3.1 Breakdown of pilot questions by subject

Birds	4OP, 10OP, 11O(P), 15OP
Culture and heritage	25T, 28O
Fish	19OP, 21T, 22(T)O, 23O
Fishing trade	3T, 5T, 6T, 8T, 13T, 14T, 18T, 24T, 27D
Not coastal-specific	1O, 2O, 29O
The sea	26T
Seaweed	9TO
Shellfish	7TO, 12T
Weather	16O, 17T, 20T(**multiple choice**)

some attempts were made to vary this method. Question 27 ('What is the difference between *gartlins* (great lines) and *smaw lines* (small lines)?'), attempted to elicit a more open-ended discussion through comparison. It should be noted that those designing the questionnaire were aware that many of these items would have a male bias. For this reason Question 6 ('How was the *farlan/faurlan/foreland* used?') was added, since the place in question was where open-air gutting of herring took place, an employment associated almost entirely with female labour.

While discussion of other elements of fishing and coastal life could also produce translation-type tasks – particularly, perhaps, with the names of fish, the focus of the communities' livelihood at least until recently – open-ended elicitation was much more possible, particularly with the use of photographs. An example of a question which lies between the translation type and the open-ended elicitation type of question is Question 19, associated with a particularly arresting picture of a monkfish. 'In English, this fish is known as a monkfish. Do you know any other names for it? (By all means give more than one.)' On this occasion the translation is not Scots to English but rather English to Scots. This might encourage a more open-ended elicitation because of the lack of standardisation in Scots and the divergence in terms for this fish in dialects across relatively small amounts of space, it was postulated.

3.8 Pilot study

Thirteen participants were recruited. The distribution by age and gender is given in Table 3.2. Eleven participants described themselves as 'from Peterhead' while two had worked in Peterhead for thirty years, but lived inland, in Mintlaw. Additionally, three participants, aged 23, 52 and 62, had lived away from Peterhead for eight, sixteen and thirty years, respectively. Three are retired fishers – all three of the men in the oldest age group. The remainder are non-fishers. All participants (except one) were connected to the fishing industry in some way.

Although no question remained without any answers, it quickly

Table 3.2 Stratified sample of participant demographics by age and sex

Age	Male	Female	
20–39	1	1	
40–59	2	3	
60+	3	3	
total N	6	7	13

became apparent that some topics were so patchily known – often by older males – that nothing could be learned about the speech of younger informants from them. After consultation, it was decided to drop nine questions from the final draft of the questionnaire.

Understandably, perhaps, the questions least favoured by the participants were those concerned with fishing, partly perhaps due to the translation method discussed above, but more likely because, even in Peterhead, the fishing business has changed so markedly in the last thirty to fifty years, both in technology and often what is fished, that the items employed and lexis used for them have changed considerably.

Breaking down this category, it quickly became apparent that words related to the fishing industry – particularly if expressed as translation tasks – had not always produced as fruitful a response. Thus Question 5, 'How would you feel if you had landed a *goshens*?', was designed to elicit a response related to a catch of considerable size and good fortune. Eleven out of thirteen of the informants had never heard of this term and were unable to generate its meaning. One male participant suggested the term might mean 'sullen goose' (possibly *solan goose*). Another male participant suggested that it meant 'pillars into the entry of a house; an architectural pillar very much in the Roman style', but then went on to say 'it's nae a word I've heard of.' A third male suggested it referred to waves on the beach. Two other participants guessed the meaning of the term, but were unable to confirm they had heard it previously. Both these participants were in their twenties, and deduced the meaning from its syntactic and pragmatic positioning on the questionnaire. It can therefore be deduced that this term is not present in the lexicon of Peterhead residents today.

Other questions met the same lack of knowledge. Question 12 ('What animal lived on a *scaup*/*scaap*?') was designed to trigger 'mussels' or similar shellfish, used for baiting lines. Only three informants knew the word. Two were retired fishermen (although interestingly another slightly younger retired fisherman was unfamiliar with this term). The other informant who recognised the word gave a less precise definition of the word, stating that it was 'where the bait was kept', suggesting that he did not have first-hand experience of harvesting the mussel beds. The word therefore appears practically moribund. As we will see with a range of words connected to line fishing, even the oldest informants, even if they were connected with the fishing industry throughout their working lives, only barely remember much of the lexis associated with that particular specialisation.

Question 13 ('What was a *halfdalesman*?') appeared at surface not much more successful. Eleven out of thirteen participants had never heard the term. Again, one participant did not know this term but her husband, a middle-aged fisher who was not interviewed, did. Two out of the thirteen participants, both retired fishermen, had heard of the term but would not themselves use it. After giving the definition of the term to participants or after they identified their knowledge of the term, four participants suggested that the term they would use would be *half share*. This term, common to the knowledge and experience of fishermen of all ages who were questioned, referred to the half wage an apprentice received and not to the apprentice himself, one informant mentioning that the half share wage lasted a period of six months. The meaning 'being a fisher with no gear, hired on a day-to-day basis' was not given by any participants, although one additional set of participants gave the term *tenth man* for the meaning given to them of 'a fisher with no gear', which would be used in Fraserburgh. One participant said that when a person goes out looking for a day of work, they'd be going *chancin*.

Not all informants connected the term with fishing, however. One participant guessed it might have an agricultural reference, mentioning Clydesdale horses. It is possible that the spelling on the questionnaire had an effect on the results here. One participant, towards the end of the pilot study, mentioned that the term would make more sense if it were spelled <halfdealsman>. Alternatively, it is possible that this term was never current in Peterhead.

An equally unsuccessful question was 18 ('What was a *snood* (*snuid*, *sneed*)?'), in reference to a central part of the mechanism whereby hooks were connected to lines. Six out of thirteen participants had never heard this term or any of its variants. Three female participants recognised the term but (correctly, although a different word) as a type of hood combined with a scarf or a tabard, associated in recent decades in the main with the early 1980s pop star Nik Kershaw. One person said it sounded like the brand name for those 'blankets with a hood and sleeves'. Interestingly, one middle-aged man claimed that the term also signified a type of hood worn by fishers, 'a polo neck jumper without the jumper'. This kind of *snood* did indeed enjoy something of a second heyday in the early 2010s.

There was, however, some residual knowledge of the term in its fishing sense. Four participants were familiar with the 'hook attachment' meaning of *snood*. Of these all were men and three were retired fishers. Moreover, at the Royal Fisherman's Mission, both *snood* and *sneed* were acceptable. One male informant went on to explain the exact number of hooks that attached to a long line versus a small line; another showed the hooks which would be attached to a *sneed* and drew a picture of one. Beyond this, one of the participants' husbands claimed to know the term, and defined it both as 'the length of the small lines' and 'what you tied the hook onto on a small line', demonstrating either a degree of extension in meaning not previously recorded or some confusion. Another participant's grandfather knew the meaning of the term: 'hook attachment for a main line'. She went on to comment, 'He's the one to know all the fishy type of things.'

It must be accepted, therefore, that this technical term was not well known in the community with the exception of retired fishers whose knowledge is the result of regular use of *snoods* in their occupation. As an occupational and technical term, we have no reason to expect non-fishers to know this term. As this study involves fishers and non-fishers alike, terms which we would expect non-fishers to know as well have to be given some prominence, so as not to discourage participants when they encounter dialect words unknown to them, but also to make the study relevant to their lives. On the other hand, it seems unlikely that we can say much about lexical attrition with terms like this, since we have no evidence that non-fishers would have known this or many other technical terms at an earlier period in history, although it would have to be recognised that women, the elderly and often children within the community did help clean and bait lines, which must have implied a working knowledge of how lines were assembled. It is possible, of course, that the almost complete replacement of line fishing by the use of nets in the post-war period has made these terms particularly obscure.

Slight variations on the translation method, such as Question 27 ('What *was* the difference between *gartlins* (great lines) and *smaw lines* (small lines)?'), were not always effective for elicitation either. Six participants were able to differentiate between the meanings of *great lines* and *smaw lines*. Three of these six participants were former fishers; fishers also provided the most descriptive definitions of these terms including that a great line with six strings contained 112 hooks, while one with eight strings had 124 hooks, and that great lines stretched for twelve to fifteen miles. The pronunciation *gartlin* was not recognized by any Peterhead participants. Two participants only knew the meaning of *smaw lines*, and deduced the meaning of *great lines*. One participant, who did not know the meaning of these terms, asked her husband what these terms meant. He suggested that *great lines* are used for halibut fishing in Iceland and the Faeroes while *smaw lines* are used in 'our shores' in Peterhead.

Interestingly, the main distinction made by participants between *great* and *smaw lines* was in reference to where the fishing took place. *Great lines* were used in deep and often distant waters while *smaw lines* were used for inshore fishing. The *Fisherspeak* corpus appears generally to suggest a technological distinction in terms of length of line and number of hooks (although it is perfectly true that these technological differences meant that they were used for different purposes, in different places, often for different fish).

Although quite a large number of informants knew the terms, and most of these could make a fair attempt at translation, there is the suspicion with at least some of them that the reason they were able to do this was because the terms are transparent to some degree to all speakers of Scots (and English). Moreover, knowledge of these terms, as with other line-based questions, appeared to be largely confined to older men who had been actively involved in the fishing trade at some point in their lives.

Question 20 ('If weather is said to be *attery*, is it: (a) good? (b) bad? (c) indifferent?') was perhaps the least successful of the questions in the pilot. Nine participants had never heard the term before, while four participants answered that this term meant 'indifferent'. Two of these four participants guessed this answer from the context. Interestingly, one participant said that *attery* was a country word. None identified the meaning of this term as 'bitter; stormy', as found in the corpus. It seems likely that it has slipped from use (or, alternatively, it was never used in a fishing context).

Question 15 was of a strikingly different type. It was not involved specifically with the fishing trade; nor was it a translation exercise; instead, it represented an open-ended photograph-based question which we would expect to be quite fruitful in terms of elicitation. It consisted of a photograph of an oystercatcher (a common coastal bird in eastern Scotland), along with the question 'What names do you know for this bird?' Six out of thirteen participants gave the term *oystercatcher* for this bird. Only one participant gave both *oystercatcher* and an additional term – *winkle picker*. Four out of thirteen other participants did not come up with *oystercatcher* but generated the following alternative names: *wader, mussel coke, magpie, and mussel picker*.

Women came up with the terms *wader* and *magpie*. The woman who said *magpie* might have been mistaken; she moved away from Peterhead after finishing school and recently returned after thirty years. Magpies and oyster catchers share a black and white colouring, even if their body proportions are rather different. As for the woman who gave *wader*, it is unclear if this more general term is for her a generic term for a class of birds, or if she uses it only to refer to oystercatchers. The former interpretation seems more convincing, however. She does not appear to know the term *oystercatcher*.

Retired fishermen came up with the terms *mussel coke, mussel picker*, and *winkle picker*. Only *mussel picker* is currently in the corpus. This former fisherman also asserted that the term wasn't the 'proper term', but rather was one he used. One fisher was quick to state that oystercatchers don't actually only eat oysters; rather they eat whatever is at the water's edge.

Some participants took some time before being able to generate a term for this bird. A few gave alternative terms which they later concluded were not correct. These comprised *tyuchit* (*teuchat*), *snipe* and *herring birds*. Additionally, one participant who generated *oystercatcher* asked a fisher friend for help with the task, and this fisher offered *tystee*.

Three out of thirteen participants did not come up with a term for this bird. Of these, one specifically said she was 'terrible with bird names'. A second person said that she knew the bird, but did not have a name for it. Perhaps in line with the use of *wader* above, all three participants who were unable to come up with a term were female. Nevertheless, another participant, a young man, only knew the word from a poem about oystercatchers.

From this evidence it does appear that the photograph of this bird did not generate too many local terms, and quite a few people struggled (in other words, took a while) to come up with a term at all. Only older fishers were able to generate local terms, signifying both that local words for this bird may now be obsolete. As this bird is commonly seen on the seashore and many participants expressed the opinion that youths do not spend anywhere as much time outdoors as used to be the case, perhaps this bird is less visible and simply less discussed by young people, which could explain why local terms do not appear to have survived. Since the most common elicited response to the question was the use of the Standard English form, it did not seem sensible to retain the question in the revised questionnaire.

Despite the challenges revealed by the pilot study in eliciting lexical knowledge, most of the questions of the original questionnaire were retained in the final version, albeit sometimes with alterations to wording and layout. Some of these were chosen, as will be explained below, even though quite a number of informants did not know the words. The distribution of this knowledge was different, however, from those questions considered to be wholly unsuccessful.

Question 3, for instance, dealing with the meaning of *arles*, the 'honour money' paid to workers – in particular in this context, *gutter lasses/quines* – demonstrated that eight out of the thirteen participants did not know the word. Of those, both of the youngest informants did not know the term; the same was true of two 69-year-olds – male and female. One person, who claimed she had heard of the word but couldn't define it, said she only knew of it because of her research as a curatorial assistant in the Arbuthnot Museum. Another person who worked at the museum *did* know the meaning of the word. She was the only person under 60 years of age to be able to do this. We can say, therefore, that the word has dropped from use primarily because the 'honour money' tradition has been quiescent for at least two working generations. Knowledge of the term, whether with knowledge of its meaning or not, does appear to continue among younger people if they are connected to the heritage industry, suggesting, perhaps, an attenuated survival of terms in a performative, heritage, context.

Interestingly, one informant gave an 'incorrect' definition of the word as a device in a herring drifter for washing herring. When asked if he ever heard of *arles* with the meaning in the Fisher Speak corpus, i.e., 'money a herring quine was paid in advance', he said 'no, because they were always paid "in the rears"'. Whether this represents a transfer in meaning or a separate word otherwise unrecorded is difficult to say from this one example.

Question 4 consisted of a photograph of a cormorant and the wording, 'What do you call this bird? Please give more than one name, if you wish.' Knowledge of words for 'cormorant' was a little patchy in the Pilot Survey, with some informants not even knowing *any* name for the bird, others knowing its English name, some knowing *scrath*, while variants of the word *duck* were also offered. One informant also called the bird a *great northern diver*. As will be discussed in Chapter 4, evidence of this type demonstrates the cognitive associations that particular words and particular birds can have for informants.

Question 6, which asks 'How was the *farlan/faurlan/foreland* used?', a mainstream translation elicitation question, produced a similar pattern of in-depth knowledge standing side by side with lack of knowledge of the word and its contexts. Eight informants defined the term, relating to the tubs used by herring gutters to keep the gutted fish, in agreement with our corpus, with one participant suggesting the spelling *farlin*. Some definitions were much less descriptive than others; for instance, while most participants mentioned women gutting herring when discussing *farlan*, one participant simply defined the *farlan* as 'a box for herring'. One participant described the *farlan* as a '*table* where women gut the fish' as opposed to a trough or box, suggesting a practice not actually seen by that participant. Even further away from the original meaning was that given by one informant, who claimed that the *farlan* was located between the high water and the splash zone and was used in the drying of fish. A fisher would put down a bed of seaweed, arrange the fish in stacks of four feet square layered with salt, and dry the fish in the *farlan*. Interestingly, the *place* for the activity suggested has some accuracy. There are some fishing historians who would link it to the Foreland in Lerwick, a low-lying, until the twentieth century uninhabited, piece of land beside the beach north of the main settlement. That this was associated with fish processing – albeit of the wrong type – may also be connected to the original meaning, although the vividness of the new definition has to be recognised.

Of the participants who knew the term, all were in the older or middle-age groups. Both women from the museum knew the terms, as well as all the retired fishers. Those who did not know the terms include the two young participants and two people who were not fishers themselves. Obviously younger people did not take part in, or even remember, the 'boom time' of the herring fishery. Given that this word is gender sensitive – since women rather than men were traditionally involved in herring gutting – it may be significant that older women as well as men could define the term. The fact that the women associated with the museum knew the word might be connected to this gender-specific tendency, although, again, the fact that they are employed in the heritage industry would at least encourage this knowledge.

More generally known was *buckie*, as in Question 7 ('What is a *buckie*? Are there specific types?'), a blend of translation exercise and open-ended question. Eleven out of the thirteen informants recognised its connection to shellfish. Six identified it as 'whelk' or 'winkle', with the latter described by one participant as a 'fancier' term for whelk. One informant specifically said that while she knows the term, she herself would merely use *whelk*. Unfortunately, this type of information was not captured for other participants. Two other participants gave semantically related definitions, of 'limpet; mussel' and 'shellfish; cockle'. Two other informants simply defined *buckie* as 'shell'. Some commentators recounted a narrative of boiling whelks in a tin can on the beach, using sea water, and using hairgrips as winkle pickers. There is every reason to suspect that similar stories would be told along the Scottish coast.

Two participants did not know the word with the expected meaning. One younger participant, in attempting to carry out his task of 'translating' the word, mentioned both Buckie, a fishing port near the mouth of the Spey on the Moray Firth, and interpreted the word as a diminutive form of the 'tonic wine' Buckfast, much drunk by young people and considered by some to be a major social problem.

Similar results were derived from Question 9, 'What is *waur/waar/ware*? Do you know any other names for it?' Eight participants knew that *ware* signified seaweed, while the remaining five were not familiar with this word. Two of those unfamiliar with the term were young; the rest were middle-aged. Interestingly, one informant had definitely heard the term used in a phrase such as '*ware* washing up on the beach' but misinterpreted its meaning, thinking it signified 'waves or wave foam'; in that sense, it might be argued that the word was on the very edge of the participant's passive lexical knowledge. Strikingly, even knowledge of the word's meaning did not signify that a person used the word. A few participants commented that while they knew the meaning of the term, they themselves would simply use *seaweed*.

On the other hand, use of the word could be stimulated by personal experience. One participant said that this is a term which she herself still uses, because her sister lives in an area where at low tide on a warm day, the *ware* emits an unpleasant smell; another participant mentioned how *ware* is malodorous in the summertime. Peterhead also has a street named Ware Road, which a small number of informants associated with seaweed and one with the use of seaweed as fertiliser on the fields around the town. This bank of knowledge must nonetheless be qualified by the fact that one informant thought the question was about the Scots equivalent to English *where*, producing the local *far* as an equivalent.

As we will see in Chapter 4, there were a number of older informants who had a fair knowledge not only of seaweed terms but also in which parts of Scotland particular terms were used.

We can therefore see that even an item of flora so visible (and odiferous) in a seaside setting may not trigger the continued use of the local terms. Unlike in relation to a seagull, perhaps, seaweed's lack of animation might not make it come to the front of someone's mind unless they were actively involved in travelling over the sea where, near shore, seaweed *does* appear animated. As with a number of words of this type, while there is an apparent cline between knowledge and lack of knowledge, the level of knowledge of a word, its variants and words for similar plants or animals among older participants is quickly replaced by an at best passive knowledge of the word among younger participants. This makes the question an interesting one to ask, particularly if different knowledge patterns were found in other ports along the coast.

On occasion, however, almost the whole sample knew what a word meant and could even make distinctions between different *types* of that particular being or thing. Questions 21 'What is a *fleuk/fluke*?' and 22 'Are there different kinds of *fleuks/flukes*? What are their names?' worked rather well in producing answers, many of which showed considerable thought and engagement in the subject. For instance, a number of participants proceeded to name 'types' of fish which would fit into this category, many times coming around to 'flat fish' at some point in their response, but not always.

In terms of which fish a *fleuk/fluke* was, seven informants defined it as a 'flat fish', either through the method of generating types of flukes discussed above or by merely saying 'flat fish'. On the other hand, two people (one from the youngest age group) identified a single fish as a *fluke*. When considered through the prism of the corpus, this is not surprising. In general *fleuk/fluke* is a generic term for flat fish. It can occasionally refer to single fish, however, although the tendency seems to be to qualify with a premodifier, so that *tobacco fluke* is reported in some parts of Scotland as the name for lemon sole. Moreover, disagreement over which specific fish is meant by the word may well illustrate the breakdown of the necessity for having different words for different types of fish when the fishing industry is contracting and employing fewer people.

Question 23 represented a series of multiple choice questions on the names used for a variety of common fish during their life cycles; in particular, perhaps, marking the boundary between sexually immature and mature fish, a division with important repercussions for the longevity of the fishing industry. In relation to young herring, the following terms were generated for a young herring: *sprat, mattie/madgie, job, britt, maizy, grillin* and *mecsked/mixed*. *Sprat* was given by two participants; *madgie* by three participants, and *maizy* by two participants. The remaining terms were given once.

The search for terms for the young of other species was rather less fruitful. With the haddock, ten out of thirteen informants were unable to produce any terms. One participant produced *chipper* (from the chip shop) and *speldin*. Another gave us *smaw haddock*. A third provided a list of terms going from youngest to oldest: *baby haddock, smaw, big smaw* and *shats*. None of these terms shows up in the corpus with the exception of *speldin*, which is defined differently as 'salted and dried herring'. One person described *speldin* as a delicacy. A few more people were able to produce terms for younger salmon. Four participants generated *grilse*, two generated *smolt*. One person produced *parr* while another offered *clear fish*. One participant offered that *smolt* was/were smaller than *grilse*. It is possible that the ongoing trade in salmon as a high prestige product encourages the maintenance of specific terms for younger age groups. The fact that these are not widely known (but generally understood by a concentrated grouping) may well be connected to the specialisation which has affected the fishing trade in the last fifty years.

Informants were also asked for terms for the young of other species. Only three produced any terms. All three participants generated *codling*, and one participant each named *warry codling, fry* and *pout*. There may well be methodological reasons why some parts of this complex question were not fully answered: there was a larger than normal amount of text necessary to elicit the terms that may have been off-putting and certainly would have been difficult for all but the most committed reader to connect with. A more pictorial response might allow informants to access the purpose of the exercise more readily, as a means of protecting the fabrics involved. Having said that, however, the exercise is still worth repeating since, again, it appears to demonstrate evidence of once widely known lexis now confined to a relatively small-scale group, often male and older.

Question 24, 'What were you doing when you were *barkin?*', refers to a now obsolete, but once prevalent to the point of near-universality, practice of treating sails, ropes, garments and, in particular, nets, with a chemical derived from the barks of a range of largely tropical trees. Eight participants knew the term and what it referred to. Of these, three were retired fishers and two curatorial assistants at the Arbuthnot fishing/whaling museum. Interestingly, one participant knew only that *barkin* was 'something they'd do with nets', demonstrating a bleaching of the original meaning. A similar effect can be seen in the response of another participant. She did not know that *barkin* referred to 'nets'; rather she was only familiar with *barkin ganjeys*, the treated Guernsey jumpers often used by fishermen until the advent of the nylon cagoule. Both probably represent the last memories of a word which – for these informants in any event – had rarely if ever been used.

The findings for these 'borderline' questions in the pilot study informed what was expected from the similar questions put forward for the main survey, as we will see in the following section and in Chapter 4.

3.9 The main survey questionnaire

The discussion above focused on some problematic questions in the pilot study questionnaire; there is rather less to say about the more successful elements of the pilot study at present. Salient points will be dealt with in the following chapter, since the questions, with a degree of rewriting, were re-used in the main study, and appropriate commentary from the Peterhead pilot study has been included in that discussion.[2] In choosing questions to use in the main study it became apparent that some of these questions were more successful than others in triggering informed commentary. For reasons which were not entirely obvious, for instance, questions about seagulls triggered more interest and response than did the question on cormorants, despite both birds being regular visitors to Peterhead. Words concerned with warmth triggered fewer responses than did those concerned with wet and cold. Rather more strikingly, however, words concerned with the fishing trade – whether perceived as male or female – were not richly attested among younger people in ways that words about weather were. It is not difficult to find reasons for this, of course, and it will naturally be discussed in the next chapter (where some interesting countercurrents will be found in the broader survey). But in revising the questionnaire for the main study, it had to be accepted that quantification of responses, while having meaning, was not in itself the centre: often depth was as important.

Table 3.3 indicates the types of questions used and topics involved in the survey. The main survey questionnaire can be found at http://fisherspeak.net. Questions which were not necessarily fishing-specific were placed at both the beginning and end of the pilot questionnaire. In the final version, however, while the initial questions remained, the question about words falling into disuse was moved somewhat earlier, largely to encourage speakers to consider lexical attrition while at the same time allowing them some relaxation before returning to the fishing-based questions. The tradition of a 'loosening' of connection to the fishing continues, however, with the last group of questions being related to the weather, a particular concern of the fishing community, of course, but one shared with everyone else to some extent.

To replace questions abandoned because they did not produce much in the way of response, the corpus was employed to find words and semantic fields similar to those no longer being used, in the hope, based upon usage patterns and distribution, that informants would be more likely to produce words and discussion. While a number of fishing-trade-specific terms were maintained, these were fewer in number and distributed widely around the questionnaire. In general, the questionnaire was made more visually attractive and user-friendly.

The questionnaire was intended both to prompt participants to speak

Table 3.3 Breakdown of main survey questions by subject

Birds	4OP, 5O(P), 14OP,
Culture and heritage	12T (but with following discussion), 19O, 26O, 27O, 28O
Fish	9OP, 15aT, 15bTO, 16O
Fishing trade	13T, 17T, 18T, 20T, 21T, 23O,
Not coastal specific	1O, 2O, 22O
The Sea	8T, 24O
Seaweed	10TO
Sealife	25TP
Shellfish	6T, 7TO
Weather	3O, 11O, 29O

about the questions in discussion with the fieldworkers and, on occasion, with other participants, and also to be a document on which they could jot down answers and fill in gaps. The use of photographs as prompts for some questions was one way of achieving this. Other questions, such as 11 on rain and 16 on stages of fish maturity, included empty grids or tables in order to encourage participants to think about an ordered set of answers for gradable concepts. While the presentation of empty boxes to fill in could potentially put off some participants, being reminiscent of a test or of school work, we think that the final questionnaire, in the context of its use during a conversational interview, succeeded in prompting discussion and generating structured answers. This will be demonstrated in Chapter 4.

4 Analysis of the data

4.1 Introduction

As Chapter 3 in particular demonstrated, capturing the lexical use and choice of any community is not straightforward. Given the historically discrete nature of the communities researched, however, it was postulated that elements of the local lexis would in the past have been locally distinctive. Parts of this difference would have been related to the fishing industry and its ancillary trades. Others, however, were related to the local flora and fauna and elements of how the local community expresses its identity linguistically, both internally and in relation to its neighbours. As discussed in Chapter 3, attempts to access these lexical (and semantic) fields were channelled through the use of various (and varied) questionnaire tasks. In the following, therefore, we will discuss the material associated in relation to a number of non-linguistic variables – primarily age and gender. A number of preliminary conclusions will be provided within the analysis, although final discussion will be delayed until Chapter 5.

A particular issue needs to be aired before the analysis begins. The material is qualitative, not quantitative, in nature. Although assumptions are made about lexical knowledge from the evidence provided, no statistical significance can be assumed. Nevertheless, in the relatively small communities covered, it is certainly reasonable to assume that group tendencies are observable along with individual choice. At times, the evidence is so rich that it is impossible to avoid reaching guarded conclusions on use. As Chapter 5 will demonstrate, general tendencies are observable across the communities, albeit with different levels of knowledge in different places. Interestingly, most of these distinctions are predictable.

In the following, therefore, the material collected through the questionnaire has been treated largely thematically, generally moving from fishing-centred vocabulary to lexis shared by the whole community, thus making sure that people from the fishing community by descent or adoption who do not have any immediate connection to the trade will still feel themselves treated as experts. Vocabulary specifically associated with female labour will be occasionally highlighted. In general, a north to south discussion of the evidence is provided, with the evidence for Peterhead being discussed first because of its status as the only fully functioning fishing port treated. On occasion this order is transgressed, largely because a clearer narrative and analytical path is made possible through the change. This change in order will not be specifically discussed unless reasons for the alternation are not self-explanatory.

4.2 Analysis

4.2.1 Fish names, species and maturity level

In this section, three basic topics are covered. The first involves the discussion of which type of fish a *fluke* (otherwise *fleuk*) is and whether informants could give more detail about types of *fluke*, thus testing knowledge of the pre-existent terms relating to the native fish typological systems. The second continues this sense of judging the level to which small-scale (but initially vital) lexical distinctions are maintained, dealing with different words for commonly caught fish, according to level of maturity (or size: the two typologies are not always the same). After this, terms for *monkfish* (otherwise known as *anglerfish*) were elicited, because the corpus suggests that quite local terms for this fish existed, but its economic importance only grew significantly in the relatively recent past. The order as described can therefore be seen as one moving from the potential elicitation of a wide range of terms to one where concentration on one term (or a small range of terms) is required, but where the words involved may be iconic for the community.

4.2.1.1 Fluke/fleuk

Flat fish have long been a staple part of the Scottish fishing trade. Although halibut, sole and flounder have perhaps dominated economically, other fish of this type have regularly been landed and traded profitably. Given that flat fish are similar to each other in looks but attract different prices according to species, it is inevitable that different names should have been found for each fish type; because of their similarities, however, it is also inevitable that some of these names should be variants of each other rather than entirely discrete.

With this in mind, informants were asked to define what a *fluke* (also spelled *fleuk*) is. According to the Corpus, *fluke*'s primary association is with the flounder, in many ways the archetypal North Sea flat fish. The *Glossary* comments, however, that '[f]luke, or fleuk, is also used as a general term for most other flatfish eg "a bag fu' o' flukes". More properly, the type of fluke is specified, eg "Tobacco fluke, silver fluke etc."' The corpus demonstrates that this is indeed the case. As a sample, evidence from the *Glossary* and elsewhere (in particular the *ST*) tells us that *prain fluke* is an Aberdeenshire word for the common dab (although *rough back fluke* is used for the same fish in essentially the same region), a lemon sole is known as a *sole fleuk* in the Moray Firth region, while in Aberdeenshire and Kincardineshire it is known as a *tobacco fluke*. It should be noted that even the flounder is sometimes recorded with pre-modification, as with *beggar fluke*, a phrase used in northern and eastern Scotland to refer to both that fish and the similar plaice (another flat fish much used in cooking, often in similar ways to the flounder).[1] To what extent is this diversity recognised or maintained in our research materials? With this in mind, a supplementary question asked, 'Are there different types of *fleuks/flukes*? What are their local names?'

In Peterhead, just over half the informants recognised that *fleuk* referred to a flat fish. All of these informants were older or in middle age (predominantly the former). A number of other informants, largely middle-aged, although with one younger female, recognised that the word referred to a fish, but could not go any further. A small number of young women associated the word solely with the colloquial English meaning of an unexpected or undeserved stroke of luck.

Informants were asked to give examples of types of *fleuk*. Almost half of the informants did not provide an answer to this question or did not know. There was, however, a sizeable group who demonstrated not only knowledge of the use of *fleuk* with a range of different fishes – in particular lemon sole, plaice and dab – but also of where these fish were to be found. Most of these respondents were older males (just as there were no older males among those who gave no answer to the questions). A somewhat smaller number mentioned the use of *fleuk* for the megrim, flounder and the witch (the last a type of flounder). Two informants (both middle-aged men) also mentioned *fresh water flukes*, one observing that, 'as a bairn' he would have caught *fresh water flukes*, the other that they were found in estuaries, were not good to eat and that animals fed off them.

In conversation with the informants it was apparent that even the oldest participants, who offered several types of *fleuk*, did not recognise the premodifying naming method mentioned above, instead using the Standard English names (or very occasionally other local names) for the fish. To some extent this may be due to the nature of the questionnaire, which focused on translation in the previous question, thus making it likely that Standard English remained the default means of describing fish of this type. But a number of 'good' older participants were quite vehement in their denial of these compound terms. It could just about be argued that Peterhead people never used the *x + fleuk* constructions, since none of the corpus sources states specifically that they were used in that town. The fact that they are apparently not known at all demands reflection, particularly since many informants knew the names of types of bird used at a considerable distance from Peterhead (see below). Is it possible that the premodified *fluke* terms recorded in the national resources (they are less common in the regional and local equivalents) represented the idioms of a small number of speakers rather than that of dialects as a whole? Or is it that the fieldwork for the *Glossary* in particular had encouraged the recording of terms of this type by the initial use of *fluke?*

In terms of which fish a *fleuk/fluke* was, seven participants in the pilot study defined it as a 'flat fish', either through the method of generating types of flukes discussed above or by merely saying 'flat fish'. On the other hand, two people (one from the youngest age group) identified a single fish as a *fluke*. Knowledge of what the word meant was not universal, however. Two people (one of whom was in the youngest age group) did not know what a *fluke* was. One informant said that a *fluke* is a whale's tail. This does indeed appear to be the case, although OED (*s.v.* fluke *n*2) places this meaning as secondary and metaphorical to a range of meanings related to the shape of a large ship's anchor. Interestingly, this word may well be a metaphorical development from the word for a flat fish, due to the shape of the anchor. Peterhead was a whaling town of some standing, of course, but this heyday is decades gone; whaling has been entirely moribund since the 1970s at the very latest. It is likely that the informant knew the term from personal interest rather than from occupational experience.

Similar findings are present for Wick, with a slightly larger proportion making the connection with flat fish than in Peterhead (and a rather smaller part of the population associating it only with 'fish'). Several informants used the diminutive *flukie*, suggesting that the word at least was part of the central community vocabulary if we believe that the use of a diminutive implies regular, perhaps even affectionate, use.[2] Interestingly, however, one younger woman only recognised the word in its flat fish associations after she was prompted, while another younger woman, who associated the word solely with good luck, informed the researcher that she had 'never heard of it to talk about fish'. One young woman claimed that she knew the word primarily from the public art installation on the Black Stairs, where local words were written.[3] Knowledge could be said to be somewhat 'frayed' among younger people.

The same is true with the 'types of fleuk' question. No one produced any of the *x* + *fleuk* type names, although many older men and women and a few middle-aged people recognised a range of different flat fish, including dab (and *sma dab*), lemon sole, meagrim, plaice, skate and witch. One older male was particularly informative, pointing out there were 'no different types of flukes', as the question suggested, but that he distinguished between flukes and plaice, turbot and halibut, which are bigger flat fish, so 'a fluke is particularly a flounder, found inshore'.

In Lossiemouth the general 'flat fish' interpretation prevailed among older and middle-aged women, although some informants also identified a number of fishes – *dover sole, lemon sole, flounder, plaice, witch, meagrim* and so on – as forming part of this set. An interesting dispute within the community concerns over how dabs were to be classified. Some older male informants claimed that dabs were *sadies* or *satties* (although one older male informant was not sure whether the two terms were mutually exclusive).[4] On the other hand a number of apparently well-informed people claimed an immediate connection between *dab* and *fleuk*. According to the corpus, *sattie* is used for the dab in Aberdeenshire and Banffshire (in the *ST*); it is given in the *LG*. From the way its use is analysed by Lossiemouth people, it would be easily assumed that it is a particularly localised word. As with all other settlements, no premodified names were elicited (although occasionally other forms were found, as in *megs* for *meagrims*, given by one middle-aged male), with the exception, as with other settlements, of *freshwater fleuks*, which three middle-aged men classified as *sewerage fleuks*, since they were found around the sewage pipes.[5] All of this implies considerable knowledge of, or interest in, fish species and the terms used for them. It should be noted, however, that practically none of the younger inhabitants gave the local meaning of *fleuk*, instead interpreting the word in relation to Standard English *fluke* 'stroke of luck', although some recognised a flat fish association when prompted. One young female informant, however, could only produce 'fish'.

Similar findings were reported from Anstruther and Eyemouth, with lower levels of knowledge than the preceding, particularly perhaps in Eyemouth. Most older and middle-aged informants knew the word *fleuk*, with many associating it with flat fish (although some informants – including older people – only recognised that it referred to undifferentiated fish). Many older informants could give the names of different kinds of flat fish, although these were primarily referred to by their Standard English names (one older woman in Anstruther did volunteer that *flukies* referred to small flounders).

We can therefore say that *fleuk* continues to be known as a word for flat fish among quite a large number of people in these communities; in particular, perhaps, in the northerly ports. What is striking is that, even in these settlements, many younger people either do not know the word at all or know it only as a word for 'fish'. The word's existence as part of the active local lexicon is apparently threatened. Similar patterns may explain the lack of knowledge or use of derivative *fleuk* forms. But such forms may never have been as common as the independent names for particular fish. A number of the sources for terms in the corpus were probably designed to be comprehensive rather than representative. But the fact that *none* of the informants either produced the forms or appeared to know them takes the argument much further. If this were the case for only one community it might be argued that forms of this type had never been found there; the fact that the absence appears universal invites further thought. There is a strong possibility that these forms were highly peripheral in all communities even when fishing was the primary employer.

4.2.1.2 Active knowledge: fish maturity and size

With the *fleuk* questions, it was assumed that someone living in a fishing community, but not actively involved in the fishing industry, would have known some discrete terms for a common class of fish. In order to counteract this likelihood, a series of questions were posed on names for fish at various stages of their life cycle (triggered by cartoon-like drawings of different sizes of fish), a terminology which, while important to the trade, was not vital to those employed elsewhere, no matter how closely connected to fishing. Members of the community with an 'ancillary' connection to the fishing might have been, at most, concerned with the size of particular fish and therefore have far fewer specific words and phrases for this purpose.

According to the corpus, not all communities present the same level of lexical diversity; nor do they always have the same number of terms for all fish. But the tendency to differentiate according to size and/or sexual maturity is present at the very least with fish which were (and sometimes are) regularly landed, such as herring, haddock, cod and salmon. It was therefore assumed that terms dealing with these economically central fish would be likely to survive in communities. With fish such as mackerel or ling, a small number of terms are reported solely in the

Glossary, a resource which provides as wide a range of terms as possible rather than primarily reporting regular use.

In Peterhead, a majority of informants were unaware of *any* terms for levels of maturity for any fish. A large minority, made up mainly of older people but also including some middle-aged informants, produced quite a few words and phrases related to the topic, including for fish which were not specifically named in the questionnaire (although these, such as the word *geet* for smaller and *black jacks* for larger *podlies*,[6] were generally produced only by a small number of older people). With the fish which were specifically mentioned – haddock, herring and salmon[7] – more variants were elicited. The extent to which these words and phrases bore similarities to the material in the corpus was patchy, however.

For a small haddock, the corpus records a limited number of words. The *Glossary* defines *calfies* as the 'smallest marketable fish', recorded in Aberdeenshire. The *ST* gives *pontie* as a 'small haddock', found throughout Scotland. In our Peterhead fieldwork, the words *sma*, *podlie*, *chipper* and *metro* were given by one informant each. The last term, a middle-aged male stated, had only started being used recently, particularly in the market. As far as can be told, no further information – local or national – can be found on this term. For medium haddock, two middle-aged men gave *seed* and *big sma*. For the largest haddock, *jumbo* was given by four participants, while one older man suggested that *big* was the term used for haddocks one stage smaller than *jumbo*. This evidence is in contrast to the corpus, where *harrowster* is a general Scottish term for 'a spawned haddock', according to the *ST*. The *Glossary* also has *cameral* for 'recently spent fish', which it places in the Aberdeenshire and Moray Firth regions.

A number of the terms recorded – *jumbo*, *seed* and *chipper* (along with *rounder* and *selected*, otherwise not recorded) – were associated by two informants with stages in the gutting process, so that *rounder* was a fish which had not as yet been recorded, while *chipper*, unsurprisingly, was intended for the chip shop. It is striking, in fact, how the sizing of fish in the gutting process, rather than their maturity (in other words, onshore rather than offshore) was foregrounded, a point to which we will return.

A somewhat different pattern applies for Wick. Few differentiating terms are found in discussion with *haddock*, for instance, with one middle-aged woman asserting that different terms for different sizes (or ages) of this fish did not exist. In general this appears to be the case. A number of informants from all age groups produced only *haddie* as a generic term for the fish. One older man discussed modification along the lines of *young haddie*, *old haddie* and *big haddie*, however. On the other hand, another older male and two younger women state that *haddie* refers peculiarly to a 'small haddock'. This last point may be encouraged by the use of the archetypal Scottish diminutive *-ie* with the word (although it has to be recognised that in Caithness an alternative pattern using *-ag* or *-ock*, derived in the main from Gaelic, prevails). *Snap*, defined by the *ST* as meaning 'a small cod or haddock', said to be used from Orkney to Ross-shire, was not elicited.

In relation to herring a wider range of terms are recorded in the corpus. For small fish, *sile* or *sill* is given by the *ST* for 'the newly hatched young of fish', in a geographical range which includes all of the centres covered in the *Fisherspeak* project with the exception of Eyemouth. *Mattie* (otherwise *maatie*) is defined as 'a young maiden herring with the roe not fully developed' by the *ST*, and placed in Shetland, the North-East and Angus. The word is also given in two Caithness sources, however, with both the CW and the *New Caithness Book* (Omand 1989) defining it as a 'small firm herring'. The *Glossary* defines the word as 'maiden herring', but gives no sense of where it might be found, suggesting that it was known much more generally than the *ST* suggests. The *Glossary* also records *nun* for 'maiden herring' in Angus and Fife. According to the same resource *shaldoo* means 'young herring' in the Moray Firth region. *Wine drinkers* refer to the same stage in the same region, while *yaulin*, the *Glossary* reports, was used throughout Scotland.

Words exist also for 'maturing herring', such as *filling* (*Glossary*), found throughout Scotland, and *halflin(g)*, given by the *ST* for 'a half-mature herring', placed in Fife and Lothian (the same word is defined by the *Glossary* as 'young herring', and said to be confined to the Moray Firth region; it is worth noting that the word primarily refers to young humans, so its extension may well be ad hoc). 'Mature herring', on the other hand, can be described as *full* (*Glossary*; a common Scottish term). *Maizy*, again given by the *Glossary* as being found throughout Scotland, is defined as 'spawning herring', while a similar geographical spread is given by the *ST* for *matfull*, 'sexually mature herring'.

With herring, the most productive area for discussion of fish terms in Peterhead was undoubtedly related not to the age or size of the fish, but rather in relation to alternative names for the fish itself. Some of these were common terms, such as *silver darlings* (put forward by a young woman) or alternative pronunciations, such as *heerin* (recorded by an older man). One, *madje*, was particularly interesting, however, primarily because, although the middle-aged woman who produced it considered it to be a generic term, she also noted that her mother classified it as a herring 'after it has been spent'. As we saw above, the corpus records a similar form – *mattie* (probably of Dutch origin) – although strikingly this word is connected to 'virgin herring', in other words herring which have not spawned. Interestingly, one older Peterhead male defined *mattie* as a 'small' herring.

Otherwise, the words and phrases elicited for various sizes of fish are not particularly rich. Two older informants – male and female – used *sprat* for small herring; an older woman used *whitebait*, both employing a similar but separate species to describe herring. The descriptive *sma* was the only other term found (from a middle-aged man), although one older male pointed out that a *mattie* was larger than a *sprat*, possibly representing a further level of identification. Only one middle-aged male informant produced a word or phrase for a 'large herring': *bonnie herring*. The medium category was also represented only by one phrase (again from a middle-aged male), the laconic *nae bad*. It has to be recognised that the Peterhead results for this fish represent fairly slim pickings, only partly because Peterhead was slightly less of a herring port than were other ports along the coast. Indeed, with one exception, any words or phrases which were elicited related to the fish on the slab rather than the fish in the net. Interestingly, one older woman could not provide size- or age-distinctive terms for herring, but could distinguish between *saut herrin, fresh herrin* and *kippers*. It might be that, given women's importance in the processing of herring, such an association is altogether predictable.

In a similar question, the participants in the pilot study presented a report on similar (although not identical) use. In relation to young herring, the following terms were generated for a young herring: *sprat, mattie/madgie, job, britt, maizy, grillin* and *mecsked/mixed*. One participant elaborated that *britt* is a term which comes from Canada as a lot of people from Peterhead worked the herring season on Canada's west coast in the 1930s and 1940s (and its salmon season on the east coast). People were paid in golden guineas. Seven participants, however, did not know or offer any terms for a young herring. Herring retains its culinary position, however. Several informants, without prompting, discussed dishes made from herring, including *hairy willies*, a dish of salted herring and boiled potatoes all mixed together with cream and milk; this dish was described as something youngsters today are unlikely to be familiar with, however.

The search for terms for the young of other species was rather less fruitful. With the haddock, ten out of thirteen informants were unable to produce any terms. One participant produced *chipper* (from the chip shop) and *speldin*. Another gave us *smaw haddock*. A third provided a list of terms going from youngest to oldest: *baby haddock, smaw, big smaw* and *shats*. None of these terms shows up in the corpus with the exception of *speldin*, which is defined differently as 'salted and dried herring'. One informant described *speldin* as a delicacy.

Unlike for 'haddock', 'herring' presented a more complex and apparently healthy set of terms in Wick. On these occasions information regularly came from female informants: male information was not dominant. This may tell us something about the gender associations of the herring fishery in distinction to other fisheries. One younger female informant produced *silver darlings* for 'herring'. This phrase is not unknown along the coast, but may have been encouraged in the far north of Scotland because of the local writer Neil M. Gunn's 1941 novel. A nightclub of that name is also one of the few 'trendy' meeting places for young people in Wick.

For younger herring, *madgie herring* was produced by two older men (one of whom used *early* rather than *small*, suggesting a terminology centred on maturity). Another older man used *sild*. Probably a variant of *sill* or *sile*, mentioned in the corpus for the very youngest fish, it is also the principal North Germanic word for 'herring'. The cultural background of north-east Caithness could make this word a survival from the Norn-speaking Middle Ages (or, given Wick's once cosmopolitan nature, a nineteenth- or early twentieth-century Scandinavian borrowing). An older female informant gave *small mattie* for this meaning (a discussion on the meaning of *mattie* within the community will be given below). It may be significant that, in a similar way to that found for Peterhead, one middle-aged woman and one younger man gave terms for 'smaller/younger herring' which derive from the names of other smaller fish – *sprat* and *dabbies* respectively. Moreover, the fact that *sprat* was used by a middle-aged man for 'smaller/younger salmon' suggests that for some informants originally species-specific terms have been generalised through metaphorical extension of names for other species (probably always present, but now becoming normal, something to which we return when discussing bird terminology). At the other end of the 'accuracy continuum' in this context was the mention by an older female informant of *matful*, referring to a herring full of roe (in other words, sexually mature, as defined in the corpus).

There was a less fruitful haul for 'medium herring', perhaps because the features which make a herring large or small, in particular sexual maturity, are bifocal and do not fit the idea of a continuum of features associated with the median. Having said that, an older woman gave *medium mattie*, while an older man gave *half-spent herring* (originally a herring which had laid part, but not all, of its eggs) for the same meaning. A similar lack of discrete terms was present for larger fish, with one older woman giving *large mattie*, while an older male informant gave *spent herring* (he was the informant who produced *half-spent herring*, another older man used the latter for 'large/fully mature herring').

As discussed for Peterhead, *mattie* regularly appears in Wick with a modifier to describe a particular stage in a herring's life cycle. But used on its own the word can have strikingly different meanings for different members of the community. An older woman and one middle-aged informant stated that the word means a mature or large herring, while another older female informant said that it was a 'small herring with no roe' (it is worth noting, however, that this discrepancy may not be as great as it sounds: the lack of roe probably originally meant more the size of the fish than maturity). In the corpus, in fact, this last interpretation appears the most accurate. One middle-aged man could only say that a *mattie* is a herring, without commenting on size, suggesting, in fact, that the reason for the diversity of the word's meanings is not one of actual change so much as a broadening and simplification of the original distribution.

The salmon presents a different set of issues. Salmon was not a fish regularly landed by fishermen in any of the communities discussed in this research (at least not in the recent past), but it was a fish many fishing communities knew well, particularly those – including most communities studied here – lying beside a sizeable river. It was also a fish associated with a number of superstitions and rituals (Anson 1950: 41 and 43; Taylor 1988: 73; taboo-avoidance terms will be discussed later in the chapter). As the *Glossary* points out, there was a widespread and detailed vocabulary for different stages in the life cycle of a salmon –important in economic and long-term ecological terms but also relatively easy even for non-specialists to recognise, given the great differences in form a salmon passes through in its lifetime:

parr   young fish before leaving fresh water (*Glossary*)
smolt fish leaving fresh water for first time (*Glossary*)
grilse fish returning to fresh water after one winter in the sea (*Glossary*)
kelt   fish which has spawned (*Glossary*)

In Peterhead, elements of this nomenclature had been retained by part of the community. The only word given for 'large salmon' by any participant (here, one older and one middle-aged male) was *salmon*. *Grilse* was produced as the term for 'medium salmon' by one older man and a middle-aged male. Strikingly, *grilse* was given by one older man and one older woman for 'smaller salmon'. The meanings suggested by the *Glossary* above, however, suggest that *grilse* could be taken as being between small and medium sized (although this ignores a number of distinctive associations). Two men (one older, one middle-aged) gave *smolt*, which is in line with the definitions given above. One older man gave *finnock* for a small salmon. In the *Glossary* this is defined as 'a white trout, in colour and shape like a salmon, usually applied to young sea trout in estuaries'. This might be mistaken identification, but is more likely to represent the transfer of terms between similar species already alluded to. In the pilot study a number of people were able to produce terms for 'younger salmon'. Four participants generated *grilse*, two *smolt*. One person produced *parr*, another *clear fish*. One participant offered that *smolt* was/were smaller than *grilse*. It is possible that the ongoing trade in salmon as a high prestige product encourages the maintenance of specific terms for younger age groups. The fact that these are not widely known (but generally understood by a concentrated grouping) may well be connected to the specialisation which has affected the fishing trade in the last fifty years.

With salmon lexis Wick was rather more like the Peterhead results than for other fish. One older male defined *kelt* (not reported in Peterhead) as a salmon which has not as yet reached sexual maturity. Two older males also gave very accurate definitions for *grilse*, referring both to its weight (under 8lb) and that it was 'on its way out to the sea for the first time or on its way back from the sea'. One middle-aged woman defined a *grilse* as a 'medium salmon'; the response was produced initially by her husband, however. According to three older men, *salmon* itself was taken to mean 'large salmon' in size (over 8 lb in weight) or sexual maturity.

Alongside these, however, a number of other size-based terms were also available. One middle-aged woman gave *spawn* for a small salmon, while a middle-aged male gave *pilchard* for medium-sized salmon. This last connection is surprising, since pilchards are members of the sardine-herring family and are therefore much more oily than salmon, but the usage is in line with the spread of terms from one species for another.

Some Wick informants were also able to present generic terms for stages in the life cycle of any (or a range of) fish. Two middle-aged males gave *tiddler* for small fish while a younger woman gave *peerie fish* for small fish. *Rose* was given by a middle-aged male informant for large fishes; *whopper* by another male of middle years for a 'huge fish'. Two older men give *black jack* for the very largest fish. The last was, according to the corpus, originally related to the *saithe* or coalfish (and recorded along the east coast). The other terms appear to exhibit the same semantic origin, although not necessarily the same forms, as the terms for *haddock* reported in Peterhead.

Informants along the coast were asked if they knew the names for different stages of the life cycles of any fish species not mentioned.

Many Wick informants commented on the life cycle and size of a fish about which they had not been specifically asked: the *coley* or *coalfish*. Yet despite the apparent accuracy of many of the terms, a similar broadening and loss of definition is also present.

For this fish's early stages the *Glossary* gives *sellag* or *sillack* in Caithness, Orkney and Shetland for its fry; the word-list in the *New Caithness Book* defines the word as 'a young coalfish'. The *ST* gives *baddock* for the same stage, saying that it is 'now' (in the 1960s at the latest) found in the North-East and Berwickshire. The *Glossary* records *comb* as a young coalfish in the Moray Firth area. *Cuddie* and *cuddin* are given for 'a young coal-fish' by the *ST*, with use 'now' confined to the North, Fife and Argyll. The *Glossary* records *cuddie* for 'young fish' in Caithness, while the *New Caithness Book* gives *cuddeen*, although interestingly only with the meaning 'coalfish'. The *Glossary* gives *geeks* for the 'young stages' of the coalfish in the Moray Firth area, while *gerrock* is recorded by the *ST* in the North-East for 'the coal-fish in its first year'.

Words for the second stage in the fish's development include *get*, 'now' found, according to the *ST*, in Aberdeenshire and Fife. The same resource records *podle* for that developmental stage in the North-East, Angus and Fife, although the word is also used for other fish, including the pollack and the lythe. Less technical terms for a less than fully mature fish include *peltag* or *piltack*, given by the *Glossary* for the fish in its second year in Caithness and Orkney. A similar meaning is given by that resource for *queeth* in Banffshire and the Moray Firth area in general. The *ST* defines this word as 'the young coal-fish', found in the North-East. *Prinkle* is given by the *ST* for the same meaning in the same area (the *Glossary* defines the word as 'small fish', placing it in eastern Scotland). In the same area, the *Glossary* tells us, *poddlie* means 'immature fish'.

Words for the mature coalfish include *saithe* or *seeth*, defined by the *ST* as 'the full grown coal-fish in its third or (local) fourth year' and found throughout Scotland. The *Glossary* gives *coalmie* for the fully grown fish in the Moray Firth area, the *ST* gives *coam* (found in the Banffshire area and probably the same word as that given above) and *colmouth* with the same meaning. Unsurprisingly, perhaps, words for the immature fish predominate. That this terminology was used systematically can be seen in the following report: 'In Caithness the first year's fish were "sellags", then came "piltags", and "cuddies" at two to four years, ending with "saithe". . . . "cuddie" is the most widespread along the east and west coasts of Scotland' (Coull, Fenton and Veitch 2008 86–7). According to the *Fisherspeak* survey's informants in Wick, the smallest variety of this fish is *sellig*, otherwise spelled *sellag* and *sellick* (in traditional Caithness dialect final voiceless plosives are voiced). This information was derived from the knowledge of three older men and two middle-aged informants, male and female. The largest coalfish were called *cuddeen* (otherwise *cudden* and *cudding*), according to two older men and the same number of middle-aged female informants. Strikingly, however, one younger man associates the terms with any *larger* fish, while one older woman associates it with any *small* fish, an older male connecting it with any *medium* one. A number of older men gave *seethe* or *saithe* as the name of the older coalfish; one of these also gave *grey-lord* as a word referring to the same stage in the fish's life cycle, a word which does not occur in the corpus.

In between these two states is *pellig* or *peltig*. Perhaps because this word was defined by a number of informants not so much as a *medium* coalfish as a *small* cuddeen,[8] confusion over the term's position in the fish's life cycle is possible. The majority who know and use the word associated it unequivocally with the middle stage in the fish's development, other informants saw a *pellig* as a small fish, one middle-aged male defining it as a 'small fish you threw away'. It is likely, however, that these distinctions are primarily concerned with viewpoint rather than discrepancy. Interestingly, while one middle-aged man defined *pellig* as a small fish similar to a haddock, he added that he did not 'know what they call them anywhere else'; an older man was able to say that *podlie* was the word used for the same species at the same stage in Buckie. These discrepancies must be largely due to differing life experiences.

We may not be able to reconstruct all the reasons why Wick informants should have a far larger range of words for 'coalfish' than in Peterhead, especially since it is likely that the fish is (or was) common in accessible waters. Coalfish, because they are abundant in-shore, have been eaten along the east coast since very early times (Coull 2008a). A tradition of 'hobby fishing' for inshore species may be present in Wick, but is likely also to be present in other parts of Scotland; the fact that commercial fishing is still strong in Peterhead may obscure what has become visible through lack of such opportunities. This interpretation may be supported by the presence of words for 'coalfish' in the southern ports.

In Anstruther many life-cycle terms elicited in the more northerly communities were also found, albeit occasionally with rather fewer attestations. In relation to 'haddock', *pouts* were given for 'small haddock' by an older and a middle-aged man; this word is not found in the corpus. Interestingly, *haddie*, normally taken for any haddock (although see the Wick discussion above), was given for this stage in the fish's life cycle by a middle-aged man and an older woman. One older male gave *halflin* for a small to medium haddock, while a middle-aged woman and an older man gave *seed* for the same stage. One older male informant produced *danny* for a large haddock (a word not found with that meaning in the corpus). A younger offered *haddock* for 'large haddock'. On no occasion was sexual maturity defined as a feature in producing these distinctions.

Like Wick, Anstruther threw up a range of terms for 'coley' or 'coalfish'. A middle-aged man gave *dergie* for the smallest coalfish (the *ST* records that while *darg* refers to a young whiting in the North-East, *dargie* does indeed refer to coalfish fry); an older female informant reported that small children 'would catch these small fish'. Slightly larger coalfish were known as *potlie*, while *saithe* were medium-sized and *collie* large. Recording these terms *is* impressive, but it must be recognised that all of them were produced by one middle-aged man.

The same man gave *par* for a small salmon, while a middle-aged woman produced *smelts* and an older man *smolt*. *The Pars* is the nickname of the nearby (but not necessarily loved) Dunfermline Athletic FC. *Grilse* as a term for a medium salmon was recorded from two men, one middle-aged, the other older, and one middle-aged woman. Each of these produced all the 'salmon' terms already discussed. The middle-aged male informant also gave *salmon* as the term for the fully developed fish. Another older man gave *red fish* for mature salmon, which may represent a taboo-avoidance term (as discussed below). One younger male informant filled in *red fish* for *all* the stages in a salmon's life cycle, it should be noted. For these speakers at least the term's taboo-avoidance associations have been completely lost.

Strikingly unlike Wick, however, only one *herring* term was given in Anstruther: *sma herring* for the smallest form of the fish. The same number of terms was recorded for 'cod' (which was not specifically called for); indeed two older men and an older woman offered *codlin* for a small cod. This is particularly interesting, since the East Neuk was a major herring fishing centre.

Features like this leave as many questions as they answer. Does this pattern of usage exist because a relatively small number of people have remembered a number of terms which were (and possibly are) not representative of the community as a whole?

The Eyemouth use pattern is similar to those already recounted, although with rather fewer informants providing terms. An older man and woman both produced *sprat* for 'small herring', while the same man gave *herring* for 'medium herring' and *bloater* for the largest of the species. The final word is also used for a specific type of smoked herring. A middle-aged woman gave *roonders* for 'small haddock', *chippers* for medium and *dannies* for large. A middle-aged man gave *small* for 'small haddock', *best small* for medium and agreed that *dannies* are large haddock. No other informants provided information on this. The term *norrie*, recorded for Berwickshire by the *Glossary*, was not elicited in 2011.

The same middle-aged man gave *fry* for 'small salmon' (a particularly interesting association since this is a regular word along the coast either for small fish or small pieces of fish of any species), *smolt* for a medium-sized fish and *salmon* for a large one. An older man also gave *parr* for a 'small salmon'.

No words were recorded for coalfish or coley in Eyemouth. But words *were* elicited for *cod*, *whiting* and *plaice*. It should be noted, however, that all of the words were derived from one source, the middle-aged man already mentioned. For 'small cod' he gives *green* and *rowpie/robie dobie*, while *heids* is suggested for a large cod. *Whiting*, otherwise rarely reported (although an economically important fish: while east-coast fish and chip shops generally use haddock as their default fish, their west-coast equivalents use whiting), with *stingoe* and *piranhas* being given for the smaller fish. Informants offered *postage stamp* for a small member of the *plaice* species, a species commonly mentioned in the corpus; none of these terms features in that resource, however. Some terms, such as *piranhas*, are very likely to be recent.

It seems therefore that what at first appeared to be a rich fund of knowledge in Eyemouth is likely only to be evidence for the retentive memory of a small number of informants. Some of the more unexpected and even eccentric results may be due to this small group therefore.

With these fields Lossiemouth is unusually placed as an outlier; a very different position from that found with other sets of questions. With generic size terms, one older man observed that there are terms for different sizes of fish, but he did not use them, preferring instead using only *small*, *medium* and *large* (he did, however, with a degree of coaxing, recognise *mattie* and *grilse*). One middle-aged woman also knew *grilse* and *sprat*. With 'herring' one older male informant commented that the only term he knew beyond *herring* was *kippers*. Moreover, despite Lossiemouth's position in a salmon fishing-intense region, salmon was hardly mentioned, with an older man commenting that his lack of engagement in the salmon fishery meant that he was not sure about terms related to that fish. With 'haddock' two older men and one young woman said that *haddie* was not used in Lossiemouth. The only other comment was from a middle-aged man, who commented that *chats* and *jumbos* were used in Peterhead, but were not used in Hopeman. The lack of knowledge in Lossiemouth is baffling, particularly given the wealth of terms for flat fish discussed above.

In relation to knowledge of these terms, older speakers who had direct experience of the fishing industry were predictably able to give a wider range of these terms than were younger informants – although some younger informants, some of whom were connected to the heritage industry in one way or another, also demonstrated a degree of awareness. What was less expected, however, was that many of the distinctive terms elicited referred not to the maturational cycle so much as the size of the fish after processing, suggesting a landward (and possibly female) basis for interpretation on many occasions.

4.2.1.3 Monkfish
In order to assess awareness of specific species beyond the historical 'canon', a question was asked in combination with a particularly striking photograph of an angler-fish (also called monkfish). This fish was chosen for a variety of reasons. In the first instance, a number of quite local words are recorded in a range of resources for this animal; moreover, the fish, while considered a delicacy, is extremely ugly and therefore memorable; finally, it is only in the last generation or so that its status has risen. Relatively recently it was considered practically without value.

For the *monkfish*, the *Glossary* tells us, *frog fish* can be found throughout Scotland. From a range of sources, it is apparent that *oof* is the common name for the fish along the Moray Firth, while BC (and, based upon it, the DD) have *caithick* as the Peterhead (and eastern Buchan) equivalent. According to the *Glossary*, *mulrein* is associated with the fish in Fife. Only the ST records words specifically for *angler-fish*, even the *Glossary* collates that fish with the *monkfish*, while maintaining a separate presence for the former in a single entry. The sole non-localised word recorded for *angler-fish* is *wide-gab* (literally, 'wide mouth'). A few localised forms are also found. the ST records *keth(r)ie*, reporting that 'now' (within the last fifty to sixty years), the word is found only in Aberdeenshire and Berwick, suggesting that the word was previously found in between, but has now retreated to more conservative enclaves (see Millar 1999). *Oof* or *wolf* is given for the same fish, solely for the north-east. What is striking is that, with the exception of Wick, all of the communities covered in this research have a name for these fish either completely or largely discrete from other places. Are these to be taken as identity markers, therefore?

In Peterhead most informants recognised the fish. Many of all ages called it a *monk*, while slightly smaller numbers gave it its 'Sunday names', *monkfish* or *angler-fish* (with apparent variants like *sea angler* and *angel fish* also being recorded; many people who said both *monkfish* and *monk* indicated that the latter was far more natural to them). The pilot study offered essentially the same distribution. In the main study, three informants – all older men – gave *oof*, although all three did not consider the term local – one associating it with Buckie, a considerable distance along the Moray Firth, one with the markets, while the last knew the word but would not use it himself. One participant in the pilot study also offered this word, without comment. *Big moo* 'big mouth', offered by one older male in the main survey, is not recorded in the corpus, but it resembles *wide-gab* semantically, which is recorded in that resource. The most unexpected *banjo* was given by two older men, both of whom claimed that the name derived from the shape of the fish. It appears that this might be a case of mistaken identity, however: a *banjo* is a strikingly ugly fish, found particularly in North American waters (where, as we have seen, Peterhead fishermen have occasionally sought temporary employment). The name is associated with sub-species of dogfish, however. A transfer from one species to another is possible, although the confusion in interpretation is aided by the fact that two other informants (a middle-aged woman and a younger man) called the fish a *dogfish* (one participant in the pilot study also gave this name). A similar gloss can be given to the name *jenny cuntie* or *jenny* given to the fish by an older male and an older female informant. This phrase is not found in the corpus, but DSL, following the SND, gives *cuntack* or *cuntie* as a word found at least in Aberdeenshire for the father-lasher, adding that its origin is doubtful, although comparing it to Shetland *konta-plucker*, which refers, significantly, to the angler-fish. It is commonplace in Scotland for the name *Jenny* to be added to animal names. In the corpus, for instance, *Jenny* (or *Jinnie*) *grey* is given as a Caithness word for a young guillemot. The loss of the second element in the name might be to do with the potential taboo nature of words with similar pronunciations to *cuntie*. The apparent confusion between angler-fish and father-lasher is explained by the similarity in looks – although not in size – between the two species. Proportions are not always obvious in photographs.

One final name given was *mock scampi*. Before monkfish became fashionable, many members of the fishing community used its tail meat only, dressing the meat as if it were scampi (since at the time the latter was considered of greater value). What is striking, however, is that *caithick*, reported by a single, but highly reliable, source in the corpus as specific to the Peterhead area was not recorded from any informant, young or old; nor was it recognised by even the oldest informants when it was introduced into the discussion. Was it ever used in Peterhead, or is it a 'ghost word' or misunderstanding?

The responses in Wick were not as rich (as we saw, no local name was recorded for Caithness in the corpus). A number of older women (one of whom failed to recognise the fish) said that they would have recognised its tail more readily than its face, with association with 'mock scampi' implied, supported by the word *scamp* given the fish by an older woman. Most informants recognised the fish as a *monkfish* (although none gave the more familiar *monk*). Some older men also pointed out that while *monkfish* was its everyday name, it was actually an *angler-fish*. Four participants gave *angler-fish*, one older male informant suggesting that there must be a local Caithness word for the fish but he did not know one off-hand. A number of informants associated the fish in the photograph with a range of other fish species, such as, predictably, *dogfish* (or *dowgfish*), from an older and a middle-aged woman. A younger man gave *hake*, a fish which shares the size, but not the looks, of the monkfish, while a younger woman offered the vague *flattie* and *flat fish*. These last two informants' views may represent the falling away of former knowledge towards default (and largely generic or non-descriptive) local forms.

A number of comments by informants possibly explain the lack of local names for the fish. Older people who had been involved in the fish trade obviously considered the fish to be largely worthless. It had, it was reported, never been landed at Wick and was regularly thrown away before a return to port. By the time its prestige grew, it might be argued, Wick people were not normally closely associated with fishing and therefore learned a name for the fish largely from external, Standard English, sources.

Predictably, Lossiemouth informants of all ages also offered variants of *angler (angel) fish* and *monkfish*. A large number from middle-aged and older backgrounds produced *oof*, predicted as the local variant, however, with a few unusual spellings, some of which (such as *ouf*, with a diph-thongal pronunciation) may represent actual differences (these include *oomph* and *oeuf*, the latter of which may be tongue in cheek). Interestingly a number of informants defined the fish as a *dogfish* but also as *oof*, sug-gesting either a breakdown of barriers or, as we have suggested before, the continuation of a less detailed nomenclature among active fishers than might have been expected. One younger woman called the fish a *catfish* (a separate species, but not much prettier than what is shown here); another young woman calls it a *flounder* (a fish which has the breadth, but not the looks, of the angler-fish). Interestingly, however, an older male informant offered *large gunter*. In DSL, *gunner-fleuk* is given for 'turbot', obviously presenting the same connection.[9] A number of informants mentioned the tail of the fish as part of its name, some dis-cussing the 'scampi' connection.

In Anstruther, most informants who responded gave only *monkfish*, with a few giving *monk*, and one *anglerfish*. One informant gave *sheet*, otherwise unrecorded. The local word reported in the corpus, *mulrein*, was not mentioned. Similar lack of elicitation was found for Eyemouth, with *monkfish*, *anglerfish* and *monk* being most recorded, although *banjo*, also recorded for Peterhead, was elicited, as was *keckie*, given by one older and one middle-aged male. This may well be a variant of local *kethrie*, reported by the corpus, which may itself in fact be a reflex of the otherwise elusive *caithick*.

It seems therefore that Peterhead is somewhat anomalous in relation to this fish. Its being a functioning fishing port during the rise of the monk-fish as a delicacy possibly emphasised the need for knowledge of, and words for, the fish. Where fishing is now minimal, however, knowledge of the fish (and coinage of terms for it) remained lower. It is noteworthy, however, that a small number of older informants from elsewhere do seem to know words for the fish (the case of Eyemouth is particularly striking), so the lack of much recent fishing may have erased knowledge of terms for what were never much sought-after fish. It is possible that both explanations are correct.

4.2.2 Fishing trade lexis

Moving on from the primary focus of the fishing trade, we will now consider lexis associated with the trade; in particular the vocabulary employed for the line fishery and the clothes worn by primary participants.

4.2.2.1 Clothing

For a large part of the Scottish fishing trade's most prosperous period, the clothes fishermen (and also female members of the community, such as fishwives) wore were highly distinctive in comparison with what their landward neighbours wore. Partly this was because, when catches were good and the price of fish reasonable, members of fishing communities often had larger amounts of available cash to buy new clothes. More importantly, years of specialisation meant that work clothes had been honed to serve a particular purpose but, until the end of the Second World War, beyond a local level, with little thoroughgoing standardisation of clothing type and manufacture. The combination of home-made and shop-bought clothing must also be borne in mind when diversity is considered: while similarity in practice did mean that similar clothing needs were found along the coast, individual and group realisations of these patterns inevitably differed.

There was something of a ritual about dressing in the fishing communities, as seen in stories of fishermen being carried onto and off their boats by their wives; a tradition encapsulated in a superstition about not wearing sea boots on land. Essentially, however, the focus was on comfort and warmth, with the use of layered clothing to achieve this. A concentration on remaining dry was also central to the clothing needs (and, indeed, effective work) of fishermen and was particularly difficult to deliver in the period before the mass production of effective and relatively cheap protective clothing, such as those made using oilskin.

The first stage in the dressing process was donning undergarments. Along the coast (and indeed inland also) the most common names for this stage would, according to the corpus, have been *semmit* for the upper body and *drawers* (pronounced in a variety of ways) for the lower. There are, however, a number of extra terms in the corpus, derived normally from relatively local sources. The ENV provides two modified descriptions of *drawers*. *plaidin' drawers*, 'knee-length drawers made of blanket cloth' and *worset drawers*, 'ankle-length pink drawers', the first at least implying home-made origin. Above the waist two features were recorded from the North-East: *fancy sark*, which Stewart (no date: 4) discusses: '[t]he undergarments [of fishermen] were hand-knitted long worsted drawers, a calico shirt, or, as it was called in Doric "a fancy sark".' The DD provides *ficket*, a 'woollen garment with sleeves and buttoned front, an undervest worn under shirt'. The latter is likely to have been used well beyond the fishing communities.

The corpus also presents a few words for overshirts, such as *serks* and *shift* (*o claes*) 'flannel shirt', both derived from the ENV. Again, it is most unlikely that these words and phrases were confined to the fishing trade only. Rather more productive, perhaps, are the words and phrases associated with jumpers and other forms of clothing worn over shirts. Perhaps the most common vocabulary item associated with this field is *ganzie* or *ganjie* (the spellings vary considerably, but two pronunciations – /'ganzi/ and /'gandʒi/ – appear to be most common). It is commonly assumed (although a number of people who use the word disagree) that the word is derived from *guernsey*, a style of woollen overgarment similar to, but distinct from, the jersey. If that is the case, then the word must have come into Scotland via a non-rhotic variety of English. Since regions such as East Anglia and Yorkshire with which Scottish fishermen had much intercourse have been non-rhotic for some time, this transfer is relatively straightforward to reconstruct. The word is found along the coast and indeed had productive derivatives, the construction *lousie gansy*, reported in the LG for a 'black and white jumper', probably only scratching the surface. The *Glossary* is rather less productive in relation to words for 'upper clothing', although the ENV does include *kersey*, a relatively common word throughout Scotland, for this concept.

Protective clothing naturally forms a major part of the vocabulary items recorded. Most likely to be remembered are words associated with particular processes or technology, such as *barkie* for a cagoule treated in bark (as discussed below) to waterproof it, recorded by Downie as a general north-east feature (while *pamzie*, defined as 'cagoule' with no (overt) reference to curing, was, according to Downie, only found in Lossiemouth) or *barkit jumper*, defined as 'brown canvas pullover' by the ENV.[10]

Barkin was, of course, replaced by new oilskin clothes, primarily in the post-war period. The fact that this technology was centralised and associated with mass production means that *oilskin* or *oilie* appears to have been the primary name for the clothes (sometimes with the Scots *ilie* pronunciation being given emphasis, primarily because it is only the pronunciation which marks it off from the Standard English form). There are, however, a few examples of words related to the new clothes which did not use the conventional terminology, such as *brooks*, reported for an 'oilskin trouser suit' by the ENV and *frock*, a word whose meaning appears to span the changeover in clothing practice, the ST informing us that it was recorded in Orkney and Aberdeenshire with the meaning of 'a sailor's or fisherman's knitted jersey', but as 'a short oilskin coat or cape' in Shetland, Caithness and Fife.

Another feature of fishing was appropriate head-gear. But although some terms, such as *coolie* for the 'woollen cap worn under a sou'wester', recorded in the CD and reported by DSL as being 'mainly Northern', or *neepyin* for a 'small head shawl', recorded by the ENV, do appear based in the fishing industry, there is largely a disappointing lack of such terminology recorded in the corpus (perhaps because of the presence of the supralocal *sou-wester*).

In Peterhead, a wide range of clothing items were offered. Some of these words and phrases appeared largely indicative of a past age rather than specifically associated with the fishing trade (although for older members of the community, these clothing items, despite being used elsewhere, were central to their experience and memory of the fishing). These included *bonnet* (offered by two older men and one younger woman), *cheesecutter* 'skipper's hat' (offered by two older men), *gallases* 'braces which held up the hairback briks' (of which more shortly, offered by one older woman), *gravit* (or *gravat*) 'scarf', offered by two older men and an older woman (a variant of this, *granaat*, was offered by another older man), *kep* 'cap', produced by three older men, one older woman and one middle-aged woman, *linner* or *lunner*, defined by an older woman as 'thin flannel, like a chemise, usually grey' and by an older man, and *muffler* 'to keep the water from going down your neck', offered by one older man.

A further set of these more general words were offered largely by younger people. These included *baffies* 'slippers', offered by one younger woman, *beets* 'boots', offered by two younger women (one of whom said that she would also say *boots*), *bricks* 'trousers', offered by one middle-aged woman, two younger women and a young man, and *sheen* 'shoes', offered by two younger women. All of these were words associated with everyday life, rather than particularly fishing-related; having said that, however, the 'old days' *were* fishing, practically exclusively, for any of these ports, and it is also possible that what had once been a general word had become associated with the most 'different' (or local) connection – the fishing. Nevertheless, at the end of this continuum are the answers given by two younger informants (one male, the other female), who gave *boiler suit* and *wellies* 'rubber Wellington boots' for what fishermen wear.

Somewhere between these two are examples such as *simit* (or *simet*) for 'vest', produced by a range of age groups and both sexes, although these informants did not include any older men. The same is probably true for *sark* 'shirt', suggested by one middle-aged and one younger woman. Other words and phrases which are part of this informed, but not entirely fishing-based, category include *mazie* 'jumper', given by one younger woman and *toppers* for 'wellies', given by the same young woman and another woman from the same age group. For the former, DSL gives *maisie n3*, which it defines as 'a "binder", a flannel undershirt', the citation dated 1911. It asserts that this is a '[v]ariant of or mistake for *mawsie*'. The second definition for that noun is 'a warm woollen garment such as a jersey or pullover', with distribution being confined to the North-East and Angus. The examples given appear to be confined largely to agriculture. It is striking, nonetheless, that a possibly mistaken citation is shown to be correct by someone born in the last two decades of the twentieth century. The same woman offers *hummel dodies* for 'gloves without fingers', a local phrase of long standing, probably originally derived from the agricultural community, where it refers to former techniques used to remove a cow's horns. *Topper*, on the other hand, appears not to have such a pedigree. It may be that the name refers to the characteristic top part of the original wellington boot.

With words and phrases which we have already discussed above as being essentially part of the core fishing lexis for fishing clothes, it is not surprising that older informants predominate. Informants from other age groups do regularly give examples, however, not least with *ganjies* 'jumpers', known by a range of people from each age group (including the younger woman who also offered *mazie*).[11] *Sou'wester*, which is probably used in all British coastal communities, was only produced by older people. A local variant – *seewester* – is given by one older man, who defines it as a 'canvas hood with a long bit at the back of the neck'. The diminutive forms of *oilskins* (again not originally a local word), are again more found across the ages and the sexes, with the most local pronunciation – *ilies* – being given by both an older man and a young woman.

A number of locally specific words are related to knitting and, barring the *ganjey/ganzie* connections, undergarments and socks. This is not, of course, surprising: well-knitted long johns and socks could make onboard life much more pleasant than would otherwise have been the case. A number of older men and women remembered *worsit* or *wushit drawers*, one older man referring to a 'warm, itchy clothing item *wyved* ['knitted'] by women', while an older woman reported that they were 'woolen [*sic*] hand-knitted underpants which were heather coloured and laced up' (the difference in perspective between maker and wearer is noteworthy). It is perhaps not surprising, given that lower prices for shop-bought woollens and, later, acrylic, underwear eventually meant that buying was cheaper than making, that it is only older people who remembered the terminology of worsted wool, although it should be noted that one young and one middle-aged informant reported the wearing of *long drawers*.

One older woman remembers *wushit socks*. Memories of the long hose produced are perpetuated by one middle-aged woman (*hose*). A younger woman offers *blue mogganers* 'socks fishers wore in Peterhead'. This knowledge would doubtless be encouraged by the fact that, as we will see later in the chapter, Peterhead advertises itself as *The Blue Toon* (it is on all signs on roads coming into town). There are a number of stories about where this name came from, but the 'blue mogganer' explanation is certainly the most popular (more discussion of this point can be found below). One older woman also adds *seaboot hose* for 'thick knitted socks'.

A few further words were collected in this field in Peterhead. These included *barkey*, from a middle-aged man, but derived from his father: 'nowadays a nylon, light waterproof jacket to keep the wind out; in [my] father's days, it was a cotton jacket made of sail cloth'. It may be significant that no mention of the *barkin* process is given (see below). An older man produced *sloppy*, 'like a sailcloth jumper', which provides a further feature – that the *sloppy* was essentially made of denim – to the corpus definitions discussed above. Finally, two older informants offered a modification of *bricks* 'breeks; trousers': *hairback bricks*. The female informant defines this phrase as 'thick woollen trousers', while the male states that they were 'moleskin bricks that were so heavy that when you took them off, they stood up on their own'. Again, we see the difference between making and using.

Similar patterns of knowledge and use are to be found in Wick. Many informants of all ages knew what were apparently central terms, such as *ganzey* (or alternate realisations) for 'jumper'. This word was not merely *known*, in the sense that informants could, with difficulty, recall it. One middle-aged male informant, who had had to think hard before producing fishing-specific vocabulary, immediately was able to give this word. Although jumpers of this sort are probably not made for the fishing any more, it was striking that a number of older informants, both male and female, could still discuss, with considerable pride, the traditional ways in which the jumpers were created.[12]

This notwithstanding, most of the traditional names for clothes specifically associated with fishing were generally only remembered by older informants. These include *barkin jumper*, produced by two older men, for a jumper treated with bark (see below) and *worsit* for woollens, submitted by an older woman. A number of older informants also mentioned the traditional underwear and socks, although largely with Standard English descriptions, such as (*knitted*) long johns, *hand-knitted drawers* and *socks* or *seaboot stockings*, with the partially local *iley wool stockings*, produced, interestingly, by an older man (the others being overwhelmingly produced by older women). Examples such as *Baltic boots* (or *seaboots* – provided by an older woman) for the long boots worn by fishermen probably represent the same phenomenon.

Small-scale exceptions to this dominance by older informants are available. One middle-aged woman produced *corsy trooisers* with the meaning 'warm trousers made of woollen tight material'. *Corsy* does not occur in any spelling variant in the corpus, DSL or OED; it appears to mean essentially the same as *Guernsey trousers*, however. But the phonological leap from *Guernsey* to *Corsy* is considerable. The same informant provided *paddie hats* for hats which had seen better days, worn by fishermen. Again the exact source for this phrase is not immediately available. The OED provides a number of examples of compounds formed from *paddy* which have a somewhat derogatory meaning; *hat* is not given, however. It is striking nonetheless that one person has obviously remembered lexical items associated with local colour, forgotten, or at least not 'accessed' by other informants.

As with Peterhead, a range of words for items of clothing not essentially part of the fishing trade were also offered in Wick. This includes *bonnad* (with typical Caithness voicing of final /t/) or *bonnet*, produced by a number of informants from all ages and both sexes. Other examples of this type include *semit* for 'vest' (offered only by two older women), *scarfie* for a scarf (produced by a middle-aged woman) and *toorie* for a 'bobble hat', given by a middle-aged man and a middle-aged woman.

There were also a number of occasions where the standard form (or something close to it) was given by informants. As we might expect, the most common of these is *oilskins*, offered by many informants from all ages and both genders. Equally expected is the local pronunciation *ileskins*. The same is true for *sou'wester*, again found across the informants (although, unlike Peterhead, with no local variant pronunciations) and *wellies*. It is very striking, however, that one younger woman produced *waterproofs*, which is neither local not fishing-specific. A number of other younger female informants gave the impression that they knew about different items of clothing associated with the fishing trade but almost entirely lacked a vocabulary to describe it.

In Lossiemouth, *gansey* also predominated in this category, being offered by both genders across the age groups, with older people discussing how they were made, the oiled wool that was used and the different patterns found in different places. This more detailed interest is represented in the words and phrases elicited, with one older man offering *dress ganzey* 'made with finer needles' and *working ganzey*, coarser than a *dress ganzey*. Another older male informant offered *faira ganzey*, referring to the highly distinctive Fair Isle jumpers. A number of older and middle-aged informants also mentioned *lunder* (with one older man spelling it *londers*), a thinner jumper, possibly worn on more 'dressy' occasions with a polo neck. Their warmth was remembered. Also mentioned by older informants was *pansie*, a light waterproof, variously described as having 'oilskin arms with a cotton jumper' through 'light, long jumper that was brown and barked and worn in the summer' to 'protective clothing that they put over everything made from sails' (the last offered by a female informant). The general sensation from this is that the garment – which appears to have been preferred in warmer weather or when close work was needed where oilskins might get in the way – was generally home-made and improvised. Indeed the name seems to be highly localised, given (in the form *pamzie*) by Downie (1983) for Lossiemouth. *Barkey* was given for a treated light jumper or jacket. Surprisingly, however, it was offered only by middle-aged informants.

A number of terms were also remembered or used for trousers, including *kersey* trousers (otherwise spelled *gersey* or *guersays*) and *serge troosers*. Two older men mentioned *fearnots* for particularly heavy trousers,[13] which one older female informant gave *moleskins*, the archetypal name for heavy trousers. A number of younger people gave only the common Scots *bricks* or *troosers*, which may, again, represent a move towards the generic among younger informants. With older and to some extent middle-aged informants, a number of words related to specialist underwear, largely related to *drawers*, with *wissit drawers* and *woorshits* being given particular prominence. In relation to the latter a middle-aged woman said that her grandfather used to wear them and that they were 'hideous to look at', suggesting both an emotional resonance and its positioning in the quite deep past. An older male informant described *warsit drawers* as coming in salmon pink or green 'with a sort of tape on the top'.

In relation to upper inner garments, a number of both older and middle-aged informants offered *flannel sark* and *fancy sark*. One older male remarked that the latter were 'fancy shirts, with stripes'. An older female informant commented that fancy sarks, as worn by her father, were black and grey. Only older male inhabitants offered *flannan sark*, however, with, as demonstrated by DSL, the more Scottish variant form of *flannel*. A small number of older and middle-aged people offered *simmit* in a range of spellings. One middle-aged woman offered *woolly semet and drawers*, observing that a 'woolly semet was button up long-johns'. One older man offered *weskets*. Three older men offered *black gravat* for a scarf.

A number of older and middle-aged informants offered *boot-stockings*. No particularly local (or even Scots) words or phrases were offered. The same is almost true for footwear, with words like *boots*, offered only by older and middle-aged informants, or more specialist types of boot, such as *leather seaboots* (with one older man commenting that 'rubber boots did away with the leather, thigh high seaboots') and *long leather boots*, offered by older informants, at least seeming to be Standard English; the same appears to be the case for *waders*, offered by one older man. The colloquial rather than dialectal *wellies* was offered by one older and one younger woman, the latter commenting that 'they basically just wore old clothes and wellies'. There were a few more local options offered, however. One older woman offers *water beets* (which she defined as 'wellingtons'), while an older man offered *widers*. These suggest that the apparently standard forms may merely be written forms masking the local spoken reality. One older woman offered *gutties* for 'water boots', a noun more commonly used for gym shoes in the eastern parts of Scotland. *Gutty* in origin refers to rubber (and at least was employed by some speakers to refer to toy catapults), so it is possible that we have evidence here of a previously unnoticed semantic association.

In terms of outer garments, many older and middle-aged informants gave *oilies* (with local variant *ilies*). The sole younger male informant also offered this (not surprising, given that his occupation involves close contact with sailors, sailing vessels and the open sea). One older man offered *frock ilies* for 'oilskins', representing a halfway house between the older and more recent styles for seaborne clothing. A fair number of older and middle-aged men and women offered *sou'wester* for 'hat', with one middle-aged woman offering *bunnet*, one older man giving *cap* and an older man and woman offering *toorie*. It is interesting that none of these external forms are specifically marine in reference, while *sou'wester* is.

There seems to be a considerable knowledge of both older and newer terms for fishing-trade-specific clothing; this is almost confined to the middle-aged and older inhabitants, however. The comment, already cited, from a younger woman that 'they basically just wore old clothes and wellies', demonstrates both lack of knowledge and (arguably) interest. It is equally striking that one middle-aged woman offered *clayse* 'clothes', whether demonstrating how central fishing was or that the local equivalent of *clothes* was associated with a niche-related past, rather than with contemporary existence.

Anstruther provides an interesting example of how an unexpected piece of history can affect the ways people relate to the material culture of their communities. The East Neuk was the home of two small oilskin manufacturers (and indeed Kirkcaldy, to the west, was the Scottish centre of the linoleum industry; see Malaws and McDonald 2009 and Turner 1957). Moreover, the Scottish Fisheries Museum had had a very successful exhibition in the recent past of traditional jumpers, called *Extravaganzey*, which toured around Scotland. It can therefore be expected that certain features of the local vocabulary for fishermen's clothes should be well known in the community; particularly since they are iconic in other communities even when there is no such institutional support.

This did indeed appear to be the case with *gansey*, although the word is generally known only by older people, with one older woman mentioning the diamond or rope patterns knitted into the jumpers. One older man says that it is a Cellardyke word, possibly demonstrating the atomisation of a previously common word, particularly striking when the two settlements run into each other. With oilskins, on the other hand, a number of older and a few middle-aged informants used the word, in its local or standard pronunciation, with most mentioning the Cellardyke factories. Two others mentioned a *dauper*, a 'smock, all in one, made in Cellardyke', or *daupers* 'oilskins', a word otherwise unrecorded, as far as we can tell. *Sou'westers* were mentioned by one middle-aged man and an older woman. Interestingly, almost as many people talked about pre-oilskin clothing in the form of *barkit jumper*, defined as 'no buttons, covered in bark' and having a 'roond neck'. Again, however, all informants were in the older age group. *Barkit* will be returned to below.

A small number of people also commented on the traditional fishing attire, including *pink drawers*, mentioned by one middle-aged and one older woman, *long drawers*, from another older woman, and *long socks*, from the same older woman. *Sea bits and hose* (/bɪts/ being the Central and Southern Scots equivalent to English *boots*) were given by one older man. As with elsewhere, a number of specifically Scots, but not necessarily fishing-centred, items of clothing were realised. One middle-aged man gave *toorie* for a knitted bonnet and *tammy* for a peaked cap. A middle-aged woman gave *bannets* or *capes*, while an older man gave *bunnet* (noting that 'if it was braw and new it was a snapper') and an older man and woman wrote *cap*, although with no indication of pronunciation. Trousers also formed a group of realisation, with a range of older men and women (and one middle-aged woman) giving *kerseys* for heavy trousers and another older woman giving *breeks* (this common word may just have been felt to be too common to be of interest to the researcher, although an older man does mention that *corduroy breeks* were what 'all St Monans boys wore . . . to school'). One older and one middle-aged woman mentioned the *flannel winser serk*, a short shirt which was also known as a *Buckie linner*. Beyond this, a few mainstream English words, such as *jumper*, *mits* and *balaclava* were all recorded from older women.

In Eyemouth fewer distinctive words for fishermen's clothing were presented or discussed. *Gainsey* or *Guernsey* were recorded from a few informants (not all of whom were older or middle-aged). *Barkit jumper* was recorded from an older man and woman (the latter of whom, it should be noted, made reference to the clothing of her grandfather's time, while pointing out that the word would not be used now). As well as *Sou'wester*, only given by one older man, one middle-aged woman gave *brat* for 'oilskins'. This may be an extension of that word's meaning, which DSL defines as referring to a rough-cut apron or other cloth covering. As with Anstruther, but with many more witnesses of both sexes and all age groups, *doppers* appears for oilskins. Two older informants (male and female) give *sea bits* for 'sea boots', the male informant also giving *sea boot stockings*. A middle-aged female informant offers *toory* for 'knitted hat', while an older man gives *gloves*. In a sense the Eyemouth material provides a microcosm of the patterns found along the coasts, although it has to be accepted that the variation in form found elsewhere is barely visible here, despite the fact that there is a Ships' Chandlery on the harbour front.

It could therefore be argued that a considerable amount of knowledge relating to trade-specific clothing subsists in our communities. But while some highly specific lexis was triggered, a large part of the material offered represented Scots words used well beyond the fishing trade or Standard English terms for fishing-trade-specific clothing, or represents a garment, such as the *ganzie*, which appears an iconic representation of the (past) fishing life. It is possible that providing information for cultural and linguistic outsiders pushed informants in this direction; it is equally possible that, if some of the older informants had been shown a number of the specific words mentioned at the beginning of this section, they would have been able to define at least some. The fact that these terms are not at the core of informants' terminology for these features is commonplace throughout this study and needs to be addressed, however.

A feature of traditional fisher preservation techniques was *barkin*, the process, often carried out by women, older children and retired fishermen, whereby nets were strengthened and protected through treatment in hot water full of chemicals derived from various types of tropical bark (often termed *cutch*). This term was of particular interest since, in the first instance, it had been productive, so that the term *barkit jersey* or *jumper*, for a waterproof woollen upper covering, was produced (as touched upon above), and, more vitally, because the introduction of nylon nets in the period following the Second World War and the introduction of plastic-based waterproof clothing in the following decades meant that *barkin* was rendered obsolete at a point which researchers can ascertain.

In the pilot study, considerably more than half of the Peterhead informants knew the term and related it to net preservation. This knowledge was shared with some middle-aged and one younger person, which suggests that memories of the process were handed on considerably after it ceased to be carried out. Nevertheless, a distinction can be made between a minimal knowledge of the process and a more thorough one. In the case of the latter, details of the chemicals used and the reasons for their use, were provided by a number of informants. Although these definitions were largely confined to older informants, the most eloquent description was given by a middle-aged male informant, who noted that the process was intended to '[protect] cotton nets from rot and rats [brought in by grain boats] by dipping them in pungent bark at the end of the fishing season, before storing them away for the season'. Interestingly, a few informants, from all age groups, associated *barkin* with the use of tar to protect nets. This alternative process did exist, but there appears to have been an elision. Many informants said little more than that the process was involved with the upkeep of nets, however, suggesting that memory of the process, except among young people with some interest in the past of the town, was becoming hazy. Those informants who did not appear to recognise the fishing meanings of the word concentrated instead on colloquial interpretations related either to coughing or to madness. *Barkin* might be said to have 'built-in obsolescence', unlike names for flora and fauna, for instance. As was noted in Chapter 3, many of the pilot study informants had rather vague associations with *barkin*, largely seeing it as having a fishing connection without being able to go any further, or as being connected to the process of *barkin* jumpers to protect them.

Having said that, for those in the main Peterhead survey who actively used the word, the question generated considerable description and discussion of as well as narratives about net *barkin*. Participants spoke about how many nets would be barked at a time (apparently 100), the smell of the bark, the brand name of the bark used – *borneo kutch* (the name itself possibly derived (by reanalysis?) from a major Borneo settlement, Kuching) – the point at which *barkin* came to an end (when nets came to be made out of nylon), that *barkin* was done onboard the steam drifters but onshore in the case of other boats (presumably because the former had the ability to produce plentiful hot water at will) and how there was/is great pride in their nets in Peterhead. One informant also told of going dancing on a Saturday night after *barkin* nets, with hands full of the substance, getting bark all over the back of the girls' dresses. The word is possibly maintained through stories like these, with memory being supplemented with a heritage-based appreciation of the word.

In Wick, again, considerable knowledge of the term was demonstrated for both older and middle-aged informants. Nearly all older informants were able to give considerable amounts of information about the process – including two older men, working together, who gave a recipe for *barkin*, some went no further than 'treating the nets'. As with Peterhead younger people (on this occasion *all* younger people) and a few middle-aged people did not know the word in this meaning, preferring instead to associate it with madness and coughing (along with meanings related to arguments and shouting). Similar patterns are found in Eyemouth, with the caveat that results were not as rich as for the other communities.

In a striking divergence from other analyses, discussion of *barkin* in Anstruther produced some particularly rich material. One older female, for instance, noted that 'We had a big boiler outside the back door, dipped nets in the bark then had four galluses (posts) to hang them on.

White nets January to April in the firth [of Forth]; summer nets up as far as Shetland.' Given the large female input into the preservation process, we might have predicted that women would give the most detailed discussions; it is only with Anstruther that this appears to be the case. It might be suggested that the East Neuk's association with the herring fishery (in comparison with the competing cod line and trawl fishery stronger in ports like Wick and Peterhead) encouraged the retention of trade-specific words, as does the local presence of the Scottish Fisheries Museum, perhaps; Eyemouth was also closely associated with herring, however, and does not exhibit the same richness, as we have seen in relation to fish names. Indeed younger Anstruther informants did not recognise the fishing meaning of *barkin*, instead giving the colloquial coughing or insanity interpretations found elsewhere.

The degree of specificity of a traditional lexical item's definition varies. Sometimes it is unclear whether this is because the participant does not know the full traditional definition or has simply not been as thorough as she or he might have been in defining it (perhaps because another person involved in the interview already gave a thorough definition, for instance). Nevertheless the pattern of decreased specificity or fullness in definition is probably a feature of lexical attrition and is worth discussing further.

4.2.2.2 *The language of the line fishery:* scull

Another feature of the lexis of the fishing trade given to being superseded over the last century and more are the techniques by which both the means of catching fish and how the fish – alive or dead – were held after being caught. The project chose not to catalogue these changes in any depth, largely because, as discussed in Chapter 3, this was something in which Schlötterer (1996) took a considerable interest. More importantly, the knowledge of the techniques would, by the second decade of the twenty-first century, have been known only to the oldest inhabitants, since even where fishing has continued techniques and technologies have become homogenised, perhaps even globalised. A few exceptions were made, however.

Informants were asked to define *scull* (in some parts of Scotland *scoo*), 'a shallow scoop-shaped basket for holding fish or baited lines', *now* confined to the North-East (*ST*). Some evidence does exist that the word was known elsewhere in Scotland; particularly, perhaps, to the south of the North-East. The ENV defines it as 'baskets-lines', while the Edinburgh School of Scottish Studies Archive records the word in 1975 from Alice Aitchison, a resident of Eyemouth. The word was also part of a marriage ritual in some places:

> At Boddam, Aberdeenshire [now incorporated into Peterhead], when lines were baited for the first time after a fisherman's wedding, it was the custom to begin with one hook, then turn the 'scull' or flat basket upside down, draw the lines across the floor, put them back again in the scull and start the work again. (Anson 1950: 35)

Despite issues about coverage, therefore, the word was chosen for inclusion in the questionnaire, primarily because the technology involved – line-based fishing – had been largely superseded more than a generation ago, so it would be an interesting test of whether words with a long heritage could survive change. Moreover, the fact that a Standard English homophone existed, related to a particular type of rowed boat or as the act of rowing itself, might tell us something about informants' awareness of the homophones and how well the local word's meaning had survived. Potential confusion with *skull* was also predicted.

In Peterhead, ten out of the seventeen participants did not know the word, including all younger and most middle-aged informants and almost all older female participants. Those who remained, however – five older men, one older woman and one middle-aged man – had often a very precise understanding of the word's meaning, including 'a woven basket used by women when baiting lines' and a 'container for keeping/shooting small lines'. Further information was given by a number of informants, one offering that the bait used were mussels or whelks, while another informant suggested lugworms. One older man remarked that, in distinction to the *scull*, the basket used for great line fishing was known only as *great line basket*. It is dangerous to make too much of one comment; this distinction might demonstrate the historical primacy of the small line. In the pilot study, seven participants knew the word with the meaning of 'basket used to collect baited lines'. All were either fishers or worked at the fishing museum (where there are pictures and an example of a scull on display). A number of informants said they knew the term from observing their mothers baiting lines, which immediately demonstrates a backward time shift.[14] Three other participants only knew this to signify 'a basket used for holding tatties'. Of those who did not know the word, two were in the youngest age group. One attempted an interpretation of the word as 'oar', relating it to *scull* 'propel a boat by oar'. An interpretation of this type, while 'wrong' from the point of view of Scots, has a certain applicability in a community associated with waterborne occupations. As with a number of words of this type, therefore, the reactions to this word are useful in demonstrating age and occupational associations, although some younger speakers may know them through the heritage industry.

In Wick, very few informants of any age knew *scull*. Two older informants knew the line-based basket 'correct' interpretation, while one other older fishing informant suggested that it was a flat basket for collecting fish. Something similar was given by an older male informant who suggested that a *scull* was a 'shovel that you shovel up the fish with, a scull or a scoop'. The word appears just on the edge of complete obsolescence, although the fact that one national scholarly resource does not record the word for this area must also be borne in mind.

In Lossiemouth a few older informants had a vivid sense of what the word refers to, some making a direct connection to lines, others merely describing the basket. A number of older people mentioned that it was a process dating from before their immediate experience (despite their often vivid impression of what the baskets were and what their purpose was). This was underlined by a range of middle-aged informants who said they associated *sculls* with heritage installations in places like the Lossiemouth Museum. None of them had ever fished with lines. A middle-aged woman recognised hearing the word with this meaning, but a male contemporary guessed that *scoo* was 'school', possibly due to the Scottish 'dark /l/'. All other informants, young and middle-aged, had no sense at all of the meaning of the word.

In Anstruther, however, many older informants, male and female, knew the word in its traditional meaning. One middle-aged man gives the meaning 'a basket (also called a *pad* or a *scull* – rather than *scoo*)', while an older woman gives 'a herring basket' and one middle-aged woman provides 'a basket type thing for tatties', both suggesting, like the material produced in Wick, a broadening of the word's original meaning. Perhaps exhibiting the same phenomenon is 'creels to catch partins (crabs) and lobsters', offered by one older woman (the same person who gave the 'herring basket' interpretation), which suggests the structure of the *scull* is being emphasised over its purpose and the material it is made of. One informant defined *scull* as a Danish fishing boat, while another gave 'to row a boat'. The fact that a fair number of middle-aged and older people knew the word is in line with what the corpus suggested.

In Eyemouth, conversely, only two older informants (one male, one female) knew the traditional meaning for *scull*. The 'oar' meaning was also offered by two older informants, one of whom was the male informant who also knew the basket meaning. These informants are younger contemporaries of the Alice Aitchison mentioned above.

4.2.2.3 Female-specific lexis

Scull represented a process carried out by all members of the community. It must be recognised that a great deal of local vocabulary has a male bias, even if women were involved in the processing and selling of fish. To redress this issue somewhat, a small number of local words associated primarily with female-dominated parts of the trade were therefore investigated.

The *faurlan* (also *faurlin/farlan* and *foreland*) was the large tub around which herring gutters worked, with the gutted herring being thrown into the tub. The peripatetic *herring lassies* or *quines*, highly skilled young gutters who followed the annual herring fishery and, in quite unpleasant and dangerous circumstances (particularly before the discovery of penicillin), made much needed hard cash for their families and communities.

In Peterhead the majority of informants knew what a *farlan* was, at least in relation to herring gutting, including a few younger informants. Some informants knew that it was a container used in herring gutting, but did not define it as the place where gutted herring was thrown. One older and one middle-aged man defined it as a container where herring was placed *before* gutting; two older females gave essentially the same interpretation, one saying that the *farlan* was 'the trough where the herring was placed for the gutting'. A number of informants knew it related to herring gutting, but gave a rather more general (or vague) interpretation. One older man defined it as a 'table for holding herring', while a young woman said it was 'the big long things for all the fish' during the gutting process. Two informants associated the word with barrelled herring, an older woman defining it as a barrel for salting herring (although, after the fieldworker gave the corpus definition, she agreed that the corpus was closer to what she remembered). A number of participants talked about the *farlan* as a place. Thus the farlan was not only the trough but also the place where gutting took place; vestigial survivals might have encouraged the extension of meaning – if the range of meanings can be interpreted in this way. An older woman and a middle-aged man associated the word with a system of measurement, the latter informant saying that a *farlan barrel* acted as a measurement of a particular amount of herring (whether confusion existed with the obsolete *firkin* measurement is impossible to say). At the very edge of understanding, one middle-aged woman said it had to do with the herring and said only that it was related to 'when they went away'. Beyond this, a relatively small number made no connection with the word at all. These were evenly spread across the age groups, although it is striking that two middle-aged women did not know the word, despite its connection with quite widespread female labour.

Similar patterns were found in the pilot survey, with most informants knowing that *farlan* referred to the gutting process. The women associated with the museum had an accurate sense of the word's meaning. This might represent gender-sensitive retention, but could be heritage industry triggered.

Knowledge of the meaning of *farlan* is still rather widespread but, as with *barkin*, many participants have only a partial understanding of the practice, suggesting ongoing loss of knowledge of the discrete meanings of words and phrases from the peak period of the fishing. Age grading is less clear here, however, as some younger and middle-aged participants did have a fair understanding of the meaning and nature of the word. The young woman's observation that it was 'the big long things for all the fish' is striking, however, because it is possible to see it as evidence that some knowledge available to older speakers, who participated in a fishing industry which used the *farlan*, including what actually went on at the farlan, has not been transferred. Indeed the way in which the meaning is described appears almost to represent the memory of something seen – perhaps in a photograph – rather than something much discussed. This could be seen as an example of how *heritage* may help maintain a word just on the edge of memory, but with limited semantic content.

In Wick only a minority knew the word. A few older men and women were aware it related to a trough, although what happened with the trough differed from informant to informant. One older female thought it was a fishing line, while an older man thought it was the ground used for spreading the nets. Another interpretation was that *farlan* was a landmark viewed at sea. This might be 'foreland', although one informant (an older woman) talked about it meaning the 'far lands' (this might, of course, be folk etymology; interestingly, the other informant who gave this interpretation, a middle-aged woman, was given the meaning by her husband).

Half the informants did not answer the question at all, with only one, a middle-aged man, attempting to achieve an answer by relating it to *farls*, the quarter slices of bread, bannocks and cakes produced in traditional baking. It would be fair to say, therefore, that the term is on the brink of being moribund in Wick. This might be because the herring fishery became less important to the town in the course of the twentieth century, but it would be dangerous to accept such a conclusion fully from this evidence.[15]

Comparable material was collected in Lossiemouth. Most older informants had an understanding related to herring processing. Some had a fairly accurate idea that it referred to a table on which herring was gutted (although fewer that it was also connected to a trough). A number recognised the fish-processing connection, but understood *farlan* to mean the barrels in which the gutted herring was cured (or held before gutting). One older female informant gave a fairly accurate response: 'long container used to hold herring ready for women to gut', but goes on to say that she had heard this from her mother. One older man remarked that 'at the farlans' was an expression used. Another old man did not define the word but mentioned that the 'herring girls' worked at it and showed a photograph of the process to the researcher. He added, however, that herring was 'done' by the time he was a boy and that talking about it was considered old fashioned.

A number of informants also define *farlan* in relation to volume measurement, a connection made elsewhere.[16] Interestingly, quite a few people connected this to the gutting process, or as an alternative. As in Wick, one older man and a middle-aged woman both associated the word with what you could see of the land from a boat, the older man being particularly detailed in stating that these sights were 'used by fishermen as a navigational aid to fishing grounds' before the advent of modern electronic devices. It must be recognised that almost all young and middle-aged informants could not offer any definition for the word, however.

Similar levels of lack of knowledge are also present in Anstruther, whose connections to the herring trade were considerable. Some inter-pretations were highly detailed: 'a herring trough to hold herring for the quines[17] to gut them' (middle-aged female informant); 'herring were tipped into the farlan and the gutters stood around in twos with a packer behind' (older male). Two informants mentioned the troughs, but at Peterhead and Yarmouth. Interestingly, one older female attempted to define the word through a half-remembered song, 'The Farlan and the Creel'. This is likely to represent a 'heritigisation' of past work, just as using the names of other places in relation to the gutting may recognise that it was at its most industrial in the larger ports. It cannot be ruled out, of course, that this apparent dislocation actually demonstrates that the word was not regularly used in Anstruther, however, in particular in recent times, despite what the corpus says. This seems unlikely for a variety of reasons. In Eyemouth, the herring-related meaning is entirely gone, with one older man relating it to *foreland*, but only in relation to the nearby St Abbs Head.

A further historical query was related to *arles*, the 'pledge money' paid to women herring gutters before the gutting season began, demon-strating the contractor's good will and solvency as well as commitment on the part of the employee. The word was also used in relation to the various quarterly agreements between employer and employee (of both sexes) in agriculture; in fishing, however, it was associated entirely with women. It must be noted, however, that this word was amongst the most patchily recognised of any in the questionnaire.

In Peterhead, seven out of seventeen participants were able to define the word at least minimally; all were older, with the exception of one middle-aged female (although two older people, one male, one female, could not define the word). As with *barkin* and *farlan*, some informants gave a 'thorough' definition, such as 'an earnest given to gutters by fish curer prior to the start of the season to secure them for the upcoming season' or '1 shilling promise that you would work for a particular man in the gutting'. Other informants gave rather less precise definitions, including 'retainer', 'a payment' and 'the money that you get, 1 shilling', the last two of which having no overt sense of a deal being struck. As was shown in Chapter 3, the pilot survey group had generally rather vague associations with the word (some of a heritage type), in particular if the informant was under 60.

In Wick, only four older people knew the word, three male, one female. All seemed to understand the concept; one male informant related it to male experience on a boat; one male used the word *feein* as a synonym or near-synonym, which most Scots speakers would associate with farming employment cycles rather than fishing. Strikingly, one older male said that he had 'learned the word as an adult' and that '*arles* is not particularly a Caithness word'.

This appears to be less the case with Lossiemouth, where older women in particular were able to define the process in detail (although one did remark that she had learned the word from her mother). One older man gave 'pay?' as his written answer. This is considerably less certain than many of his comments on fishing methods. Despite female knowledge of the word, an older man observed that it was 'Not Lossiemouth. More farming. Fisher town vs Country Town.'[18] A male contemporary made the connection between seasonal hiring of labour in fishing and farming communities, although he was unsure if *arles* was the correct term for the latter. An older woman attested, however, that seasonal agricultural hiring took place in Elgin and the term used for the 'honour money' was *arles*. Very few middle-aged informants and no younger ones recognised the word.

Even fewer Anstruther informants knew the word. One middle-aged woman knew it meant 'payment for women', while an older man defined it as 'money paid to herring lassies'. Interestingly, one older woman said that she 'did not know [what *arles* were]', but in discussion said that it 'was very doubtful that anyone would get any money in advance'. In Eyemouth no one knew the term.

Probably the word was either only fully used in the North-East of Scotland or memory of its use remains strongest in that area. Historical evidence suggests that the former explanation is unlikely (although the lack of knowledge in Wick, which took part in some numbers in the herring trade, argues against this). It may be that the continuation of large-scale fishery in Peterhead (albeit without *arles* being distributed) may make its continuation in the memories of older speakers more straightforward and potent (although this is not something which could be proven). Moreover, and somewhat surprisingly, there is no evidence that the word was better known among female informants than male, despite the word's connection to women within the trade. This is in marked contrast to *farlan*; this distinction may, perhaps, be due to the less personal nature and much longer duration of the latter, along with its preservation in photographs and other physical evidence.

4.2.3 Cultural lexis

As was noted in Chapter 2, the Scottish fishing communities not only differed culturally from their landward neighbours; they also shared much with their sister communities. A central feature of this connection was the development of taboo-avoidance strategies which involved substituting one word (or phrase) for another which would be more acceptable either aboard ship or under any circumstances than the original word(s) were.[19]

One taboo-avoidance strategy identified along the coast related to 'salmon'. As with many superstitions, it is difficult to see exactly *why* using *salmon* onboard a fishing boat is unlucky, although a fish based in salt and fresh water at different stages in its life might be deemed inherently *unchancy* to those seeking purely sea-fish. Some knowledge – whether as a memory or a continuing practice – remained in all of the communities analysed, although knowledge levels differed geographically. In the first instance discussion was triggered by a question about the meaning of *cauld iron*, a common term for 'salmon', probably deriving from the touching of metal onboard ship when an unlucky word or concept is used.

In Peterhead, most informants recognised *cauld iron* as a term for 'salmon', most being aware of that fish's supposed bad luck. Those who recognised this point included young women. On the other hand, two informants were also aware that *cauld iron* was a more umbrella term, used instead of a word or phrase unlucky at sea. Interestingly, one informant was a young woman. The other, an older woman, commented that someone might say 'Don't speak of that, that's *cauld iron*.' Another older female informant said that *cauld iron* referred to 'pigs', another 'unlucky' animal. This interpretation is likely to share the original umbrella sense, but with the loss of the central prop.[20] It is likely that originally *cauld iron* was used to avoid any taboo term. Over time, most people interpreted that as purely salmon, while others specialised the term for other central unlucky creatures. Similar evidence was derived from the pilot survey, although strikingly one younger participant did not realise the term was a taboo-replacement term, stating that it was called this because a salmon is 'a strong fish'. No memory of taboo appears to have been maintained, therefore.

In Wick, knowledge of *cowld iron* (as would be the pronunciation there) was still considerable, but confined largely to older men and women (and also some middle-aged people). It was striking, however, that those who *did* know the word tended to be voluble in their discussion. One older man commented that 'if you say salmon they shout "cowld iron" back at you. It still happens', in marked contrast to another older man who said that he had 'never heard anyone using it deliberately, so it was already pretty rare by the 1950s'.

Strikingly, one middle-aged male informant, when prompted about the taboo, observed that 'I always says "salmon" til them; I like winding them up. See, if he says "salmon" it's supposed to be bad luck.' This must be viewed alongside another middle-aged informant (a woman), who observed that the taboo ran deep within the community, with memories of only tinned salmon ever being eaten by people associated with fishing in Wick. In Wick an understanding of the taboo may be more remembered than invoked, while in Peterhead it is known and used on an everyday basis, by at least some members of the community.

In Lossiemouth, a considerable number of informants did not know what *cauld iron* referred to, although a number recognised the phrase when it was explained to them. This group included an older man and woman. A considerable number of older people (and one younger woman) knew that the phrase was used instead of 'salmon' or when 'salmon' had been mentioned. This interpretation is starkly different from that given by another middle-aged male, who commented that 'salmon [was] unlucky at the fishing and if someone said the word, you'd tell them to touch cauld iron, which he says is just like when you say "touch wood".'[21] One older man made the association of *iron* with 'blood', although it was difficult to say whether he was referring to the dangerous aspects of the fishing trade or to the living nature of the fish. Two older men offered *red fish* for *cauld iron*, perhaps suggesting that they prefer to use other taboo avoidance strategies even when encouraged towards a 'mainstream' interpretation. A further two older male informants offered *queer fish* for 'salmon'. One younger woman noted that she was not allowed to say the word, that neither her father nor grandfather would ever say it and that they would let the fish go if caught. The strong remaining connection to fishing practice should be noted here. On the other hand, another younger woman thought that it was 'another name for a fish'.

An unusual variant on the taboo-avoidance strategy, associated with two older male informants, was that the word *salmon* was never used in public because it was illegal to fish that species from a fishing boat. Using the alternative term was a means of avoiding problems with the Crown Fishery Agents in Lossiemouth (it is worth noting that the River Lossie and to a greater extent the nearby River Spey are major salmon-fishing rivers). As has been suggested, publications like the *Glossary* may actually have been designed to help inspectors from various government agencies to avoid being bamboozled with local terms for species. A bleaching of the original superstitious associations of the phrase may have taken place, partly due to a wish not to appear superstitious, in relation to modern practice and the views of evangelical tradition. The final result of this process can be seen in the example given in the previous paragraph.

In Anstruther *cauld iron* was not as well known as in the more northern communities; instead a larger number knew *red fish* as the taboo avoidance form for 'salmon', suggesting that something like an isogloss passes between this community and Peterhead (where one informant, it should be noted, knew *red fish* – although note also the evidence from Lossiemouth: this would suggest more 'patchy' distribution than actual isoglosses). There may be something more going on here than this, however, since a number of older informants knew *cauld iron*. What is striking, however, is that few if any of them actually associated it directly with 'salmon'. One informant stated that the phrase was used to 'ward off superstition, touch cauld iron after saying salmon, pig, etc.' Two informants saw its use in a more general sense of protection from ill chance, one observing that '[t]ouching cauld iron would negate the effect of something which would bring on bad luck.' As already suggested, this may well have been the original use of the term.

Two other comments might be taken to imply at least semantic change and perhaps even a bleaching of meaning. One older woman suggested that saying *cauld iron* was 'lucky' (although she could not elaborate on what she meant). There was no link to protection from ill luck. Another older female informant noted that the phrase was '[s]omething that's said when something's not true', suggesting that *cauld iron* has been reduced to a sense of mock surprise. There may also be a touch of disapproval in 'something not true'.

Cauld iron did not elicit much discussion in Eyemouth. Although many seemed to know it as a means of avoiding taboo subjects, its connection to salmon, while occasionally mentioned, was not strongly felt. This may again be dialectal, since other taboo avoidance terms, such as *red fish* or the various names for rabbits and pigs were still well known by at least some older members of the community.

Superstitions are, of course, regularly held up to ridicule in modern Scotland (although most Scots will have at least one ritual which they feel they must perpetuate). Fishing communities, often considered as rather inward-looking by outsiders and also connected to a dangerous profession which encourages beliefs of this type, may have become particularly careful either *not* to say much about these traditions in front of outsiders or to make light of them, portraying them as 'rubbish' and thus distancing themselves from the past. In the northern communities in particular evangelical Christian traditions naturally disapprove of superstitious practices and, in theory, encourage their rooting out (although in practice rituals continue because they are engrained). This last point may make their continuation all the more shameful for many and may discourage their discussion except in the most condemnatory way. Views of this sort were commonplace in our survey. What is striking, however, is that where both tendencies would be expected to be strongest – in the north – is where memory and use continue most.

4.2.4 Non-fishing-related flora and fauna: moving beyond the community and its central occupation

In relation to the communities as a whole, attempts were made by the project not to be too fishing-trade specific. One such avenue in this avoidance was a discussion of seaborne and coastal flora and fauna which were not immediately connected economically to the fishing trade. Even when fishing was the hegemonic trade in the communities, some local people were not connected immediately or in an ancillary fashion to it. From this point of view, therefore, an awareness that the life on the coast and its specific vocabulary was not entirely connected to fishing was necessary. The flora and fauna of the common environment therefore had to be recognised.

4.2.4.1 Shellfish

All coastal districts need words for shellfish, whether edible or inedible. Old stories told around the Scottish coast and beyond associate shellfish with times of want or even famine, sometimes encouraging taboos against their use. But shellfish were also important as bait for the line fishery and were harvested in large numbers and then processed, often by women and children. Neither association is likely to have been active in living memory, although an awareness of the importance of a ready supply of shellfish to a community has remained with some informants. Many remembered (or at least recounted) the archetypal childhood experience of harvesting shellfish and then boiling them in a can on the beach for an impromptu feast. It was important to find out whether *local* words were associated with these memories or (possibly discrete from this) the present diversity found on the coast.

In the corpus, a range of words for different shellfish are present, some only found in a relatively circumscribed area. One which the sources attribute to the whole coast, however, is *buckie*, which the ST defines as 'the whelk, edible or otherwise; its shell; sometimes applied to other molluscs'. This more general sense is supported by the *Glossary*, which defines *buckie* as 'any spiral shell'. The DD, conversely, is more specific in its definition (although this may represent a situation where the full denotations and connotations of a word have not been thought through: 'periwinkle; spiral shell of winkle; *as fou's a buckie* drunk'. Schlötterer (1996: 61) agrees with the 'whelk' meaning for the word, recording it for the fishing villages around Eyemouth (but not for the Fife ports he also studied; he does, however, recognise that the word is common along the coast, backing this up from the SND).

The *Glossary* provides a number of premodified forms, such as *roaring buckie* (found along the coast, it says), *horse buckie* (found in northern Scotland) and *black buckie* (found in north-east Scotland), all referring to 'winkle'. The ST adds *rair/roaring buckie* 'a kind of whelk shell which, when held to the ear makes a roaring sound thought to sound like the sea', observing that it is now found in Angus and Fife. That resource also gives *John o Gro(a)t's buckie* for the cowrie shell; the DD presents a shortened form, *Johnny Groatie*, which refers to the same mollusc (John o'Groats is a small village to the north of Wick which is traditionally considered the most north-easterly point on the island of Britain; for fishermen, its importance lies in its being the point where the currents and tides of the North Sea meet those of the Pentland Firth).

The word *buckie* appears well known, but is also capable of being analysed as referring both to one mollusc species and to all (edible) shellfish. The fact that modifications are possible, with some forms referring to specific types of shellfish, also makes the word attractive for research designed to test knowledge of what had been common words in these communities. In order to do this, two questions were used. The first was a traditional dialectological-style enquiry, seeking a translation for *buckie*, the second a more open-ended request for information on whether the informant knew any further kinds of *buckie*. Before administering these questions we were aware that for many informants – perhaps particularly the young – the chief association of *buckie* was as the diminutive form for *Buckfast*, a 'tonic wine' whose use among the young is considered a problem in many communities (and whose consumption is also taken as a badge of pride among some young men). This connection was indeed active for many informants (although patchily: our Wick informants seemed less inclined towards the wine connection), as was, for some, the connection to the Moray fishing town. These did not mask the knowledge of the fishing-specific term, however.

In Peterhead a large majority knew that a *buckie* was a mollusc; quite a number associated it with 'whelk' or 'winkle' and sometimes both. Many older men and women associated the word with molluscs with grey and black shells, although one older woman said it was a 'little grey whelk, not very attractive'. This sounds as if it is related to a different kind of shellfish, but it is difficult to tell. A small number of middle-aged informants associated it with a 'creature in a shell', one actually equating it to a hermit crab. Interestingly, two younger female informants said that they knew what the word meant, but had never used it themselves. As was demonstrated in Chapter 3, around half of the pilot survey group knew the shellfish connections of *buckie*, although some appeared able to be more accurate in their definitions than others. A few younger informants offered Tonic Wine or the Moray port as their first association.

Most Wick informants of all ages knew the mollusc meaning of *buckie*, although a small number, again across the age groups, defined it as a shell (the reason for associating with the discarded carapace of an animal rather than the animal itself will be explained in the following). A number associated it with 'whelk' (usually with the Scots pronunciation /wʌlk/), although one informant associates it with a 'wee cowrie shell'. Most of the informants think of the word as being an integral part of *groatie buckie*, a point to which we will return.

While some younger Lossiemouth people did not know the shellfish meaning for *buckie*, many of them giving meaning related either to the alcoholic drink or the nearby port, many informants were able to make the connection to shellfish, offering a range of different associations – *whelks, periwinkles, winkles, cockles, mussels*. The shells and sizes of these molluscs demonstrate considerable difference, which could suggest either that *buckie* is the umbrella term, or that speakers no longer have a strong sense of distinctions between the different species. Three older informants, two female, one male, associated the word with a sea snail which 'clings to the rocks'. Unlike the previous example, this *does* suggest a local association. One older woman said that big shellfish were also called *buckies*, if a great many of them were found, you might say that there was 'a world of buckies the day'.

Rather less rich pickings were present in Anstruther. A fair number of middle-aged and older informants associated *buckie* with shellfish (although only one with whelks). One younger man said it was a scallop shell (a very different shape of shell indeed). On the other hand two older informants (one man and one woman) actually distinguished between *buckies*, which were large whelks, and not good to eat, and smaller whelks, which were delicious.

Despite Schlötterer's findings discussed above, *buckie* was hardly known in Eyemouth. Those who did know it as a mollusc were at least middle-aged. Strikingly, almost every informant had a different conception of the animal's colouring and size (although one middle-aged informant very specifically defined it as a *dog whelk*).

In relation to the 'other words for *buckie*' supplementary question, the northern communities were much more productive than the southern. On this occasion, it was Wick which produced the most discussion. As we have seen, most informants answering the first question immediately used the phrase *groatie buckie*. If, as has been suggested, this term has a local connection, this is not surprising. What was striking was the amount of narrative inspired by the word. *Groatie buckies* were prized more for their look as shells than as a food resource and many informants spoke about looking for the (empty) shells as children. Strikingly, Peterhead informants who mentioned the *groatie buckie* (or *Johnny groatie*) largely saw it in the same terms (while adding that they were no longer to be found in Peterhead).

Wick informants produced an impressive discussion of other type of shellfish, including a definition of the difference between *whelks* and *buckies*. These included *buck*, 'big edible shells', *tinkler whelks* 'dog whelks' and *spoots*, 'sword shells', although the older male informant who gave this example said it was 'already an uncommon word in my youth'. This experience is somewhat different from the occasional appearance of *spoot* in the conversation of Caithness speakers heard independently of this research. It should be noted that, with the exception of *bucks*, known by a middle-aged man, all information derives from older people. All the other communities produced rather less discussion, with Peterhead producing, along with *Johnny groaties*, only one mention of *whities*, poisonous buckies. Lossiemouth informants offered a range of English equivalents – *periwinkles*, *winkles*, *whelks*, and so on. A number of variants were offered, however, including *horse buckie* for bigger, white buckies (offered by an older man and woman) and *sewage buckies* (offered by an older man). No mention of *groaties* was made. Anstruther informants largely produced standard words – *scallop shell, whulk/whelk, limpets, periwinkle,* Eyemouth informants were similar in what they produced, with the exception that they also provided words for crabs along with shellfish lexis.

There is a possibility that Wick people remember these terms better than other communities because their fishing tradition was associated with the use of line in ways that the others were not, this being the opposite argument to the community's lack of knowledge of herring-based vocabulary described above. But it runs further than this. In Wick, Peterhead, Lossiemouth and to an extent Anstruther the word *buckie* is still meaningful (although it must be accepted that the precise meaning is a little 'frayed'). To a considerable extent Wick speakers appear to have continued a sense of *buckie* and its near synonyms; the fact that *groatie buckie* has local associations (in a similar way to *scorrie* 'seagull', as discussed below) no doubt encourages the strength of this survival. Peterhead informants were less productive, but local traditions of nomenclature obviously survive. In Anstruther (and even more so in Eyemouth), this tradition is practically moribund. All that are left, it would appear, are a few common words. This is important because words for shellfish were never as closely connected to the fishing trade as, say, words related to gutting. Anyone who lives in a coastal community will come into contact with the animals involved. The fact that informants in Eyemouth place crabs among the shellfish demonstrates the perceptions of someone who does not connect fully with the sea, particularly striking when it is remembered that, unlike Wick and Anstruther, Eyemouth still has some professional fishing. Even in Peterhead, however, evidence suggests that the youngest informants have little or no interest in the use of local terminology, even when they know it.

4.2.4.2 Seaweed

Seaweed is omnipresent in coastal communities (to the eyes and the nose, whether involved in fishing or not), but not, for obvious reasons, found elsewhere. Different species of seaweed look different and smell different. Until very recently, moreover, seaweed was used for fertiliser and in the production of iodine. Several species were also regularly eaten, although other species are poisonous. The kelp beds in particular were associated with the habitats of a range of shellfish and fish. It was therefore necessary for dialects to distinguish between the different species in ways that more mainstream varieties would largely consign to technical registers.

A considerable number of words for seaweed turn up in the corpus.

Some refer to separate types of weed, while others are geographically constrained. Among these, the most prevalent appears to be *ware* (variously spelt *waar* and *waur* and pronounced as /wer/, /war/ or /wɔr/, depending on the region). The ST defines it as 'a kind of seaweed, *chf* for use as manure', giving as its present provenance Shetland, Orkney, East Central and West Central dialect areas. BC, however, demonstrates its use in the North-East, while it is also recorded in both the CD and the CW. Its distribution can then be said, at least in the recent past, to include all of the east coast. *Warry* is given as a derivative, defined by the ST as 'covered with, living among or generally pertaining to seaweed'. The CW also gives *waarie midden* for a 'bank of seaweed', the smell involved implied by *midden*.

A number of variants on *ware* were also identified in the ST, largely in relation to the more northern regions. For Caithness, *bell waar* and *henny waur* are recorded with the meaning 'seaweed' in local resources (the latter, recorded for Kincardineshire – considerably further down the coast – by the ST is defined as 'an edible seaweed'). The CD also records *bougie-waur*, which it defines as 'kelp'. In the north-east, *bellware* or *beliwar* is also recorded by the ST as 'a course seaweed'; the same resource records *seaware* for the same region, as 'seaweed, esp[ecially] the coarse kind washed up by the tide and used as manure'. No extensions of form and meaning are recorded for the southern communities.

Another common word for weed is *wrack, wreck* or *wreak*, defined as 'seaweed and miscellaneous flotsam washed up by the sea' by the ST for everywhere in Scotland except the Northern Isles (indeed a subsidiary meaning relates it to freshwater weed, thus making its occurrence possible throughout the country). It is, of course, related to forms present in, but now marginal to, Standard English; interestingly, no derivative forms are found in the corpus.

Other terms for seaweed are also represented in the corpus. *Tangle*, for instance, is recorded by the ST along the east coast, with the sense of 'the long stalk and fronds of large, coarse seaweed growing above the low-water mark'. The same resource provides *brook* for 'a deep layer of seaweed cast ashore by stormy weather', frequently as *brook o ware*, recorded in northern dialects. *Keys* for the type 'badderlacks' is also northern.

For Caithness, *kefans* is recorded by both local resources with the meaning 'green seaweed'. The ST records *slake, sloke* as the name for 'one of various species of edible fresh- and saltwater algae', with its present distribution being Shetland, Orkney and Caithness. The CD presents *swarthead* for the root of seaweed. The DSL gives *swart('s)heid* for the edible top of the large tangle, with a purely Caithness provenance. The

CW gives *swart* for the thick stem of kelp, while providing two possible Old Norse etymologies for the word. There is every chance that these three words are related to each other, although it is difficult to see precisely what the connections might be.

Dabberlacks (probably a variant of *badderlacks*) is, according to the ST, a kind of edible seaweed, recording for Moray and Banff. Other North-East words include *carlers* 'heavy seaweed of tangles, used in cosmetics and medicines' (recorded by the DD, derived from BC), *currack,* another word for 'tangle', recorded for Banff by the ST, *dallie's cleysies,* 'doll's clothes; coloured seaweed' (recorded in the DD, derived from BC) and *green gaw* 'green slimy seaweed or green algae', which the ST records for Aberdeenshire. The same resource records the word *raips* for the 'stems of seaweed, specific[ally] of the oar-weed' for the North-East. The LG gives *tangles* for 'kelp' as a local word; it appears rather more widespread, however. Schlötterer, for instance, records *tangles* for almost all of his communities, from Crail and Anstruther in the north to Burnmouth and St Abbs in the south. He observes that '[s]ome informants mentioned *kelp, weed* or *seaweed* next to *tangle(s)*. They always insisted on *tangle(s)* being the local word, however' (Schlötterer 1996: 40). *Reid, red* or *rid ware* was given by the ST for 'the seaweed *Laminaria digitata* from its red colour', its distribution being from Shetland to Northern dialects and also in Fife.

Given the wide distribution of some terms – such as *ware* – and the fairly localised use of other terms, the questionnaire was designed with two seaweed questions: one dealing with knowledge of *ware*, the other with other terms informants might know and use. In the following analysis, the first will be dealt with separately from the second.

In Peterhead, all of the older informants, most of the middle-aged participants and one younger woman connected *ware* or *waar* with seaweed. A number of them could give a more specific interpretation for the word. These included: '(black) tangles', 'small, green seaweed washed up on shore' (all provided by older informants, male and female) and 'seaweed that is washed up on the shore' or '*the waar:* seaweed that's washed up when tide is out and smells horrible' (given by middle-aged participants, the first male, the second female). The unpleasant smell given off by the seaweed was remarked upon by a number of informants, many using the phrase *the guff o ware* (with one older woman saying that this was the title of a book about seaweed in the Moray Firth). One middle-aged male informant gave *kofi* (*kafe*) *waar* for 'a fine, perfume smelling seaweed of which you'd get a lot while fishing near corrals'. Those participants who did not recognise the seaweed meaning were divided between those who did not recognise any meaning for the word

ANALYSIS OF THE DATA

and those who saw it as Scots *waar/waur* 'worse'. One younger man somewhat optimistically related the word to *haar*, the cold summer fog which affects the coast. As Chapter 3 demonstrated, a sizeable minority of informants did not connect *ware* with 'seaweed'. Some of those who did know demonstrated considerable connotations for the word, however, often associated with smell.

Although, as we will see, Wick informants gave a range of words for seaweed, only a few knew the *ware* meaning. This may be due to the multiple spellings given in the question, with *waur* 'worse' and *wur* 'our' being given by a number of informants of all ages and both backgrounds; other interpretations being, as in Peterhead, 'where' (one younger woman saying 'we don't pronounce the [h] in *where*') and even a common surname in Canis Bay. A number of older participants, particularly older men, knew the word, defining it as 'brown seaweed' or as 'a generic word for seaweed; there were various types of *waar*'. Another older male informant noted that '*ware* is not so commonly used now. We'd use it among ourselves but it's not a common word'. One informant adds *hennywaar* 'the green one you can eat'. A number of older and middle-aged informants referred to *waar-blockie*, a (red) cod which lives among the seaweed. An older male informant added that '*waar blockie* is a cod which lives in the *waar*; not a Caithness term; . . . they're red . . ., like goldfish, . . . people catch them . . . a word not known by many, nor is it known in Fraserburgh', a point belied somewhat by the number of people commenting upon the usage. Why *ware* is not commonly recognised by Wick people cannot presently be established, particularly since the word and its derivatives are well recorded for the region in the corpus. In Wick the word was known by some older informants, and one middle-aged man. Few if any younger people knew the word. Many people associated it with the equivalent to English *worse*, with one middle-aged man claiming that it was *where*. Interestingly, a number of Lossiemouth people of a variety of ages say either that it is not known there or that they do not recognise the word at all. In Anstruther, a number of older informants knew *ware*, although it did not appear to be widely understood (even one older male gave 'worse'). In Eyemouth, no seaweed connection was given, with some older and middle-aged informants giving 'worse' or 'our'.

With relation to other words for seaweed, two older male informants in Peterhead give *carlas* (*carlers* in the corpus). One of the informants said that children used to fight with this type of seaweed. An older man and woman gave *delce* for a type of (red) edible seaweed. One older woman gave *gaar* as the word for seaweed in Portsoy (a considerable distance along the Moray Firth coast), while an older man suggested that it was the 'small stuff' (this form is not recorded in the Corpus, although *gaw* is). *Raak* (*wrack* in the Corpus) represented 'seaweed with bubbles' to one older man. The most common other name for seaweed found in the community, including one younger woman, was *tangles*, often seen as the generic term (rather than *ware*). At the other end of the recognition continuum, some, normally older, informants recognised alternative words for 'seaweed', not found in Standard English. Participants gave the terms *tangles* (six participants), *dulce* (three participants), *curly seaweed* (one participant), *kelp* (one participant), and *loonies* (one participant). *Tangles* were described by one participant as a specific type of seaweed different from *ware*. The former are thicker and browner. Another person mentioned that *tangles* were edible. One participant suggested that the term *tangles*, pronounced 'tunnels' was only used on the Moray Firth coast (in distinction to the North Sea coast represented by Peterhead). One older man defines the word as 'thick seaweed with leaves; washed ashore during storms'. Lossiemouth informants offered a fair range of words, including *bladderack*, a type of seaweed with 'pimples' that you squeeze and pop (offered jointly by two older men), *dulce* a reddish, edible seaweed, offered by several older men and women (two of whom mentioned *dulce pudding*). A number of older people offered *lacers* or *laces*, for a long seaweed which got tangled, dangerous to swimmers and boats. One older man and one older women offered *wire*, in some senses appearing to produce a word similar to *ware* (which one at least did not know well), possibly to accommodate the research. This particular seaweed is long and thin and may be called *wire* by metaphorical extension. The most commonly elicited local word for seaweed is *tangles*, however. As the name suggests, these were large weeds which easily became tangled in nets (often meaning that the nets needed to be cut). Both older and middle-aged people offered this word; no younger person did, however. In Wick, *dulse* was also recorded by older and middle-aged people; *tangles* is also common for the same age group. Interestingly, neither word is defined further than 'seaweed'. In Anstruther, even less variety was available. Most older people knew *tangles*, with one older woman giving *carpet on the rocks* and the same person and another older woman giving *green*. In Eyemouth, only one middle-aged man gave *tangles*. It may be that the great changes in use of seaweed over the twentieth century, as its industrial applications and regular use in food (in Scotland) collapsed, led to an growing 'amnesia' in relation to seaweed species and perhaps even of seaweed itself, quickly spread among the coastal populace. Unlike birds or fish, of course, seaweed cannot really 'do' anything. It cannot interact with humans and can therefore be readily ignored.

4.2.4.3 Seabirds

A good example of the ranges of use, as well as the survival and loss of lexical forms and features along the coasts, can be found by comparing words triggered by photographs of a seagull and a cormorant, both regular visitors to (indeed, often inhabitants of) coastal settlements even if, particularly with the first bird, they are not universally loved. These birds are likely to be amongst the most recognisable wildlife in the communities, even without a fishing connection. Moreover, prior research had demonstrated that words for 'gull' were often badges of local pride, with communities within a very short distance of each other using strikingly different words for the birds to the extent that the name often became a nickname, as discussed above. With the decline of the old coastal connections between communities, it was considered interesting to investigate the extent to which these designations have survived.

In Peterhead, Downie and other scholars demonstrate, the local form for 'seagull' is *scorrie/scurrie*. Overwhelmingly this has remained the case, with a number of informants commenting that the Standard English equivalent was one associated with outsiders. Three out of the seventeen participants also referred to *myaave*, the local form of Scots *maw* (cognate to archaic English *mew*). Two of these were older men, interestingly, who considered the word to be 'local'; the other was a younger woman who came from St Combs,[22] a village between Peterhead and Fraserburgh, a point which may be of some interest, since *myaave* had non-native connotations for some Peterhead informants. Similar findings were present in the pilot study, with *scorrie/scurrie* being dominant. Two other words were given by two retired fisherman: *mallie* and *pewlie*. The first is striking because, as we will see in our discussion of the Lossiemouth material, the word refers, according to the resources available, not to a gull, but rather a fulmar. This may be less a 'mistake' than a generalisation of names according to habitat and habit rather than species, a point to which we will return.[23] The observation by an elderly minority that *pewlie* is a *Peterhead* word for 'seagull' when it is largely seen as being the term preferred in fishing communities to the west of Fraserburgh (as we will see below, Gardenstown/Gamrie in particular) again points to a time when these terms were less rigidly attributed to particular places than is now the case. It is noteworthy that one pilot study participant said that Aberdonians did not know *scorrie*. Interestingly, one younger woman offered *scurry* as the normal word for 'gull' in Fraserburgh, with concentration, perhaps, on the difference of pronunciation of the central vowel.

Peterhead people were also often aware of the words used in the fishing communities relatively distant from them, as well as those who lived in the immediate neighbourhood, as we have seen. Gardenstown/ Gamrie and the nearby Pennan were associated with *pule* by a considerable number of people, including one younger woman. That this was not merely a neutral designation can be seen in the story recounted by a middle-aged man about his grandparents. When they were fighting, his grandfather (from Rosehearty, in the rural hinterland) would call his wife a *Gamrie Pule*. She would retort that he was a *Rosehearty Ingin* 'onion'. We will return towards the end of the chapter to the use of these toponymic near-insults. One middle-aged woman produced *gow* for people from Moray.

As can be seen, most informants associate *myaave* with the villages between Peterhead and Fraserburgh, or even with Fraserburgh. That two older men associated it as a native form with Peterhead might suggest that these distinctions were not at one point as clear-cut as they are now. Nevertheless, it is the passive knowledge of a range of terms which remains in the mind, their survival due to the need to distinguish closely nearby and often related communities from 'home'. In the pilot study the term *pewlie* was recorded by three informants, two associating it with Gardenstown/Gamrie, the other with Buckie, a port further along the Moray Firth coast. Two participants offered *gaw* for 'seagull', one in Buckie, the other Elgin. It may be that by 'Elgin' nearby Lossiemouth is meant, but it is impossible to be certain about this.

Interestingly, the Peterhead word for 'cormorant', *scrath* or *scroth*, was produced by rather fewer informants – eleven out of seventeen. While this still represents a majority, it should be noted that no young informants volunteered the word (most preferring standard *shag* or *cormorant*), two called it a *gannet* (normally a term for a species distinct from, but often conflated with, the gull) and four people (one older, one in middle age and two younger) produced no name for the bird. All, strikingly, were female. While it is probably to be expected that fewer people would know the local name of the cormorant than the gull (which has both iconic and identity-bearing characteristics), it is still a common bird, regularly seen in harbours and along the coast, with a range of stories and superstitions historically attached to it.

Answers to this question in the pilot study were rather more varied. They included *cormorant, scrath, duck, mallie, juke,* and *northern diver*. The most frequent term given was *cormorant* (by eight people) followed by *scrath* (given by four people). All four who said *scrath* were men in the oldest or middle-age group; no women or young people were familiar with this term. Three people who gave *scrath* had also identified the bird as *cormorant*. On the other hand, one participant who named this bird as 'a *scrath* or a *duck*' explicitly said that he did not recognise the bird as a *cormorant*. One participant's grandfather, whose responses are not tallied here, produced both *scrath* and *juke*, the latter probably representing the local pronunciation of *duck*, /djuk/.

Four people did not give any terms for the bird, including Standard English *cormorant*. Of these, two said they were not good with bird names. Interestingly, one informant could not think of any terms, but recognised *cormorant* when that word was used for the bird in the picture. As mentioned above, one young male guessed that this was a *gannet* (a word normally associated with the seagull, although actually a similar but discrete species), but was unsure.

Interestingly, there was also some confusion among those who knew words for the bird over whether some words actually referred to *that* bird. The older fishers who participated in a group interview were unsure whether or not to also call this bird a *mallie* (a word which does not seem to be recorded in DSL). One older male, who produced both *scrath* and *cormorant*, also gave us the term *northern diver*. He was the only one to generate this term. It is unclear if he used *northern diver* for cormorants or for a different bird altogether (the Great Northern Diver is largely black above the water, but is rather more plump – almost duck-like – in comparison to the cormorant), but the former interpretation is the most convincing, since he gave us this term as apparently equivalent to *scrath* and *cormorant*.

The sole local term for this bird that is known with any regularity is *scrath*. It should be noted, however, that *scrath* is known by middle-aged and older men alone. Youngsters and women use the standard term, *cormorant*, or no term at all. It can therefore be postulated that both age and gender, as with other terms, is central to their survival. Other features have to be borne in mind, however.

A person's ability to generate an appropriate term depends in part on their familiarity with (and interest in) birds in general, an explanation given by some participants who were unable to name this bird. Also, some people appear to have mistaken the bird for some type of duck. Why this was the case is less clear (see also the discussion of the Great Northern Diver above). It could be because of the bird's resemblance to a duck, the photo being ambiguously a duck or a cormorant, or their semantic referent of the terms cormorant or *scrath* to include or exclude ducks. There was also a hint of ambiguity when it came to *scrath*, with one participant suggesting that a *scrath* was not a cormorant, while the remaining three people who gave us *scrath* equated it with that bird. It might be argued – although it could not be proven – that *scrath* lies at the edge of retention, barely being maintained within the local lexis.

In Wick, on the other hand, the greater part of informants know the local name for 'cormorant', *scarf(ie)*. Even on this occasion, however, four people did not produce *cormorant* or *shag*, two of these were young women. As with Peterhead, two names associated with other sea birds were given for the cormorant photograph by one middle-aged woman: *gannet* and *skua*. Why this falling away and disassociation is taking place is difficult to judge from such a limited amount of information.

With the seagull photograph, however, the knowledge of the local word – *scorrie* – was universal; indeed, it tended to be the first word elicited from an informant, even before *(sea)gull*. A number of informants mentioned that the local football team was nicknamed the Scorries. In a sense the weekly appearance of the word in a range of media must encourage its retention. *Maa/maw* was known only by the older informants; many saw it as a separate species (or sub-species) whose nesting took place on the hills behind the town (they were often termed *hill-maas*) rather than on cliffs and buildings nearer to the sea.[24] Historically, these two words refer to the same bird; that does not mean, of course, that local people, faced with synonyms, have not developed a distinction.

Despite being geographically discrete from the other Scottish fishing ports, some informants – normally older – were aware that Peterhead people also called their gulls *scorries* but that the people of Lossiemouth called them *gows*. Understandably at that distance only the usage of the larger ports is known. A number of Wick informants knew that *maa* was the main word for seagull in their sister town of Thurso on the Pentland Firth. This raises the question of whether Wick people are aware fully of the proposed split they have made which their neighbours have not.

Similarly, in Lossiemouth almost all informants immediately offered *gow* for 'seagull', a form which is given as Northern in the ST, and as north-eastern by Downie, but as associated with Buckie (a port not far to the east of Lossiemouth) by the DD; it is specifically referred to in the LG. One middle-aged female informant in Lossiemouth observed that her children used either *gow* or *gull* depending on who they were speaking to, but she used *gow* solely. Two older men agreed that *gow* would still be known in Lossiemouth by young people. One young woman said that she now mostly used *seagull* rather than *gow* because, when at university in Glasgow, she had had to adjust in order to be understood. One older female said that *seagull* is the 'right word' for the species, but that she and her husband use *gow* universally.

Several further terms were offered. Many older and middle-aged people said that the bird in the photograph was a *blackback* or *black backer*. Technically this was not the case (the bird was actually a white-backed herring gull), but the level of response for this form may demonstrate a generalisation of the term. One older male informant did define the bird as a *white gow*, which suggests that some speakers maintain the distinction.

A number of older and middle-aged informants of both sexes identified the bird as a *grey willie*, many of them saying that they did so primarily because the bird appeared young. The ST associated the term with Northern dialects, while *grey wull* is given for 'seagull chick' in both the CD and the LG. Downie reports *gru willie* with the same meaning in Hopeman, Lossiemouth's near neighbour to the west.

A small number of older and middle-aged informants offered *jockey* for 'seagull', some associating it with black-headed gulls. This term was also used in Peterhead as an affectionate term for gulls. But the LG associates the word with the *fulmar* (a similar but distinct species), while Downie associates this meaning with Lossiemouth. A number of informants did associate *jockey* with 'fulmar', however, one adding *malley*, which Downie suggests is the Peterhead word for 'fulmar' (interestingly, DSL does offer this word for a range of birds, but never for 'fulmar'). A number of other informants gave variants of *kittiwake* (and one of *tern*) as a word for 'seagull', suggesting that many of these terms were regularly used interchangeably.

In relation to the word for 'gull' used elsewhere along the coast as perceived from Lossiemouth, it was striking that a considerable number of informants of all backgrounds did not know any other words; indeed, one older man and an older female informant acknowledged that other words are used, but could not remember any. A middle-aged man and woman offered *pewl(ie)*, the latter saying that she associated it with Whitehills, a small port to the east of Buckie (not far from the Gardenstown/Gamrie region associated with the word in Peterhead; interestingly, one young female informant gave the word as the Lossiemouth form). A small number of older informants, all men, associated *scurry* with Peterhead or (on one occasion), Fraserburgh, suggesting, perhaps, that the usage of the two large fishing towns considerably to the east has been conflated (although note the observation above that the oldest informants in Peterhead may not have such a categorical distinction of terms between the sister towns as is now the case). One older male informant associates *scorrie* with Wick.

The knowledge of words for 'cormorant' is rather less impressive than for 'seagull'. Many people knew only *cormorant*, while others offered *shag* (although one older man did note that this was a separate species, albeit similar in looks). Three women (one from each age group) offered *heron*. Three words *were* offered by a number of informants, mostly older, but with some middle-aged people. *Scarf(ie)* is widely known, although some informants view it primarily as a word used elsewhere. *Neckie* (an appropriate name given the extent to which that part of the bird is central to its appearance) is treated by a considerable number of informants as *the* local term (something noted by Downie, the only external source to mention the word). Finally, two older men give *baggie* for 'cormorant', although one pointed out that it was the name for another diving bird. The DSL defines the word as 'greater black-headed gull', but only in Shetland; the LG defines the word as 'sea bird', with an annotation that it refers specifically to 'shag' or 'cormorant'.

Healthy knowledge of the local word for seagull is also prevalent in Anstruther, with most informants providing the local form *cuttsy* or *cutty*. Some volunteered that the former was normal in Cellardyke and the latter in Pittenweem; Anstruther, we assume, being in the middle, and therefore sharing in elements of both usages, has both. There was some knowledge of *(sea-)maw*, which was identified as Anstruther or Cellardyke usage by an older woman from Pittenweem. Some persistence of knowledge of non-local words for 'seagull' was also present (and not necessarily for older people: one middle-aged man knew the term *scurry* in relation to Peterhead, for instance).

Some informants – largely older and with some prompting for a few – knew the traditional local term *scoot* for 'cormorant'. The same middle-aged man who knew *scurry* was also aware of this word, demonstrating that he is well-versed in local tradition and usage. Interestingly, some of the informants – none young, but all female – used words otherwise associated with seagulls or similar species (including *seagull* itself, *gannet* and even *cuttsy*). It might just about be possible to say that the picture triggered words associated with a black-headed gull; such an association would imply a striking lack of experience with what either cormorants or gulls looked like, however. It is interesting that this 'mistake' runs parallel to one found among some Peterhead women.

The material from Eyemouth is strikingly different in terms of quality and quantity. The normal word given for 'seagull' was *(sea)gull*. Any further local terms tended to be highly derogatory (and were occasionally found as secondary forms elsewhere along the coast). These included *flying rats*, *shite hawks* and *scunner* (the Scots word for something unpleasant or irritating; this last word given by an older woman).

Four informants knew *scoot* for 'cormorant' (one with prompting). An older woman gave *coot*, a word normally used for a rather different (although still water) bird, which may have been intended as *scoot*. One informant gave *wagtail*, a term also normally associated with another bird (on this occasion, not seaborne or black); another gave *nark*; this word has defeated searches in a range of dictionaries beyond our corpus. Three informants immediately gave *cormorant*, while two gave *shag*.

Other local usages may be retained because of cultural resonances (although naturally attrition of localised culture in the face of globalised (and even regional and supralocal) practice inevitably encourages the diminution of this type of tradition and of the words and phrases offered. The taboo-avoidance tradition discussed above is a striking part of this culture; one, also, which, at least for a time, we could assume to be continued even when commercial fishing ceased.

4.2.4.4 Marine mammals

When constructing the questionnaire, it was decided that at least one question should be included on marine animals which do not have an *immediate* connection to fishing but which would have some resonance for coastal dwellers and, in particular, those who use boats. The decision was eventually taken to include a picture of a porpoise with a request for local words for the animal. It was expected that many informants would not distinguish between porpoises and dolphins (although some would); since both animals are regular visitors to the Scottish east coast (in particular, perhaps, the Moray Firth), this was not considered a major issue, particularly since the corpus suggests that local words are used for both species.

In the corpus, *pellock* is given for 'porpoise' by the ST, with the suggestion that it was originally also used for 'dolphin'; no distribution is given; the *New Caithness Book* gives *peelag. Peenick*, which may be related to this word, is given by Downie for the Moray Firth, while the LG also records the form. As it stands, it does not appear to be given in DSL. Downie gives *louper dug* (literally 'jumper/jumping dog') for the coast from Buckie (towards the upper end of the Moray Firth) to Peterhead. The ST gives *puffie (dunter)* for 'porpoise', saying that the phrase is now used only in the North-East. Downie goes further, saying that it is prevalent only on the east coast of that region (that is, from Fraserburgh south, with a strong concentration on Peterhead). From this information it could be predicted that speakers of the northern dialects would be most likely to know local words for this mammal.

In Peterhead, around half of the informants, all older or middle-aged, knew local words for porpoise. *Louper dogs* was given by seven participants, no distinction being made by many between dolphins and porpoises. One middle-aged man suggested that the name came from the animals' habit of playing in the wake of boats. *Puffy* was given by five informants, including one older woman (the only female who gave local names). Three participants considered *puffy* to be a word for small dolphins or porpoises. Three older men knew another term, variously spelt *mulldon*, *mullden* and *mull don*. Two informants stated that these were larger than porpoises. In DSL, *muldoan* is defined as 'basking shark', the large plankton-eating member of the shark family regularly found in Scottish waters (with the cited *Fishery Board Glossary* of 1930 saying that the word is used in Aberdeen and Ayr). The origin of the word is given by DSL as 'doubtful, [perhaps] a corruption of Gael. *maol dobhran*, the otter, transferred in sea-taboo language to the shark'. It is highly probable that some confusion has taken place over which term refers to which aquatic creature; it is not impossible that the taboo-transference term has been passed on to another animal, however, possibly for similar taboo-avoidance reasons. It is striking that this word also turned up in our discussion of monkfish names.

In Lossiemouth the local words *pellag* and *peenick* (in a range of spellings) were offered by a considerable number of older and middle-aged informants, as was *louper* and *loupin dowg* (with the characteristic local pronunciation of *dog*). Older men offered *pinhead* and *porbeagle*. According to OED the latter originally meant 'shark'; in particular an edible species of shark (the word itself is probably of Cornish origin). This is very similar to the *mullden* example found in Peterhead (one other older man in Lossiemouth offered *shark*). The same resource suggests that one of *pinhead*'s meanings relates to small or young fish, this meaning being particularly common in Scotland and the United States. Other animal names offered include *sea hare* (according to OED, used for a particular mollusc or the lumpfish) and *sea coo*, which may refer to the walrus or morse (a secondary meaning in OED to the better known manatee association with *sea cow*). One younger woman sees the animal portrayed as a whale. This is probably due to a lack of recognition rather than transference, probably situating this word with all the offerings of *porpoise* given by younger people in particular as their only word for the animal; many people could not decide whether the animal shown was a dolphin or a porpoise, moreover. Despite two older men not knowing any other words for 'porpoise' than the Standard English one, there is no doubt that a fair amount of knowledge persists among middle-aged and older inhabitants of Lossiemouth. Partly this is probably due to the fact that both dolphins and porpoises are regularly seen in that part of the Moray Firth. One older man noted, however, that salmon fisherman do not like porpoises because they take one bite of the fish and spoil the catch. Such an unfortunate association may reinforce the old words for the animal (particularly because, perhaps, of the 'new age' associations *dolphin* now has).

In Wick, fewer forms were given, but one form, variably given as *pellig, pellag* and *pealtag*, expected because of corpus evidence, was known by a large minority of informants, including one younger woman. Most informants gave *dolphin* in the first instance, however; two younger women gave *whale*, while one younger man expressly said that he did not know any local words for the animal. In Anstruther, four informants, middle-aged and older and of both sexes, gave *puffy* (although one older woman had to be prompted). The fact that this is known in the East Neuk of Fife brings into question the distribution suggested for it by the ST, discussed above. One older man produced *baffy*, which is likely to be a variant of *puffy*. One younger man gave *porpiss*, which suggests an attempt at eye dialect. Results for 'porpoise' in Eyemouth are not rich, but, again, three informants – two women (one older, one middle-aged) and one middle-aged man – gave *puffy*.

A knowledge of words for 'porpoise' and by extension other marine creatures must have been widespread in fishing communities fifty to sixty years ago, but that lack of experience of being on the sea on a regular basis has largely stopped transfer of words. Although the northern (particularly Moray Firth) concentration predicted is present, there is no doubt that a number of words – *puffy* being the most obvious – are (or were) more common than some resources suggest. Whether this is due to the words' being native to the communities or having been spread and maintained through regular contact with the areas where experience of porpoises and dolphins was commonplace is beyond the remit of this discussion.

4.2.5 Weather and the sea

Although not confined in its effects to the fishing trade, weather is a set of phenomena central to the good (or bad) running of that occupation; indeed, on occasion, it is a matter of life and death. If you are not immediately connected to the trade, your tie to the weather is probably less visceral, but its effects are considerable on how you conduct your day, what your mood is and what clothes you wear. Unsurprisingly, therefore, the corpus produces a considerable number of local vocabulary items on different types of weather. Although all types of weather associated with the east coast of Scotland (and possibly the fishing grounds to which local people sailed) are represented in the corpus, it was assumed that unpleasant weather – cold and damp in particular – were more likely to occasion the use and perpetuation of local words and phrases than would good weather. This assumption was made on a number of grounds. The nature of the weather in the area under observation is generally not given to high temperatures and summer is more associated with the *haar*, the cold fog common on the coast in that season, than with great heat. Moreover, good weather does not demand the same discussion as does bad in relation to the fishing; high pressure zones, with long periods of similar weather, do not need to be spoken of in the same way as dangerously variable weather does. Fishermen and their communities had a fear of jinxing good weather by speaking about it too much or in too enthusiastic tones. As might be expected, the actual evidence from the corpus is on a large scale, covering a broad range of different weather types at different levels of strength and hardship, as well as providing a sense of overlapping dialect use. So rich is this information that it could not be illustrated well without warping the sense of the book's primary concerns.

With this diversity in mind, the questionnaire did not ask for translations of specific lexical items, instead concentrating on encouraging multiple elicitations in a manner reminiscent of the mind-mapping techniques discussed above. At one level this decision made a great deal of sense – almost all informants in all of the communities produced a number of alternative words and phrases for each weather situation or phenomenon. At another level, however, the material which this methodology threw up was strangely at odds with most of the information derived from the corpus, even in those communities – such as Wick and Peterhead – where locals generally exhibit retention of many local and cultural lexical items.

This can be seen most strikingly when the informants were asked to give words and phrases for cold weather. Much of the material elicited is essentially Standard English, such as *terrible*, suggested by an old woman, albeit with local pronunciations, such as *affa caul* 'awful(ly) cold' (examples of this type were found in both youngest and oldest age groups), *blain a gale* 'windy' (from a young woman) or *freezin* (again found with all age groups). Sometimes the local pronunciation was sufficient to make the word opaque to outsiders, such as *snavy* 'snowy' or, to a lesser extent, *coorse* 'cruel' (where the meaning of the word is at odds with its Standard English cognate). Nevertheless, there are some inherently Scots phrases and words found in the answers. These can go from specific phrases, such as *thin wind* the 'northerly wind that comes right through you' (from a middle-aged man; known as *lazy wund* elsewhere in Scotland) and *jeel* (otherwise *jeelin* or *jilt*), a word found throughout Scotland for the sensation of cold on the body. Despite this, however, the level of local lexical use in this sphere appears rather limited. Whether this means that much of the material assembled in the corpus is no longer known by the local population is almost impossible to say. One young man in Peterhead pointed out while carrying out the task that 'a lot of the words he ends up using are English words with Scottish pronunciations.'

Similar patterns were present in Wick, with variants of *cowld* and *freezin* being found in all age groups. Judgements such as *grim* or *hellish* are found as much with older informants as with younger, some of them representing colloquial usage throughout the British Isles and beyond. Occasionally, meanings different from the mainstream one (but with the same pronunciation) are also possible, such as *wicked* for winter weather, used by a middle-aged woman (not one which appears in the corpus). Occasionally it is possible to gain an insight into the internal lives of the community, such as the phrase *harsh morning the day*, elicited by an older man, who added that 'fishermen would say this.' Something like the characteristic litotes of the community appears to be being expressed here. Even more can be made of the phrase *Auntie is on her bike today*, given by another older male informant, referring to a situation where an anticyclone ('Auntie Cyclone') has moved away and been replaced with bad weather, thus increasing the dangers of fishing significantly. The fact that this is dealt with mockingly is somehow typical of the fishing communities (who dislike, like many Scottish people, making too much of a situation). Beyond this, however, little local material appears for Wick. Interestingly, one middle-aged man observed that 'there's other words [for winter weather]; I canna just catch it now.' Other words and phrases might have been elicited if questions had been asked in a different way.

As with elsewhere, the adjectives *coorse*, *caal* 'cold' and *dreich* were regularly elicited in Lossiemouth (*dour* was only elicited once, forming part of this set); the adjective *affa* was regular as well, as were *jailed* and its equivalents for 'frozen', 'chilled'. A number of middle-aged women offered *fashous* 'irritating, upsetting'. This emotional connection in relation to the weather can also be seen with the use of *foosome*, offered by a number of middle-aged people. The foulness inherent in the last word is also present in the word *scabby*, common in Scots as an expression of disgust on a variety of topics, offered by one middle-aged man in relation to a 'gale of wind'. The opposite – a use of litotes – can be found in *nae bad*, offered by a middle-aged woman. Beyond this, however, many of the words are local forms of mainstream English words, such as *freezing* or *perishin*. While it is true that a large part of the community felt empowered to offer words on this set of topics, it needs to be recognised that its younger members do not have the local breadth of knowledge and use their elders do.

Similar, but less impressive, findings were found for Anstruther (although *braw cauld* for 'very cold' had a poetic turn to it), with variants on *cold* being common, and other colloquial usages, such as *miserable, perishing* and *brass monkey weather* occurring. As elsewhere, *coorse*, meaning 'bad, unpleasant', was also elicited. The one striking feature is the elicitation of *scurry*, in relation to wind and rain. This word does not turn up in the corpus, but DSL, on this occasion deriving material from the SND, defines *scurry* as 'a hubbub, bustle, to-do, tumult', with attestations from the early nineteenth century.[25] Anstruther usage probably represents an extension in meaning from a sense originally associated with a confused coming together of moving elements. Beyond this, however, there is little to say.

The same is largely true with the informants from Eyemouth, although some words and phrases, such as *stervation* (the informant's choice of spelling) and *waesome* demonstrated the sense of Scots being used to describe the weather. The use of *haar* and *dour* in these contexts represents a rather idiosyncratic employment of local vocabulary, the former being offered by a middle-aged male, the latter by an older female informant. It is worth noting, however, that, before it was associated with the summer fog, *haar* was generally connected to cold winds, so that this may represent a survival.

Members of each community offered up *shite* or other scatological descriptors (such as *keich*) to describe winter weather, as well as *dreich*, the Scots word famously 'untranslatable' into English, referring to dreary, drab and grey weather (and other situations).

Was the lack of 'rich' material elicited due to the questions being created and implemented by outsiders? Or is it because dictionary makers tended to look at the micro-usage? Was the way the question was put not conducive to the elicitation of 'rich' local vocabulary (or even particularly descriptive or impressive turns of phrase)? Or is it that there was a localised lexicon for these phenomena which was supplemented by a koine-like vocabulary used by people from different ports? In order to answer this, further weather questions need to be considered.

A perennial issue in the lives of the coastal communities is rain. With this in mind, informants were asked to give words or phrases for light, medium and heavy rain, the idea being that splitting the concept of 'rain' in this way would encourage more fine-grained distinctions. To some extent this is indeed what happened, but only to an extent.

In Peterhead, for instance, a mixture of mainstream colloquial usage and quite local features was found. With 'light rain', colloquialisms such as *spittin* or *drizzle*, were often elicited, as were words with wide currency, but with local pronunciation and a typical local diminutive, such as *shoory* 'a little shower'. Alongside these are quite local words and phrases, however, such as *drappin drucht*, offered by an older male informant, literally 'dropping drought', where rain falls in insufficient amounts to break a drought. This is much more of a landward term than a coastal, since fishing communities have little immediate need to worry about whether crops are growing in optimum conditions or not; transfer from one community to the other, whether personal or collective, is likely to have happened therefore. A further intriguing suggestion is *sparkin* (*rain*), elicited from an older man and a younger woman. This word does not appear in the Corpus. In OED, however, s.v. *spark* v[1], the fourth meaning (defined as Scottish and northern dialectal) is given as

a. to spatter *(dirt, etc.)*;
b. To bespatter or spot with mud, etc. Also *fig*[urative].

With this in mind, the suggestion of light 'spitting' rain does appear an extension of this meaning. The *Dictionary of the Older Scots Tongue* (and therefore normally representative of Scots usage before the eighteenth century), as found in DSL, gives the following definitions under *spark* v:

a. *intr*[ansitive];
b. *tr*[ansitive] To (cause to) spatter with a liquid, etc. Also *fig*[urative];
c. *intr*[ansitive] Of water: To spatter.

On this occasion the connection to water is much greater, although it is important to note that all of the examples given are from the seventeenth century at the latest (although more modern examples are present in OED). Nevertheless, the evidence suggests a lengthy Scottish pedigree for the usage.

With heavier rain the same distribution is present, with supralocal usage such as *peltin doon, poorin* or *lashin o rain* rubbing shoulders with *slooshin, teemin* and the evocative *washin rain.* Of these, interestingly, *poorin* was suggested largely by younger men or women, while *slooshin* only turned up with older people. Along with these is the phrase *scabby day*, elicited from a middle-aged man, which was defined as being a local term. Generally in Scots *scabby*'s meaning, mentioned elsewhere, has been extended beyond its original connection to (suppurating) scabs to mean anything unpleasant or tawdry (in a similar development to that of English *poxy*). Neither the corpus nor any local or national resource carries a weather-based meaning for *scabby* along with *day*, but it is a logical extension. Whether the extension is confined to Peterhead or Buchan is impossible to say, however.

Fewer words and phrases were elicited for medium rain, perhaps because it falls between two extremes. Indeed a number of words and phrases, such as the Scots *dingin (on) doon* were found for both medium and heavy rain, as was *poorin*. *Drizzle*, on the other hand, was used for both light and medium rain. *Fool day* 'foul day', which we would expect to refer to heavy rain, was given for medium rain. Perhaps the most striking usage at this level, given only by women but across the age groups, was *rain* for medium rain. This may be the case because *sma rain* was produced for light rain, so symmetry demands not three but two alternatives, although it is noteworthy, perhaps, that *sma rain* was only elicited from older men.

Similar patterns are present for Wick, with standard or supralocal colloquial usages such as *drizzle* or *lashing down* being elicited alongside specifically Scots words like *smirr* or *coorse* (for heavy rain). One striking usage (volunteered by one older man) for 'heavy rain' was *spoot*. This word does not occur with this meaning in the corpus, but *spout* is associated by DSL with the heavy outpouring of liquid, often via a drain. The extension to heavy rain is natural. An opposing process can be found in *thunderplump*, for a sudden stormy downpour. This is a common word in both Scotland and (northern) Ireland, a point reinforced by OED. In Wick, however, while it is well known among older and (to a lesser extent) middle-aged informants, it is only discussed by one young woman, who points out that it was a word her mother would use, but she would not.

In Lossiemouth a number of mainstream words, often with local pronunciations, such as *showery* (which, as *shoorie*, is often a noun with a diminutive), *drizzly* (*dreezly* to one middle-aged man) and *damp* being common across a wide range of age groups. *Dreeps* and *threatenin* also turn up among older or middle-aged people, as does *seeking*. *Dreich* is offered by a number of informants, for young to old (it is, as any native speaker would agree, an all-purpose word). *Scotch Mist* is offered by one older man. Interestingly, *shoory*, *smaw rain*, *drizzle* and *dreich* all occur for 'medium rain', possibly because, as has been suggested elsewhere, the primary distinction is between heavy and all other kinds of rain. A number of apparently marked forms include *comin and gawin*, given only by middle-aged people, *weet*, given by both young and older informants, and *weeting stuff* by one older man (obviously in distinction to the Scotch mist form of rain; another older man give *afa wetting*, without the characteristic overt expression of the /i/ vowel), as well as *smoorachie*, given by an older woman and man, a diminutive form of *smoorach*, a Gaelic-derived word (itself possibly borrowed from Scots *smoor*), confined, according to DSL, to Caithness and Moray. Originally used to refer to coal or peat dust, it implies a close and oppressive atmosphere (as also suggested for *smoor* below). One older male informant suggested *scabbie* which, as we will see in relation to sea conditions, involves metaphorical transfer. It is striking, however, that other informants use downplaying terms, such as *rainin* or *rainy*. One younger woman gives *poorin*. Unsurprisingly, more words are found for heavy rain. These include fairly mainstream words and phrases, such as *buckets* or *cats and dogs*, *blustery*, *poorin (out)*, *dounpoor*,[26] *teemin* or *lashin doon*, as well as *pissin* or *pishin it doun*. Rather more Scots are *drooken rain*, *firin doon*, *stottin* and *washin*. Other examples include *hale watter*, *bougin weet* (the adjective possibly being equivalent to Central Scots *boggin* 'unpleasant; disgusting') and *dingin doon*. Value judgements are represent by *fool* (and *hale fool*), as well as the inevitable *coorse*, while litotes is represented by *heavy shoor*. More unexpected is *fissim*, probably related to *fiss*, which according to DSL, means 'to make a hissing, fizzing noise', the small number of examples connecting it to the North-East of Scotland (it should also be noted that the same resource notes a *noun* referring to slight rain, which is only recorded for Orkney). If these connections are correct, then this usage is likely to be ironic, in some ways similar to *nae takin time (tae come doon/stop)*. One of the older men said that it was raining *stair tods*, since *tod* is Scots for 'fox', this is more likely to be *stair rods*, which, while never prevalent, was certainly used widely in these contexts. *Thunderplump*, used throughout Scotland (to the extent, perhaps, that it is considered English), was mentioned by two older people, although on both occasions the person needed to be triggered to produce it. One of the informants was obviously pleased by the memory of the word, saying 'oh, we're diggin them up now'. This does not suggest much in the way of currency. It needs to be recognised with Lossiemouth that although older people might offer more words and phrases related to rainfall than younger, the knowledge is fairly well spread across the community (which is perhaps unsurprising, given rain's omnipresence).

In relation to specifically Scots words and phrases for 'light rain', a number of older informants and one middle-aged woman offered *smaw rain*. Another word could either be *smoory* (from Scots *smoor*, 'smother', often in relation to a 'close' atmosphere) or *smirry* (from Scots *smirr*, a description of very limited rainfall in the air, probably derived from *smear* (Millar 1994)), or both. The latter in particular is a common word in a range of Scots dialects, so it is striking that only two older people give the word.

Anstruther and Eyemouth informants provided comparable material. While words like *smirr* and *plashin it doon* regularly occur, non-local usages are as common, such as *rainin cats and dugs* (in Anstruther; strangely this was given for 'medium rain'). Eyemouth usage, while, as could be predicted, not copious, was on this occasion more interesting than other parts of the coast, with the highly local word *drow* (and *drowie*) being given by an older woman and middle-aged man, defined as a damp mist in the corpus. Another phrase elicited (from a middle-aged man) for 'heavy rain' was *hoyin it doon*, a construction which most Scots speakers would understand but consider northern English; this is striking when placed beside the archetypically Scottish *stottin* (the first expression was volunteered by a middle-aged male, the latter by an older woman). Inevitably the Eyemouth dialect is transitional between the closely related Scots and Northumbrian dialects (as in Berwick-upon-Tweed, just to Eyemouth's south, where both forms are also present according to Kennington (2006)).

We can say, therefore, that many local words for these weather phenomena remain in use, particularly, but not solely, among middle-aged and older people. These are supplemented or replaced by non-local, often colloquial, usages, however.

The final task concerned with weather conditions was an open-ended question on hot weather. We had postulated before applying the questionnaire that this question would elicit fewer answers than was the case for poor weather conditions. The east coast of Scotland is not inclined towards dry and warm weather, even at the height of summer. Fewer occasions for coinage and use would therefore be available. A number of informants commented on this, making the point – in jest – that local words for these phenomena did not exist because that type of weather was unknown in the neighbourhood. All of this is, of course, true, but only to a certain extent. What can be said is that, while fewer examples were given, rather more of these examples were local than at least appears to be the case with the more commonly discussed types of weather.

As experience would lead us to expect, many supralocal forms are found; in particular *roastin* and *scorchin*, perhaps (and variations on *het* or *hot*). But words like *mochless*, elicited from middle-aged and older people in Anstruther, defined as 'helpless because of hot, sticky, weather' in the corpus and placed all along the east coast, represent the opposite tendency. Indeed this sense of closeness, even oppression, through heat also turns up in other words and phrases elicited elsewhere, such as *scomfished* (found in Peterhead) or *scomfishin* (found in Eyemouth). On many of these occasions it is the personal reaction to heat which is central, such as *meef* (given by an older man in Wick), a word not found in either the corpus or any dictionary, but obviously representative of the personal sense of oppression through heat experienced in buildings designed to retain heat and keep out cold. Lossiemouth offered *plottin*, a typically North-East word for extreme and oppressive heat, strangely *not* recorded for Peterhead (this word produces the local joke where people claim they're *conspirin*, both a malapropism for *perspirin* and a near synonym of *plottin*, making them sound pretentious, Anglicised or 'big hoose').

It is dangerous to derive quantitative conclusions from qualitative material. Nevertheless the rarity of hot weather in the region might actually encourage the retention of local vocabulary. Most of the words and phrases referring to less pleasant types of weather tend to the external, perhaps even communal, experience of the weather; many hot weather words and phrases are personal in their orientation and therefore more inclined to encourage retention of words and phrases at a personal level.

4.2.5.1 Sea and wind conditions

Both weather conditions and the behaviour of the sea are, of course, central concerns of all mariners. Since, as well as being a matter of safety, weather conditions affect where and when fish can be found, fishing communities are particularly concerned with describing and attempting to forecast them; moreover, such an interest probably encourages a plethora of different words for different weather and sea states. With this in mind, informants were asked in an open elicitation task for words related to calm, rough and in-between seas.

In the corpus, a number of words and phrases were found for calm seas. These included *lown*, meaning 'calm', in particular when used in relation to the wind. This word has patchy recording, the ST states, across the southern parts of Scotland as well as Ulster. On the other hand, a number of words – *sma watter* (to which we will return), *sma(ll)* 'a period of calm at sea' and *smelt* or *smilt* 'a calm patch at sea' – are all defined by that resource as being recorded throughout Scotland. As was predicted, the findings for this category were not particularly rich: logic would dictate that stormy seas would trigger more vocabulary items because of their danger.

In Peterhead a number of words and phrases were elicited, although only one (*sma watter*, given by an older male informant) corresponded to material in the corpus. Within the material offered, three tendencies appeared to be present: words or phrases would 'orbit' round an adjective, such as *quiet* (found once in the response from a young woman), or calmness would be expressed in relation to a negative, such as *nae a breath of air*, given by one middle-aged woman or, finally, as a simile, such as with *like gless* 'like glass', given by one younger woman. In each case, some elicited words and phrases were more Scots than others (although it is dangerous to make too much of this: all of the informants were primarily literate in English, which means that more anglicised pronunciations might be represented by the spelling than what a person would actually say). With adjectival use, *calm* was given by two female informants, one middle-aged and one younger. Variants on *flat calm* were found with middle-aged informants (one of whom gave a more expressly Scots variant with *flit calm*). One older woman gave *calm a day* (as with the example below, *a* here probably stands for Scots *aa/ aw* 'all'), while three older men gave *breath calm*. *Still* for a calm sea was given by two younger women. In relation to simile use, an older man and a middle-aged woman gave *millpond* for a calm day, while three older informants and one middle-aged man gave *like a millpond*. With the negative expression, all the phrases suggested included the North-East Scots negativiser *nae*. These included, as we have already discussed, *nae a breath of air*, along with *nae a funk o win* (from an older man) and *nae a trickle in the waves* (from an older woman). The last two are rather more densely Scots than the first. This difference may be due to age difference and experience of the sea. To a lesser extent it can be argued that older informants in general with this semantic field tend to produce turns of phrase which are considerably further away from Standard English usage than do younger participants.

Similar patterns (although possibly less fruitful) are to be found in Wick. *Calm* was among the most common elicitations, found across the age and gender spectrum, even though it was actually given as the word to be 'translated' in the questionnaire. *Mill pond* was also common. *Fine day* also had a considerable distribution (with one older man saying he would also use *fine sea*). *Nice day* was offered by a middle-aged woman; interestingly, the more Scots *nice a day* was reported by a young woman. *Still sea* was reported by an older male informant and a middle-aged woman. One simile usage, *like a sheet of glass*, was given by an older female informant. It has to be said that, with the exception of *quiet*, with the local /ei/ pronunciation, what was elicited was not particularly local. It is worth noting, however, that a middle-aged female informant, who gave *millpond*, pointed out that this was 'not Caithness'. The eternal (and often brutal) mutability of the seas of that region is proverbial.

In Lossiemouth, *smaw water* was offered by a number of older informants, with variants like *small waves* also being offered. Along with this a number of fairly mainstream *calm* variants were offered, with others focusing on the unnatural flatness of the sea, such as *ilie sea* (offered by an older man), *jist like gless* (offered by a number of older and middle-aged informants), quite in line with the standard *like a millpond*, only offered by middle-aged and younger informants. Two older male informants produced *nae a lipper*, using a Northern and Insular Scots word for a small wave, while a middle-aged woman offers *cauk*, which may be the same word as that defined by DSL as 'to make one pay dear for anything, to exact ruinous interest' (along with other meanings related to writing something up), in which case a negative is probably missing. A number of understatements are also on offer, such as *a bitty motion* (offered by one older man), with the meaning 'fairly calm'. The common bringing together of water and day can be seen in *quiet day* (offered by an older woman and a middle-aged man), which is most certainly not related to having little work to do, and *bonny day* (also *bonny sea*) offered by a range of middle-aged and older people. The use of *silver* for 'calm' or 'bonny', offered by one middle-aged man, may refer to the colours of sky and sea in particularly calm situations. It is certainly poetic.

Away from these often positive descriptions of calm seas, one older man and one older woman offered a phrase which was variously spelled *cal' mi'rble day* or *caul rible*, roughly transliterated as 'cold miserable day'. It is unlikely that they misunderstood the question; much more likely is that calm weather was associated with winter high pressure phenomena.

Similar points could be made for Anstruther, although the level of knowledge and use appears considerably lower. With the exception of *sma watter* (of which more will be said shortly), offered by an older woman, most of the words and phrases provided were essentially identical to those used in Standard English. These include *calm* (admittedly with the local variant *flet calm*), offered by one younger female informant and an older man. One middle-aged man offered *millpond* (glossing it as 'flat calm'), while an older woman gave *good day* for the meaning 'calm'). In Eyemouth very few words or phrases were elicited for this field. One younger and one older female informant gave *mild* for a calm sea, while an older man gave *fine*. An older female offered *flet calm* (the Scots spelling being her own choice).

On two occasions, *sma watter* was elicited for the meaning 'calm sea'. The ST suggests that this is a common phrase for these conditions around Scotland. In the construction of the questionnaire it was decided to extract this usage and set it up as a translation exercise type question. The primary reason for this was that its meaning is apparently transparent ('small water'), but the reference to calm seas is not. If the phrase is not known by an informant, he or she would be just as likely to think it meant 'low tide' or even 'light rain' (particularly if the common *smaw rain* was known). It therefore might stand as a means of judging when an old meaning has become moribund. In Peterhead seven out of the seventeen informants knew the 'correct' meaning (all older or middle-aged men), with as many giving 'low tide' (all the older and middle-aged informants being women, but with one younger man). Three informants (one middle-aged and two younger, all women) did not know the word at all. In the pilot study, most of the participants suggested interpretations which might represent some understanding of what the phrase originally meant – 'small waves', 'low tide', 'calm day'. The extent to which this is luck is difficult to say, however, since both elements of the phrase would be transparent to everyone taking part in the survey. In this preliminary study, it became apparent also that participants' knowledge of a term's meaning did not parallel their use. One informant stated that while local people know the term, they would never use it. Instead she would say, 'It's a mild day.' It could be argued that a person's life circumstances and experiences result in great individual variation when it comes to knowledge of attriding lexical items. One participant said she knew the term only because her grandfather lived in a house where the waves would splash on the windows on rough days, and apparently he would speak of *smaw watter* as well.

Similar evidence was produced in Lossiemouth, with a number of older people interpreting it as 'calm sea' or 'shallow water' or, less explicitly, in *refuge from bad weather including a lee shore* and *rough water off shore, sma water in shore*. A number of references to safe water are given by older and (in particular) middle-aged informants, a particularly explicit definition, *in a sheltered area, e.g., the Sound of Mull, the Narrows or at the leeward side of a headland*.[27] This reference to Mull is interesting, since a range of middle-aged informants consider it a common fishing term, especially on the west coast of Scotland. A few people from all age groups interpreted the phrase as relating to low tides. A number of younger women, however, saw it as relating to a puddle (even 'tiny puddle') or a rock pool; this sounds like a guess, as does *small rain* (offered by an older man) or *small stream (maybe)*, offered by a middle-aged woman.

In Wick, however, rather fewer people seemed to know the phrase. One older man gave the 'correct' interpretation, but said he did not use the phrase himself; another older man also interpreted it that way, but said he *did* use it. An older woman did offer the mainstream interpretation (although she also presented 'low tide' as an interpretation, perhaps suggesting that she was making surmises). Most other informants either did not know the phrase or said that it related either to tides or the size of waves (the last possibly representing the sense of a calm sea, in contrast to the typically large waves off Caithness mentioned above). Two young female informants suggested that it related to a 'small glass of water'. In Anstruther, on the other hand, a core of older men and women (and a few middle-aged people) knew the 'calm' meaning (with one middle-aged man saying it meant 'the opposite of bad weather'). Several older informants produced a tidal meaning, however. One younger man associated it with rain or drizzle. It may be significant that an older female informant noted that it was 'used a lot round here'. At least with the older and middle-aged informants its use appears fairly healthy. In Eyemouth, however, none of the informants offered the 'calm sea' meaning, although a number gave the tidal (and one middle-aged man the 'drizzle') association. If it was ever used in Eyemouth with its original meaning, *sma watter* has now been forgotten.

It would appear a fair assumption that rather more words and phrases about stormy weather and seas would have been used in the past and have survived to the present. For active fishing populations, most of the danger of seafaring came from bad weather. For modern coastal communities the unpleasantness (rather than the danger) of poor conditions would probably be central; as a talking point, however, conversation on the topic must certainly continue, no matter the purpose.

To an extent the expected wealth of words and phrases is present in the corpus. Interestingly, however, almost all of the material recorded derives from specific places along the coast, rather than being general, exceptions being *waver*, '*of water* rage, be furious'; *gowstie* 'wild, stormy' and *grumlie* 'sullen, surly, grumbling' (all from the ST). That resource says that the last is 'now local'; the same distribution is given for *lift* 'a rising swell in the sea'. It makes sense, therefore, for usage associated with particular areas to be treated with individual ports.

Given that the North-East of Scotland is a region bounded on two sides by sea, the ST surprisingly offers only

kav [*Shetland*], kaif [*North-East*]　*of a stormy sea* foam in breaking, throw up a spray.

in relation to storm-tossed seas, as a locally circumscribed word. When asked about rough conditions on the sea, the Peterhead informants did not offer this word, but did realise a considerable range of other words and phrases. It should be noted that a few more words are recorded for waves; these will be dealt with if they are part of a description of a stormy sea.

The two most common words or phrases triggered by the idea of 'rough sea' or 'bad weather' were *coorse* and *roch*, both common Scots words relating to something unpleasant (and both regularly used to refer to rude or 'uncultured' human behaviour). An interesting distinction can be made in relation to usage, however, with the latter being exclusively offered by younger informants while the former is recorded mainly by older informants, with a few middle-aged participants, along with one younger woman. Again we can see that what appear to be separate phenomena – weather and water condition – are essentially viewed as one by members of fishing communities.

In general two types of description appear to be used to provide a picture of a stormy sea. The first represents an attempt to describe the whole sea. Some of these, such as *sore sea* for bad weather (provided by an older female; it is noteworthy that she provides English *sore* rather than Scots *sair*: the phrase would be meaningless to speakers of English) and *all swall*, provided by the same informant, which describes the dying down of the waves ('all swell') after a storm, are at the Scots end of the continuum of use. Others, such as *choppy* (provided by two younger women), *fearsome* (provided by one of these younger women), *howlin gale* (given by an older and a middle-aged man), *stormy* (provided by an older female informant) and *wild* (provided by one older man and a middle-aged and a younger female informant) are words which are regularly used for this type of weather throughout the English-speaking world.

The second tendency is to use an element of what can be seen or felt with a stormy day and employ it synecdochically to refer to the whole experience. Inevitably the possibilities for describing different parts of the same scene mean that there are more words and phrases recorded, but with fewer informants mentioning each one. Some have some currency, however, including (*blaain*) *marlan specks* (recorded for two older men) and a similar construction, *blaain smoke*, recorded for two middle-aged men. On both occasions the image presented is of wave tops so wild that the spray from a range of them blends together, making it look like smoke.[28] Although this 'smoke' analogy is not given by any resources for the north-east, Schlötterer recorded it for Pittenweem in the East Neuk of Fife. Something of the same meaning might adhere to the more general *rikkin storm*, given by a middle-aged informant as a term his father would use for really windy weather and heavy rain, although the Standard English meanings for *reek* related to unpleasant smells needs to be borne in mind. One older male informant offers *lump o water* for big waves. This type of image is not recorded for this part of the coast, but is certainly common in other parts, as we will see. One older man and an older woman offered *cookit and houkit* as an expression used to describe the sensation of a great deal of motion on the sea. This phrase does not appear to be recorded anywhere else.

With the small number of examples involved, rigid conclusions about Peterhead use are dangerous. There are indications, however, that older informants tend less to attempt a description of the whole 'picture' involved in a storm, instead preferring to use *pars pro toto*. The difference between *coorse* and *roch* in terms of apparent age distribution is rather more difficult to explain, although it may be that *roch* represents a somewhat more condemnatory description.

In Lossiemouth, *roch* (on one occasion *hale roch*) was common among older speakers, with *fool day* and *foosome* also being common. *Coorse* was also often offered, largely from older and middle-aged people, as was *heavin*. *Gale o wind*, normally with local pronunciations, was also recorded. The synecdochic usages mentioned for Peterhead also turn up further west, with *jabble, blowin reek, in a stooer* and *heavy swall* (or *win*) also on offer. A middle-aged man and woman offered what they spelt *scarling* or *skarwing* for 'rough, wild'. This is likely in fact to be Scots *skirl*, normally associated now with the particular sound of the bagpipes, but also, according to DSL, associated with the shrieks and howls of a great storm. *Plenty white horses* and *sheepies' backs* are both highly pictorial and also somewhat self-deprecating. Something similar can be found with *dodging*, defined by an older man as referring to 'dodging big waves in open sea when you could come into smaller waters'. A more immediate and pictorial representation is *sea at the mooth o' the harbour*, offered by an older woman for 'large sea breaking over the harbour'. While there is only so much that can be made of one person's offering, it is interesting that it is a woman who perceives the storm from its landward expression; indeed this is a feature which occurs regularly in the material.

In the corpus, a range of words and phrases referring to rough seas are connected specifically to Caithness. A small number of these, such as *mither o the waters*, recorded in both the CD and the CW, refer to a feature specific to the region, on this occasion the permanent onshore swell found on the east coast. Others refer to phenomena found around Scotland's coast, but where the word or phrase is prominent in or confined to Caithness. Such a word is *chabble*, which the CW defines as 'choppy water on the sea'. The DSL places this only in Orkney and Caithness, while noting that *jabble* is much more widespread (although largely as a verb; the *CD* gives *jabble* with the same noun meaning as *chabble*). An unusually large wave is given as a *tide lump* in the *Caithness Wordbook*, although DSL makes only Shetland citations. *Graith* is given in the CD as a word for foam on the sea. No other resources appear to mention this word in this or any other meaning.

The returns for Wick demonstrate a rich resource of words for stormy weather associated with the sea; none of the corpus materials appeared, however. As with Peterhead, the most commonly triggered words and phrases were *coorse* and *roch*. Unlike in Peterhead, however, there is no age-based distinction between the two adjectives, both of them being used by all ages and genders, although with more middle-aged and older informants using them. A number of other words and phrases were offered, generally by one or two people. These are generally descriptive of features of a storm, such as *hashy* (given by one older female; probably related to the verb *hash*, which DSL would define in a variety of ways in relation to hard and long-lasting labour or activity, often related to mixing, with chaotic results) or *bilin* ('boiling', given by a younger male informant), which produces a similar image. Others refer to the wind, such as *howlin* (given by a younger woman), while others represent judgements on the weather, such as *hellish*, (given by an older female informant), or *wild* (given by two older men and one younger woman). These value judgements are similar in nature to *coorse* and *roch*; they are at, or very near to, the standard end of the dialect–standard continuum, however.

Because of the work of Schlötterer, words and phrases for rough seas are well recorded for the East Neuk of Fife. Some of these, such as *bank* and *bar* for 'rough water' are recorded only for Crail (again portraying waves as solid objects); *eddy* and *shallow water* for Pittenweem and *edge of the bank* for Anstruther. The same holds true for words related to waves, such as *big seas* and *froth* for Crail; *foam* and *smoke* for Pittenweem and *shallow water* for Anstruther (this last also recorded for St Abbs on the Berwickshire coast). Such a neat split in distribution is possible but, given the extent to which East Neuk residents come into daily contact with people from the other villages, it does seem unlikely. Predictably, the questionnaire returns present an alternative (but on this occasion not entirely different) picture. *Coorse* is found from a number of people from different ages; *roch* is not recorded, however. One older man defined a *coorse day* as 'pretty bad'; another older man concentrated on the nature of the wind, for which he used the phrases *gey strong* and *a gale o wind*. Others focused on the nature of the waves, including their apparent solidity – *a lump of water* (from an older male informant, who described the force of a big wave hitting the boat by smacking his fist into his other hand; solidity was central to his explanation) – or the spindrift of a wild sea – *blowin smoke*, defined by the informant, an older man, as 'full gale, storm force 10, 11 or 12' – the last example being connected to the corpus material. A few returns also demonstrate the litotes characteristic of the fishing communities, with bad weather being described as a *poor morning* (from a middle-aged man) or a *workable gale* (from the same source). Many of these words and phrases are, of course, close to the standard, with only intonation or connotation moving beyond the mainstream. Even this claim cannot be made for *stormy day*, offered by an older female informant.

With Eyemouth the corpus is also indebted to Schlötterer (1996). For 'rough weather' he records *reef* for Burnmouth and *shallow water* for St Abbs. For 'spindrift' he records *bow* for Burnmouth and *spume* for St Abbs. Naturally, since he did not expressly look at the language use of Eyemouth, we cannot absolutely say that these words were used in that town, although the proximity of the villages studied to Eyemouth would naturally make this quite likely. In the present study, one young man gave *coorse*, while *rough* was given by two women, one younger, one from the older age group. Other informants referred to the nature of the waves, going from *smoking* (from one middle-aged woman) through to *white horses*, given by two women, one older, one middle-aged, and a younger man. One older male informant used *fly round to [direction]*, referring to the rapid movement of the weather vane, a sign of rapidly deteriorating conditions. The same man gave *gale* as his word for 'very stormy'. The returns on this topic were not rich.

The corpus provides very few words for the medium between calm and storm, largely because it is weather conditions near to the extremes which are likely to demand specific words and phrases. But because entirely calm weather may not always be desirable for fishing, it was decided that informants be asked to give any words or phrases for the mean between the extremes. Interestingly, quite a few instances of these middling descriptors, often showing quite small-scale gradations, are to be found. In Peterhead, an older man gave *girny* for neither calm nor rough (*girn* refers to whining rather than actual crying). A middle-aged man gave *chavy kinda day* for 'a bit more than the middle of calm/rough' (*taw* – locally *tyaave* and common in the North-East – refers to actions which are difficult and physically or mentally draining). Another middle-aged man gave *white horses* for this stage, which represented heavy storm elsewhere. There were also relatively slim pickings in Lossiemouth. As well as *blustery, breezy, choppy* and *hashie* ('nae a lot of wind, maybe a fresh wind, bit of movement in the sea') were offered. *Good* was used as a premodifier in *a good bit lift* and *a good swell*. One older woman offered *ribal* for 'miserable'. One older man offered *scully kind a day* and *tashie wither*. *Scully* could be derived from the verb *scull*, defined by DSL as relating to moving in a zigzag manner; while *tashy* is likely to derive from *tash*, meaning stain or blemish. It should be noted that these examples were offered overwhelmingly by older or middle-aged people, demonstrating that apparently rich lexical expressing in Lossiemouth is retreating into the past. In Wick a fair number of participants of all ages and sexes gave *choppy* for this type of sea. One young man gave *fair swell*, while *swell* was given by a younger woman. A middle-aged woman gave *high tide* (the opposite, perhaps, of *smaw watter*) for sea conditions closer to the stormy end of the continuum. It is interesting that many of our informants describe the waves in particular encountered in poor weather as if they were actual physical obstructions, such as *bank* or *bar*. On this occasion, however, an everyday experience of the sea's rising and falling is compared with a rather more worrying event, possibly as a form of litotes. In Anstruther, an older man gave *a bit of babble* for 'a confused sea'; another older man provides *licht wind* for 'light wind'. In Eyemouth, *blawing* was given by a middle-aged woman for a 'choppy sea'. An older man gave *wind's swinging round* for 'choppy'; an older male informant gives *breezy* for 'less calm'. Interestingly, he is the same informant who used terminology from the actions of a weather vane to describe stormy weather. With many of these we can see both the litotes already discusses and the need for fairly precise distinctions. But again we can see that most words and phrases elicited lie at the standard end.

Many different, indeed partly contradictory, points might be made about the above material. Three central issues can be observed, however. In the first instance, many of the more localised or particularly Scots words recorded in the corpus were not recorded in the surveyed ports (although a small number, such as *smaw watter* were. Scots words which can be used in a range of contexts – *roch, coorse, reekin, scabby* – regularly occurred, however, to describe both weather and sea conditions. As has already been suggested, it is likely that local people do not recognise a true distinction between the two. Finally, many local forms represent something close to the (Scottish) Standard English form but with a local pronunciation, a point proven regularly in this research.

4.2.6 Local identity and the naming process

Given that all fishing communities are involved in a trade largely shared with all other fishing communities (at least in the same basic ecological setting), given that all fishing communities feel themselves to a degree discrete from their landward neighbours and given that, because of the common endeavour in which the community is involved, even the smallest communities had (and have) a sense of themselves as a unique entity in contrast with (and opposition to) all other communities, it is not surprising that nicknames both for the home community and its inhabitants and also its neighbours, whether near or in equivalent communities, should have been created in many fishing communities. With this in mind, contributors were asked two questions:

26. Is there a nickname for people from this town?

and:

27. Do you know any nicknames for people who come from other places?

With both questions, space was given to suggest that this was an 'open-ended' task, encouraging multiple answers. In the following analysis these two questions will be treated separately in the first instance, community by community, before a comparison between internal and external naming practice and between communities will be attempted.

In Peterhead, thirteen out of seventeen informants gave *blue moggan-ers* as the name for people from Peterhead. This term was produced by all the older men (although only one older woman offered it); it was also provided by all the middle-aged informants and by two out of the three younger women. The variant *blue tooners* was given by seven out of seventeen informants, including two older women, one each of the middle-aged men and women, two out of three of the younger women and by one younger man. Interestingly, no older men gave this form. One younger woman gave *(Peter)heeders*; an older woman gave *Buchanhaveners*; one older man gave *birds of passage*.

Obviously the two terms containing *blue* are best known within the community. A degree of folk etymology has been applied to the purpose of the colour epithet. One middle-aged man said that Peterhead was associated with the colour blue because that was the colour the street lights appear to have when approaching the town from the sea. Another middle-aged male apparently simplified this explanation by saying that all the street lights in Peterhead were blue at one time. Whether these explanations are well founded or not is not the purpose of this study, although the slight blue tinge which gas lamps and some early electric street lamps had was not, of course, a peculiarity of Peterhead. One older woman connected the blue with the home-produced *touries*, woollen caps, associated with the area. The fact that *moggan*, according to DSL, is the word for stockings or stocking ends, and that home-made caps of the type envisaged were very similar in construction and looks to these stockings, makes this identification possible (although an association with blue socks is rather more likely). The variant with *toon* has its own issues. There is no doubt that Peterhead is known as the *blue toon* by quite a few people locally, and that *blue tooner* is a natural derivative of this. But it should also be noted, as mentioned above, that a sign with *The Blue Toon* is provided on all roads entering the town. This ongoing presence may explain why this name is more common with younger informants and also, conversely, why it is not used by older men (although again this is an apparent distinction which may not be supported by the overall knowledge of the community). But one younger woman who offered *blue mogganers* stated that she would not herself use the term and thought that she had learned it at school. Simple (even simplistic) ideas about *knowledge* and *use* need to be revised and tempered by our understanding that local culture has become to a degree commodified and perpetuated outside traditional acquisition patterns.

There were also three 'outlier' terms, each produced by one person only. *Buchanhaveners*, given by an older woman, appears to refer only to the village of Buchanhaven, now physically part of Peterhead. It is impossible to tell from the context whether the informant was associating herself with her own home village or whether she believed that the term had come to express the most 'fisher' attributes of Peterhead identity. A younger woman gave *(Peter)heeders* as the name given by local people to themselves. This is undoubtedly true; it is also the name often given by other people from the area to people from Peterhead. What is striking, however, is that this term should have been seen as being a particularly marked, external, 'English', name. At least until very recently, most inhabitants of the town would have pronounced the final syllable /hid/ rather than /hɛd/, the latter being the marked form. That this appears to have been reversed tells us a great deal about competition of norms and change in the local dialect.

The last 'outlier' is *birds of passage*, given by an older man. This informant said that Shetlanders called Peterhead people this because 'we had no home'. Other older fishermen taking part in that interview said they had never heard this, a number of them laughing at the suggestion. No other authority gives the phrase, but the fact that the informant gave such a clear description of how and why the term came into being suggests that its use was more than fancy, albeit representing idiolect rather than dialect.

In Wick less diversity was present, but more breadth. Twenty-four out of the twenty-seven informants used variants of *dirty/durdy Wicker/Weeker*; these responses were almost instant, which suggests that the identification with the name was real and contemporary for those producing it. It was in fact possible to buy *Durdy Weeker* t-shirts in the town; the expression was also one which Wick people recognised that people from 'down south' (by which may well be meant North-East Scotland; it is unlikely to imply England, which would be the case in the south of Scotland) used about them as well.

What was striking was the way in which the unpleasant implications of *dirty* were dealt with. One middle-aged man said that it was a term used originally by Thurso people because Wick herring fishers always had fish scales on their hands or clothes. A more striking interpretation is that *durdy* is a separate word meaning 'hard working' (a view given by two older men and one younger male informant, suggesting that it may be widespread throughout the community). Unfortunately there is no evidence in any Scottish or English dictionary for such a word (or even sub-meaning of *dirt*), but it is straightforward to see that a semantic elision has taken place whereby dirt accrued through honest labour might be seen as something admirable (*where there's muck there's brass*, as they say in northern England); this does not mean that that is why the adjective was originally used with *Wick*. That there is a sense of its being somehow inappropriate can be seen in the suggestion by one middle-aged man that it was a Thurso, rather than Wick, usage, not just in the past but also now, despite all evidence to the contrary.

One older man also offered the phrase *Wick in a matchbox*, apparently the response by people from Keiss (a nearby village) to the Wick expression *Keiss in a certie*, suggesting ritualised (and not particularly serious) insults about importance and connection to modernity (although the cart mentioned might actually be of the old-fashioned, home-made, *bogie* kind, as mentioned by a number of older male informants). The 'dirty' epithet may well represent just such a (jocular) insult eventually taken on as a badge of pride.[29]

The most common nickname reported by all age groups in Lossiemouth for inhabitants of the town is *Lossie Codheads* (with a middle-aged woman giving *Lossie Fishheads*). This is still highly current, suggesting that the name continues in the town despite the catastrophic decline of fishing. It is, in fact, quite a common nickname for inhabitants of towns of this type, another example being Fleetwood in Lancashire. That does not mean that it is universally popular, however, with locals considering it to be external, deriving from Burghead people or 'Elginers' (as was said in Chapter 2, 'the corn and the cod dinna mix').

The other striking name given to people from Lossiemouth and described by quite a few inhabitants was *(Lossie) gollachs*. *Gollach*, a number of informants suggested, may derive from a Gaelic word for 'beetle', and is generally associated in North-East Scots with the phrase *horny gollach* 'earwig'. One middle-aged female informant observes that the name come from there having been an infestation of the creatures at one point in the town. Others observe that it is derogatory (given the subject matter, but perhaps not as bad as *Codheads*) and that it was coined externally (the external attribution seems to be particularly strong among middle-aged and younger informants). One older man gave *forkietails*, which is a common word for 'earwig' in many other parts of Scotland. Whether *gollach* is in origin derived from the Gaelic word for 'beetle' or whether it is related to the word for 'foreigner' discussed for Caithness below is impossible to say. A few informants also offer the rather anodyne *Lossie folk* or *Lossie loons/quines*. Unexpectedly, only one older man offered *Doggers*, a name closely associated with Lossiemouth in both written experience and local (hi)story. Not all of the Lossiemouth fishing community were doggers (indeed two middle-aged men identified *dog walkers* as an external term), however.

Anstruther, by its size and location, is inevitably both at one level highly discrete from its neighbours (and highly aware of its own identity) and also aware that it is part of a collection of places – the East Neuk – where different settlements have more in common with each other than with outside communities. It is striking, however, how few people identified words of this type (in particular in comparison with the amount of words produced for other communities by Anstruther people). Nevertheless, two older women and one middle-aged female participant used the expression *Anstruther/Anster Daws*, where *Daws* could be a (now somewhat archaic) form of *John*, or possibly refers to crows (given the Dutch-style architecture found in older buildings in the East Neuk, with its archetypal 'crow's steps' gables and roofs, this might be an appropriate term). One middle-aged man gave *cod heid*, demonstrating the regularity with which this epithet turns up for fishing communities, while a younger man produced *coasters* (this last in particular apparently demonstrating an identification with a unit somewhat larger than Anstruther, as postulated above). One older woman gave a written representation (*Anster*) of the local pronunciation of the town's name. As with the *Peterheeders* example above, the standard pronunciation may be becoming the norm within the community (particularly because well-heeled outsiders, attracted by the undoubted beauty of the East Neuk settlements and their relative proximity to St Andrews and its university, regularly settle there), its old name becoming a nickname of sorts. Unlike Peterhead's younger inhabitants, however, it is an older woman who appears to have made the connection in Anstruther.

Eyemouth presents a less productive, but similar, pattern to Anstruther. Most of the informants of any age group who produced a name produce variants on *Eyemouthers*, with older people being more likely to produce extremely local forms, such *Hymoothers* or *Hiemoothers* and younger people producing forms closer to the standard pronunciation of the name of their town. One middle-aged female gave the name *gulls* for people from Eyemouth, interesting when we remember the association with gull names found along some parts of the coast; it is a pity that no one else suggested this type of name here.

We can say, therefore, that all of the communities covered have a means of describing themselves, although we need to recognise that some communities – Peterhead and Wick, for example – choose to do this rather more than do others. This may mean that local identity is particularly strong in those towns (a point which would, of course, be difficult to argue against, but impossible to prove), with Wick also being relatively isolated. But the possibility does present itself that other communities may define themselves more in relation to their neighbours than of themselves. What is striking, nonetheless, is the way that the local names and pronunciations of some of the communities appear to be becoming interpreted as secondary rather than primary.

In relation to names given to inhabitants of other places, Peterhead informants produced an abundant supply, largely for towns and villages near to the town. Indeed, only two informants did not provide any names; many informants supplied a number of names for one place and its inhabitants; it was obviously a significant way of expressing Peterhead identity, no matter the informant's occupation. Table 4.1 gives a sense of the diversity of names and places. What is immediately obvious is that, unsurprisingly, inhabitants of places relatively close to Peterhead are most commonly referred to. Only one of these near neighbours – New Pitsligo – is not on the coast. The other names mentioned relate to two rather more distant places – Buckie and Aberdeen – with whose inhabitants Peterhead people had considerable contact (and with whom a rivalry largely related to fishing existed). Inevitably, given the town's size and proximity (and the normally friendly competition between the towns), informants mentioned names for Fraserburgh inhabitants most; nevertheless, it should be recognised that even small settlements, such as Inverallochy, were mentioned by three informants, offering two names.

The names offered appear to offer four different types. The first is essentially a version of the place's name, with a suffix along the lines of -er – Brocher – or -ian (Aberdonian). The second refers to traits or customs of a place, such as kwitees for people from St Combs (according to informants, a term associated with a particular types of protective clothing – a coat, perhaps, although locals suggested a kilt – worn over the midriff and upper legs). Some of these – such as cyakkers and bazaders – are still commonly used, as a trawl through any internet search engine demonstrates, but the original meaning is difficult to ascertain (cyakkers appears to represent the local pronunciation of cake plus the -er suffix, but that does not take the investigation much further). There is also at least one example where inhabitants of a place are associated with an animal or bird: Gamrie/Gardenstown inhabitants are called pules 'seagulls'. As we saw above, names for this particular bird are highly localised in this area; people associate themselves – and are associated by others – with the local name for the bird (the corollary being, of course, that knowledge of terms for 'seagull' in other places are known along considerable stretches of coastline). The final category involves terms which are at least at surface level derogatory, such as puddlestinkers for people from Fraserburgh, which a number of Peterhead informants recognised as

Table 4.1 Names given by Peterhead respondents to inhabitants of other communities

Place	Names	Age and gender of participants providing response
Fraserburgh	Puddlestinkers	Five older men; one older woman
		One middle-aged man; one middle-aged woman
		One younger man; three younger women
	Brochers	One older man; one older woman
		One middle-aged man; one middle-aged woman
		One younger man; two younger women
Cairnbulg	Bulgers/Belgers	Two older men; one older woman
		One middle-aged man; one middle-aged woman
	Goolies/Goonies	One older man; one older woman
		One middle-aged man; one middle-aged woman
	Combers	One older man
St Combs	Combers	Two older women
	Kwitees	Three older men; one older woman
		One middle-aged woman
		One younger woman
	New Tooners	One middle-aged woman
Gardenstown/	Gamricks	One older woman
Gamrie		One middle-aged man; one middle-aged woman
	Pules	One older man
		One middle-aged man
		One younger man
Aberdeen	Aberdonians	One middle-aged woman
		One younger woman
	Dons	One younger woman
	Townie	One younger man
Inverallochy	Cottoners	One older man
		One younger woman
	Tellies	One older woman
Buckie	Blethers	One older man
New Pitsligo	Cyakkers	One younger woman
Rosehearty	Bazaders	One younger woman

being not particularly neighbourly. Possible equivalents include *blethers* for people from Buckie: most Scots speakers would surmise that this refers to loquaciousness, perhaps even a less than honest turn of phrase (although it could also refer to particular types of seaweed). *Townie* for an Aberdonian may represent something similar; the fact that the ortho-graphic representation suggests the English diphthongal pronunciation rather than the Scots monophthongal one is also intriguing, as is the fact that *toonser*, the word for (working-class) Aberdonians used in Aberdeen, was not elicited. It is likely that some of the apparently impenetrable forms given were also in origin derogatory. That they are used regu-larly by people from these areas tells us a lot about the seriousness of the original insult. Interestingly, at least one name – *Combers* – is used not just for people from St Combs, but also for people from Cairnbulg. That such an epithet, so obviously coined from one community's name, should be used for people from another community may seem strange to most outsiders. It should be noted, however, that these communities are very close to each other geographically (forming part of 'greater Fraserburgh') and that the distribution presented is that of an outsider: it is unlikely to represent the nomenclature insiders use.

Even if we accept that the coast around Peterhead has a large number of communities associated with the past or present fishing trade, the Peterhead informants nonetheless present an impressive 'psychological map' which is largely associated with its coastal connections rather than its hinterland.

Given that Wick is situated in a far less populous region than Peterhead, it might be predicted that fewer names for fewer places would be found. Moreover, like Fraserburgh for Peterhead, it would be very likely that Thurso would loom large in Wick people's perception of the other. To some extent these prior assumptions are correct, but only to some extent, as Table 4.1 suggests.

In relation to Thurso, many Wick informants – including, interestingly, a number of younger informants, produced *tea in a bowla* (or variants such as *teenabowlies*). Several informants (and the corpus), suggested that the phrase stems from the Thurso habit of adding *-a* to nouns; the implication may be that Thurso people, in not using conventional means to drink tea, may not be entirely 'civilised'. The fact that the 'tea' associations are less obvious in some versions of the name may suggest that young people in particular are not as aware of this connection than older people; conversely it might also suggest that the tea interpretation is an example of folk etymology. Indeed the phrase looks a bit like 'mock Gaelic', particularly with the *na* (a form of the Gaelic definite article) in the centre, making it reminiscent of a number of Gaelic place names in the vicinity. All of this suggests that *tea in a bowla* is an insult of sorts, but of a particularly obscure nature.[30] Three older people (one male, one female), recorded *soor sellags* for inhabitants of Thurso. As the corpus demonstrates, *sellags* are the fry of the *saithe* or *coalfish*, a fish for which, as we saw, Wick people have a considerable vocabulary. *Soor* is, of course, hardly a compliment, particularly in relation to an internal lack of warmth in a person. When coupled with the lack of size of the fish mentioned (and the implication of the insignificance of Thurso people), this could be seen as a genuine, in some ways offensive, description of the local rivals.

Most other names were associated with other places in Caithness, including some, as those for people from Keiss and Auckengill, which are not coastal. Most, such as *Stackers* for Staxigoe people, are versions of the name and bear no editorial content (as far as we know). Others, however, present a degree of contempt within, such as *Yowlies* for people from Auckengill, or *Neep dockers* 'turnip dressers', used as a nickname for a non-specific country village' (given by an older man who is likely to have been an active fisherman).[31] An interesting interjection is *Gollach*, for people of Caithness origin, given by one younger man, who related it to Gaelic *gall* 'foreigner, Norseman'. This may well be the case, although Scots *gollach* 'beetle, beastie' must also be borne in mind, as was discussed for Lossiemouth. An unexpected feature in these expressions of rivalry was the use of names associated with national or racial groups in other parts of the world as epithets for other inhabitants of Caithness. *Kaffir* was used by one older man for inhabitants of Staxigoe, for instance; he associated it with the aftermath of the Boer War: an Arabic word originally signifying 'non-Moslem', it came to mean 'black, non-white' in South Africa and was used at least until recently as a racist epithet for non-white people in many parts of the English-speaking world.[32] Why people from a small village in Caithness should have been associated with it is entirely unclear, as is the association of *Persian* for an inhabitant of Canisbay by one middle-aged male. There may be a similarity between the use of these terms and the common but essentially inexplicable use of *Arab* /ˈerəb/ to describe Dundonians (and, in particular, supporters of Dundee United FC), as well as the use of *Sanddancers*, employed by inhabitants of Newcastle-upon-Tyne and Gateshead for inhabitants of the communities at the mouths of the Tyne and Wear. Inevitably the most dismissive term is retained for people from Pulteney, over the River Wick from Wick proper, termed *Backsiders* by one middle-aged woman.

Finally, a number of places external to Caithness are also mentioned, some of these being population centres on the only road south from the county (the A9), such as *Helmy* for Helmsdale (the first town across the frontier in Sutherland) and *Invershneckie*, a common name for *Inverness*, the nearest large town (interestingly, neither of these names are those of the people of the towns; instead they refer to the town itself). The inhabitants of a number of large fishing towns on the other side of the Moray Firth also receive a mention. One older woman calls people from Buckie *Buckers*, while another names them *Soothsiders* (an appropriate name from the point of view of Wick). Two older informants, one male, one female, and a middle-aged man, mentioned Fraserburgh people as *Brochers* or Fraserburgh as *The Broch*. One middle-aged man called Peterhead the *Blue Toon*, while two older men called its inhabitants *Peedies*. None of these names is particularly derogatory, with the possible exception of *Peedies*, particularly marked since *peedie* (or *peerie*) for 'small' is iconic as a lexical item peculiar only to Caithness, Orkney and Shetland (all other Scots speakers use *wee*). Beyond this only two terms are mentioned: *Weegies* for Glaswegians (supplied by a younger woman – this term may not have been in general use until the success of Irvine Welsh's *Trainspotting* in the mid-1990s) and *Sassanach* for English people (supplied by an older woman).

In Lossiemouth, as elsewhere, it is nearby communities and their inhabitants who were most often named in the survey. People from the twin community of Hopeman are most regularly referred to. Older informants identified Hopeman people as variants of *Gunticks*, *Genticks*, *Juntiks* and *Jintucks*, older people know them as *Hopeman dollars* (which one older woman considered derogatory to the point that, she claimed, Lossiemouth people would not use it). Other middle-aged informants offer *Cavers*. Variants on the name of the settlement – *Hopemaner*, *Houdmaner*, *Howpers* – were reported across the ages and genders, with one middle-aged woman pointing out that young people generally use the monophthongal /o/ pronunciation rather than the historical diphthong. Although there was one report of these terms being offensive, it is difficult to say exactly why; the amount of usage reported suggests a long and close relationship, in fact. The same is probably the case with the nearby village of Cummingston, with one middle-aged man offering *Collacher* for its inhabitants (one older woman offers the same word, but for people from the Collach, the area in which the village is set; this bears some resemblance to the relationship between the use of the names *Gardenstown* and the *Gamrie*).

More criticism goes into the discussion of other close neighbours, however. Along the coast, Burghead seems to be getting off lightly, it being called *the Broch* by many informants (with Fraserburgh being *Fradies Broch* when differentiation is necessary, according to one older man) and its inhabitants *brochers*. One middle-aged woman referred to them as *Brochery Dowdies*, the latter part of the phrase perhaps referring to a blast of wind or even a large amount of something, as DSL suggests, which may be derogatory in ways which are difficult to reconstruct. Referring to them as *heathens*, however, as one middle-aged female informant did, remembering her mother's turn of phrase, may now be taken in a jocular manner, but, in the evangelical environment of Lossiemouth, this type of criticism was probably not originally minor. Indeed the informant claimed that the name was given to Burghead people because they burnt the *clayvie*, a ritual related to the cleansing of a boat or set of boats from ill luck. A more jocular term for Burghead people is *sprats*, offered by three middle-aged men.

Terms for people from Buckie were much more overtly critical, most of them – *(Buckie) Blabers, Blaubers, Blauers, Blavars, Blebbers* and *Blethers* (each offered by at most two older informants, mostly male) – referring to a talkative, probably boastful, disposition on the part of the inhabitants of the town. One older man also offered *bolsters* or *bobsters*. The fact that these names derive only from older informants possibly relates to the lack of contact between the two towns, both accessible only by relatively long roads branching from the main A96, when fishing ceased to be central to their existence. One older male referred to people from Macduff as *dullers*.

Moving away from the coast, the most common epithet offered for local places and their inhabitants was *(Elgin) Skiters*, offered by people of all ages and both genders to the extent that no alternatives were offered. *Skyte* may refer to diarrhoea, to being buffeted or hit (or, indeed, both); it may also refer, as with Buckie, to a predilection for boasting and exaggeration. It is certainly not complimentary. The same is true for people from Keith, a town to the south-east of the Spey, its inhabitants being referred to as *cyaards* (and its variants) by four older men and one younger male informant. Two older informants defined *cyaard* as a 'stirrer upper, troublemaker'; it can also mean cheat or thief. What the inhabitants of a town at some distance from Lossiemouth have done to receive this epithet (beyond alliterative possibility) is difficult to say. Inhabitants of Nairn, a former fishing port and holiday resort, some distance to the west of Lossiemouth, were referred to by one older man as *fudge babs*, for unknown reasons.

Outside the immediate environs of Lossiemouth a number of further places are mentioned: *Bluetoon* and *Bluetooners* for Peterhead (and its inhabitants; offered, surprisingly, only by only one middle-aged woman and one older man); more often, *brocher* for inhabitant of Fraserburgh, on the Moray Firth like Lossiemouth, and also given to confusion with Burghead people, as discussed above; and inhabitants of Wick, referred to by one older male informant as *Dirty Wickers*, while two older people (one male, one female) offer *Wicker* and one older woman offered *Weeker* (thereby demonstrating knowledge of Caithness pronunciation). Too

much can be made of the evidence of these two older women; the connections along the coast due to the herring fishery must be remembered,
however. One older man offered *the Clyde men*, for people (probably
fishers) from Campbelltown, a former fishing port on Kintyre in Argyll,
at the mouth of the Firth of Clyde, only some thirty kilometres from
Ireland. The fact that Lossiemouth is close to the Caledonian Canal,
which allows eastern fishing vessels to go to the west coast without
braving the Pentland Firth (and western vessels to do the opposite), may
have encouraged connections which are now barely remembered.

Given the number of communities which lie cheek-by-jowl on the
East Neuk of Fife, a (normally friendly) rivalry between the communities is unsurprising. Inevitably this has led to the development of a
considerable number of nicknames for neighbours. In fieldwork these
words and phrases sprung rapidly from informants, suggesting that the
rivalries (and old friendships) which underlie them are still very much
'live'. Interestingly, however, no names for neighbouring communities
were offered by younger informants.

In relation to St Monans, a number of informants gave versions of
the name of the village, possibly with local pronunciation marked,
and inhabitant marker *-ers. St Minansers* or *St Minaners*. Most informants who mentioned the village offered *St Monans Droners*, particularly
attractive because of its near-rhyme. Whether this name has anything
to do with the fact that, as was mentioned by a number of informants,
St Monans was called *The Holy City* because of the number of churches
there, is impossible to say.

A considerable number of informants mentioned that Cellardyke
people were known as *(Cellardyke) Dykers*, while one middle-aged woman
offered the (very) mild *Daft Dykers*. A fair amount of people offered the
rather more powerful *Pittenweem Torn Arses/Erses* (indeed one older
woman said *torn ones*, since it was 'not fair' to say *arses*). A number of
people offered *Pittenweemers* as a rather more anodyne epithet. The
mention of *torn arses* may be related to perceived (lack of) wealth: one
older female St Monans resident referred to Anstruther people as *toffs*.
Moreover, one older female Anstruther informant mentioned *Elie Toffs*,
referring to a community a couple of kilometres west of the East Neuk
which, while fishing had been common, had also been associated with
coal mining and linen work and, most importantly, had become since
the 1960s a major golfing centre, attracting well-heeled visitors from
Glasgow and Edinburgh; Elie was considered both separate from and
different to the East Neuk. That there was a pecking order within the
East Neuk is not surprising, although it is difficult to see how this can be
squared with the egalitarian nature of the communities.

It is striking that the only other name offered by Anstruther informants was *teuchters* (spelled *Choochters* by the informant), defined, as it is in most of the Scots-speaking world, as 'country people'. It is dangerous to make too much from the contribution of one older man, but it does seem that a binary relationship between the well-defined relationships of the fishing communities of the East Neuk and 'everyone else' exists.

Similar features occur for Eyemouth, although a number of younger people contributed names. These generally concern the nearby smaller communities, such as St Abbs (*shore gulls* or *shore people*. St Abbs is right on the North Sea, while Eyemouth is up a relatively long inlet; one older female also called them *craws* 'crows', which, while not exactly a compliment, is not particularly offensive either). Burnmouth people are, according to another older woman, *Burnmouth Batties*, which may refer to eccentricity veering into madness; two men, one older, one middle-aged, called Burnmouth people *sheip heids*, which appears rather more insulting. The same middle-aged man named Coldingham people *Cowdning/Cowdjing Hummers*, where there may be a suggestion of a strong and unpleasant smell emanating from them. Moving away from the coast, a number of younger and older people referred to inhabitants of the village of Duns as *Duns Dingers*. Scots *ding* implies 'hit, throw'. To *ding dung*, however, is to spread manure; there may be some connection intended. It can therefore be argued that close neighbours are treated with a degree of (largely jocular) disdain. The use of puns and other word play is central to this; the reference to the (perceived) unpleasant smells associated with the farming trade is no doubt entirely intentional.

There is no single word, as there was with Anstruther, for those from beyond the immediate neighbourhood. Indeed only Dunbar, traditionally Eyemouth's main rival herring port to the north, is name checked. One older woman refers to its inhabitants as *Pock Windaes*. It is striking that no name for people from nearby Berwick-upon-Tweed was offered, almost as if it was being ignored.

The memory and use of local names for other communities and groups continue fairly well (although with some falling away for younger informants). In all communities a central focus is on the neighbourhood and particularly coastal, but also landward, neighbours, treated with a degree of jocular contempt (the informants would no doubt expect exactly the same treatment from their neighbours. The jokiness of these names perhaps obscures what were originally means of defining where a community stood in size and cultural and economic standing. The larger communities have names for the larger fishing communities at a remove, which may be coupled to and complemented by knowledge of communities not concerned with fishing.

It might be suggested that this awareness of related, but often distant, communities would have been much more widespread in the period before the Second World War. Smaller communities generally confine their naming practices to near neighbours, perhaps most often when a number of fishing communities exist in close proximity, as with both Anstruther and Eyemouth. In many ways Lossiemouth lies mid-way between these tendencies – a community with considerable connections outside the immediate area but also situated on a crowded part of coastline which contains both smaller communities and possible rivals. Many of these names – particularly, perhaps, those which do not have an immediate relationship with the names of the communities – are largely confined to older people (and perhaps more to their memories) rather than their active use. Equally striking are those occasions where young people appear to treat the local form of a town's name as being the nickname, as being marked.

4.2.7 Vocabulary learned by incomers; perceived loss of lexis

Although most of the questions on the questionnaire were primed to retrieve information about fishing-based lexis or, at the very least, vocabulary about coastal life, two questions were designed to extract lexis of a more general nature, couched in an open-ended way. In the original planning process it was felt that questions of this type would help informants relax a little and also act as moments of reflection within the information-gathering procedure. Interestingly, the first question in the questionnaire, which asked for words and phrases learned by incomers to the region, designed to put informants at ease, was often so difficult to discuss that it was not the first topic addressed by researchers in conversation. That these aims were not always translated into reality was surprising, but did not affect the quality of what was offered.

In Peterhead, a range of different semantic and pragmatic fields were evinced in relation to words and phrases which incomers to the region readily learn. There are a number of ways in which the information collected can be displayed. The following represents one which can be employed across all the information gathered.

A number of words to do with greetings and everyday expressions were prevalent across the age groups. These included the archetypal North-East *fit like* 'how are you', along with some similar expressions, such as *foos your doos?*, which (probably) literally means 'how are your pigeons?', a surreal greeting common (jocularly) across the region, although strikingly only offered here by a younger woman. Less colourful are *fit ye doin/deein?* (offered by a middle-aged man), *foo you*

deein? (given by the same young woman who provided *foos your doos?*)
and *whoo are ye?*, offered by an older man, where the <wh> spelling is
unexpected. Although historically the <wh> words included *how* at
least occasionally, /hu/ (or even /həu/, in particular when the word
is used with the common Scots meaning 'for what reason, why') is the
normal pronunciation in most of Scotland where the change to /f/ is not
normal.[33] It may be that a degree of hypercorrection is at work here, due
to the informant being aware of usage outside of his immediate environs. The stereotypical response to these questions, *tyaavin* (or *chavin*)
awaa 'struggling by' was only presented by one older man and one
younger woman, the latter of whom being the same person who offered
the questions mentioned above. She also produced *nae bad* 'not bad', in
consort with a small number of older and middle-aged informants. The
relatively low level of production of phrases related to this context is
perhaps surprising, since, from experience, these are among the most
common phrases outsiders learn from an early point in their residence
in north-eastern Scotland.

Times of day – *aday, amorn* and *anextday* – the <a> probably standing for /i/ or /ə/ regularly found for *the* in the Northern Scots dialects,
were offered solely by one younger woman. This suggests that the forms
are current for her generation and that she suspects that they are specific
to her community (which in fact they are not: the phrases are found
throughout Scotland); it may be that she is stressing the traditional
nature of her own dialect in comparison with those found elsewhere in
her immediate experience.

One older woman offered *fa echts you?*, which the informant translated
as, literally, 'who owns you', although it is now taken to mean 'who
are you related to?'. This phrase is, according to a range of local and
national resources, a widespread usage, although not necessarily always
regularly used (indeed one other fishing port investigated also realised
this phrase). In a situation where personal relationship, by blood and
friendship, is central to the local community and its safety, it is striking
how far this is supported by pragmatic expression. The same woman
also produced *far do you bide?* for 'where do you live?', against representing the ways in which a community of this type constructs itself.

Kinship terms and other terms for people were also regularly
expressed in relation to words and phrases incomers regularly learn.
The following were offered by a fair spread of older and younger
informants, male and female. Strangely, however, there was no input at
all from middle-aged people. The relationship terms include: *auntie* (not
uncommon elsewhere, but with the local pronunciations, either /ɑn/
or [ʌn], as first syllable), *dauther* 'daughter' (with the archetypal Buchan

change of /xt/ to /θ/), *dydie* 'grandfather', *grunie* 'grandmother' (with north-eastern /a/ + nasal > /ʌ/ + nasal, a sound change of which both native speakers and resident non-natives are very much aware) and *man* 'husband' (strikingly the rather archaic semantic equivalent to Standard English *wife*, *gudewife*, was not recorded, nor were any alternatives, despite the fact that *wifie* was recorded with its Scots meaning of 'woman of a certain age', although *(auld) mannie* was recorded beside *man*). *Sen* 'son' was also offered, probably representing Scots /sɪn/. Other people terms without relationship implied include *loon* 'boy', *loonie* 'little boy' and *quine/quinie* 'girl, young woman'. Less north-eastern is *lassie* 'girl, young woman'. The final female term is *blon*, referring to someone's girl-friend, even if – surprisingly – that person's hair is not blond; unlike in English, there is no suggestion of limited intelligence. This archetypal North-East word was elicited from a young woman (the same person who produced a range of answers above).

A number of informants also offered words related to local foodstuffs, such as an older man offering *hairy tatties* for a smoked fish and milk recipe, mentioned above, along with *hard fish* and *dried fish* for different kinds of preserved fish. The same person offered *breed* for 'oatcakes' and *stovies* for the classic winter dish made from beef and 'tatties' (the same informant also produced *tatties*, which, from experience, is indeed among the first words that non-Scots learn). Other somewhat miscellaneous offerings included *bike/bikie* 'little bike', displaying the diminutive so common in this dialect of Scots, offered by the same older man. The same is true of *howkin* 'digging up something', *cairt* 'cart' and *berset* 'stressed'. A younger woman offers a range of words held pretty much in common with Standard English, but which are divergent phonologically: *affa* 'awful(ly)', *aul'* 'old' , *caul'* 'cold' (which the older male inform-ant represents with *caal*). She also offered a short list of words – *doon, roon, toon, hoose* – where the Scots monophthongal pronunciation is markedly different from the (Scottish) Standard English pronunciation. The older male informant offers *gweed* for 'good' (although he questions his spelling). This example is interesting, since it is unlikely that many younger speakers still use – although they would recognise – this and related pronunciations. Basic verbs were also given in their local forms: *gie* 'give', *ging/gan* 'go', *hiv/hae* 'have', *ken* 'know', *tak* 'take' and *telt* 'told', all offered by the younger female mentioned above.

Function words and affixes were also put forward, largely (except for *disnae/dinnae* 'doesn't/don't', and *fit*, *far* 'what, where', given by another younger woman) given by the same younger female informant. This was particularly the case with the <wh> words, the /f/ pronunciations rep-resenting arguably the most immediately noteworthy of the Northern

Scots features, given in almost exhaustive detail by this informant. She herself remarks that she does not use *foo* much, however.[34]

Full discussions of the issues thrown up by these questions will be given at the end of the section. Some preliminary discussions are possible, however. Despite the relatively low response rate with this question, it is striking, in the first instance, how only one directly fishing-related set of words turned up; even this was related to eating the product. Many of the words and phrases elicited were related to common words or words with an obviously different pronunciation from their (Scottish) Standard English equivalents. No words about weather or the sea were recorded, but the <wh> words were given some prominence. It is interesting that with these last examples in particular, it was young people who were particularly likely to produce these pronunciations. It may be that the encroachment of non-local pronunciations with these words are more obvious to younger than older informants.

In Wick, similar, but different, evidence was also present. Some greetings were given, including *What's 'e crack 'aday?* 'what is the news today', given by a younger female, or the variant *Crack 'e day?* or variants, produced by four young women and one young man, while *How ye doing 'e day?* and *How ye getting on?* were offered by one woman from all three age differentiations. The third group in particular does not appear particularly local, although local pronunciation would make it rather more so.

Apparently local words were also offered, including *aine* 'lady' (offered by a middle-aged woman), *bairn* (offered by two younger women), *aye* (offered by two younger women), the truly local *bowg* 'stomach' (given by a middle-aged woman and a middle-aged man), *boygie* 'boy' (given by a young woman), *chiel* '[male] child, [young] man' (given by one middle-aged and one younger woman), *dreich*, from a younger female, *foosome* 'dirty', offered by one middle-aged and one younger woman, *greeting* 'crying' (from a younger woman), *lassgie* or *lassie* 'young woman or girl', given by the same woman, as were *minging* 'ugly' and *blether* 'talk at length' and *wifie* 'woman',[35] also given by a middle-aged woman. Other words offered included *neeps* 'turnips' (from a middle-aged man), *peedie* 'small' (from a middle-aged woman), *tatties* (from one middle-aged man) and *til* 'to', given by a young man, who also commented on its Norse origin.[36] The local identity marker *scorrie* 'seagull', as discussed above, was offered by a range of young and middle-aged informants of both sexes.

A number of words were also offered where it was the pronunciation that largely distinguished the word from its (Scottish) Standard English. These included *'is and 'at* 'this and that', representing the common

Caithness feature (although it is not confined to there) of 'th-dropping' (offered by an older man', *dowg* 'dog' (offered by a younger woman), *doon 'e street* (offered by a middle-aged woman), *heid* 'head' (from an older woman) and *jecket* 'jacket', *glesses* 'glasses' and *ferm* 'farm', all offered by the apparently prolific young woman discussed above. A subset of this class were alternative pronunciations for place names, such as *Week* for Wick, surprisingly only given by one older woman, and *Poltney* for Pultneytown, where the older woman who offered it was placing particular stress on the use of a rounded vowel (very much a local feature and not confined to this one example).

Other miscellaneous material included the /f/ for /ʍ/ phenomenon, with *fit* 'what' being singled out. Somewhat surprisingly, since this is a feature with strong local connections, this is only mentioned by two men and one woman (the latter of whom, oddly, claims that words of this type are not local but rather connected to Buckie, across the Moray Firth). This lack of exemplification and discussion is highly marked in comparison to Peterhead, where the same phenomenon applies. One older man also mentioned the retention of a pronunciation difference between participial and gerund *-in*, a feature in Caithness dialect and a few other 'marginal' Scots dialects.

What is striking about these is how much material is offered by young people. Partly this is due to one young woman being particularly willing (and able) to show her knowledge, but it is also possible that, in the first instance, there was considerably greater residual and indeed active knowledge among younger speakers than elsewhere (although the evidence contained in this book suggests that this is patchy at best) and, moreover, that, unlike Peterhead, there were fewer incomers to accommodate and incorporate and that these were largely dealt with by younger members of the community.

Lossiemouth informants presented a similar pattern for words quickly learned by outsiders. In the first instance there were greetings, such as *are ye fine?* (from a middle-aged woman), *arite?* (offered by a younger woman: it is noteworthy that it is the English pronunciation for *right* which is found here, rather than the Scots equivalent, containing /x/), *come awa in* (offered by a middle-aged woman, who also noted a difference in vowel fronting in *in*, with nearby Hopeman having a more front pronunciation), *aye aye*, with the meaning 'hello', offered by a range of people of both genders across the age groups, alongside *aye aye fine day* (from an older man; *fine day* was offered by a middle-aged woman) and *aye aye, fit like* (from an older woman) and variants. *Fa yacht ye?*, meaning 'where are you from; what people are you from?', was offered by one older man and a range of middle-aged people, *foo ye a' dein?* by a middle-aged woman. *Foo's yersel?* was reported by a range of older and middle-aged people. Unexpectedly, however, a range of people from the same age groups also reprted *who's yersel*, while others offered *hoo ye doing?* This apparent retention of /ʍ/ and /h/ variants for *how* is most unexpected. Even more surprising is the reporting of *woo's all your cruddie today?*, with *cruddie* being interpreted as 'crowd', only reported by two older men, and the <wh> in *how* (see above) being represented in, in Scottish terms, astrikingly abnormal form.[37] The use of /f/ for the <wh> words largely in relation to *fit like?*, was regularly recognised by informants, often being used by non-locals as a sign of having 'arrived' (interestingly, one middle-aged man offered a response to this phrase, *yersel?*, which captures the laconic speech ways of the local community and their attraction to incomers), but the other <wh> words also get a number of recognitions by the whole range of informants, including *far ye fae?* 'where are you from', recorded by one older man.

A number of lexical items are also reported including a number of mentions of *ken* 'know', a feature of local speech particularly marked to anyone from outside of Scotland. One older woman noted that her neighbour, who is from Yorkshire, had picked up this word, in particular in the phrase *d'ye ken?* Words for different stages of the life cycles of men and women were offered by a range of informants across the age groups, including *bairn, loon/loonie, loons, quin(i)es, mannies* and *wifies*. Many of these include the diminutive *-ie*, commented upon independently by two older men as a major feature of local speech. Other lexical items includes *bide* 'live, reside', offered by a younger woman, *doon by* 'down the road and round the corner' and *up by* 'up the road and round the corner' (from the same older man), *inoo* 'just now', from a younger woman, *hale*, 'extremely', as in *hale bonnie* 'very beautiful', offered by two older men and *wee*, provided by a younger man. A set of words – *noo, ony, oot* and *weel* 'well', all offered by the same younger man – represent where the meaning of a word in Standard English and the local dialect is essentially the same, but the pronunciation is marked, particularly perhaps in situations where the (Scottish) Standard English pronunciations are becoming increasingly commonplace. Some examples of verb negation phenomena, such as *dinna* for 'don't' (from one middle-aged and one younger woman) most likely represents something similar.

A striking discrepancy appears to be demonstrated by the realisation of both *g(a)neppin* (offered by a range of middle-aged people) and *bra bricht moonlicht nicht the nicht*, defined by the older male informant who offered it as a 'standard general Scots greeting'. The latter is highly stereotypical – it may in fact be derived from Music Hall tradition. It does, however, contain the Scottish /x/ shibboleth, a phoneme unknown in the speech of the majority of people who came to work in the nearby RAF base, but one which some incomers at least would try very hard to acquire. *G(a)neppin* is quite a technical term, on the other hand, referring to the use by local people of highly standardised, often rather anglicised, forms of speech, something much frowned upon in the community. Nowadays this verb is geographically patchy in the Scots-speaking world (*pittin it on* would be the norm elsewhere), with this part of Moray and Shetland (where it is realised as *knappin*) being the places where its use is most healthy. It may be a word that not only those from outside Scotland but also people from elsewhere in the country would find intriguing.

Far fewer material was produced by far fewer people in Anstruther, although, as found elsewhere, *wha's acht you?*, is also present, given by a middle-aged woman. Another greeting, *whaur are ye fae?* was given by the same person. Archetypal *aye* 'yes' was given by this woman and another woman from the same age group. Lexical items offered included the general Scots *wee*, *dreich* and *messages* 'groceries' and the more local *baffies* 'slippers' (all given by one younger man) and *ben* 'inside', as in *I'll bring it ben to you*, was given by a middle-aged woman. One middle-aged woman presented *Anster*, the local name for the town. This suggests, perhaps, that it is now the local pronunciation which is marked, with the mainstream form becoming the norm, for insiders and outsiders alike.

A relatively small number of words and phrases were produced in Eyemouth, including *aye*, from a middle-aged woman and a younger man, *ken*, offered by informants of all age groups, the use of *gey* in *gey bothered* given by a younger man, to mean 'I'm not bothered', a good example of ironic use, since *gey* normally means 'very' and *baigie* 'turnip', a form localised to Berwickshire (although *baggie* is more widespread in the South-East of Scotland according to DSL). The pronunciation *Jeck* for *Jack* was also mentioned. A middle-aged man offered *windrams*, which he explained as 'sea breeze'. Although this is an uncommon surname and the formation of the word is at least partly transparent, neither DSL nor OED mention this word. It is heartening to see a word with seaborne associations considered to be one passed on to incomers. In the same vein, one middle-aged man offered the knowledge that some fishing families were known (including by new arrivals in the town, it would appear) by the names of their boats, so that the Aitchesons were the *Heathers* and the Jamiesons, *Pamfy*.

As is readily apparent, this task had rather mixed results. It was striking – although not entirely surprising – that pronunciations marked to the incoming population, such as /f/ for the <wh> words, should be given emphasis in such a discussion. The same is true for local greeting patterns and certain lexical items – *ken*, for instance – which are both somewhat exotic to incomers and readily comprehensible after a limited exposure even if you have never used (or even heard) them before. 'Unexpected' lexis, lexis associated with emotions or things or forms of behaviour, is also, our informants tell us, acquired by immigrants. But so are rather hackneyed turns of phrase which would not naturally be used by local people, but may be being used to make some kind of point.

Later in the questionnaire participants were asked to record any words which they had not heard since they were children. This question was inevitably designed in such a way that older informants would be more likely to be able to offer much material. This indeed proved the case, although a number of younger people did offer both material and interesting commentary. At heart the question was designed to see whether people would explicitly classify lexis connected with fishing to a past age. As we will see, this was only the case to some extent.

In Peterhead a fair number of words and phrases were offered, mostly, as would be expected, by older people (although this was not always the case). Some words related to passed or passing aspects of domestic life, such as *chubby* 'umbrella' (a word whose origin is obscure), offered by an older man, *chumla* 'mantelpiece', given by two older people and a younger woman, *chuntie* (or *chantie*) 'chamberpot', given by an older woman, *quite* for 'underskirt', offered by an older and a middle-aged woman (the latter saying that she would still occasionally use the word) and *watery* 'lavatory' (offered by an older woman). Words were given for parts of the body, such as *fazoog/fazog* 'face' (interestingly, offered by a younger woman), *crannie* 'little finger', offered by another younger woman, *(k)napper* 'head, forehead' (offered, again by a younger woman), *thoomb* (offered by the same younger woman) and *kyte* 'stomach', offered by this and another younger woman. Descriptions of personal states, such as *dammart* 'dizzy', offered by a younger man who had heard it from his mother', *orraster* 'of bad repute', *plowtert* 'overcome by heat' and *scomfeeshed* 'upset by a bad smell' (these last three from the same older woman), were also prevalent. Unlike for the question asked about incomers' language use, the /f/ for <wh> words were only touched upon by one older female informant, in relation to *fit wye* 'how'. This suggests that, for older insiders at least, there is nothing to comment upon in this usage (the same might hold true for the parts of the body words whose markedness is really only pointed out by younger people, perhaps because these are the default forms for older people[38]). No other function words – *div* for 'do', for instance – were offered.

A range of other words were offered, include words associated with food and drink, such as *bree* 'thin broth', offered by an older man, and *mealiks* 'crumbs', offered by an older woman, directions and time references, such as (*en*) *ablow* 'below', *up abeen* 'above' and (*y)estreen* 'last night', all given by the same older female informant. A number of other words strongly associated with local traditions and folk ways, such as *bide* 'stay, live' (offered by a middle-aged woman), *mishanter* 'accident' (from an older man) and *sheepy maaes* 'clover' (from an older woman) were offered. A sub-set of this phenomenon is represented by the use of *weaving* (in a variety of pronunciations) for 'knitting', offered almost inevitably by older women. A number of participants also offered examples where the primary difference with (Scottish) Standard English is pronunciation. Examples included *dewg*, given by an older woman as the pronunciation of *dog* in Cairnbulg,[39] *saat and spice* 'salt and pepper', from a younger woman and *scweel/skweel* 'school', given by one middle-aged and two younger women.

A few fishing and seaborne words were offered. These included *drytle*, defined by an older female informant as 'to go out on a little boat and not be too concerned about whether or not they brought in fish', *ganzey*, offered by one younger woman who said that her father would use it for any knitted jersey, *hairy tatties* 'a dish made from dried fish and potatoes' (from an older woman) and *waar* 'seaweed' (from the same older woman). Interestingly, one younger woman offers *by-names*, one of the terms given for the practice of using nicknames to distinguish different families and individuals with the same (or similar) name. She did not give any examples, however. Does this mean that she understands the concept but has limited experience of its use?

In Wick, on the other hand, *div* (in a variety of spellings) was given by a range of older and middle-aged informants, sometimes along with archetypal verbs such as *ken* or *mind* 'remember'. One middle-aged man gave *fit* for 'what', but went on to add that he still heard this. Apart from this discrepancy, however, many of the same semantic fields represented for Peterhead are also found for Wick. Words offered include *strannie* 'pavement' or 'kerb', produced by two older woman, one of whom went on to say that her sons do not know the word, even though she uses them'. *Laskie* 'girl' (offered by a young woman) represents a large field, as does *kaitlins* 'kittens (produced by a middle-aged woman), while *gurshle* 'messy eater or untidy person' is quite a specific term. *Twilt* (for 'quilt') was produced by one middle-aged woman, who added that people from Newcastle-upon-Tyne know this word.[40] Domestic or childhood words like *hurley* 'boxcar' or *cra'er* (where <'> is likely to stand for a glottal stop) 'creature; an affectionate term for someone' rub shoulders with *cownin* 'crying, howling' (from one middle-aged and one younger woman). As with Peterhead, the Wick informants also offered a number of variants based primarily on pronunciation, such as *aes* /es/ 'ashes from the fire' (from a middle-aged man), *mate*, given by an older woman with the meaning 'meat' and *powder*, given as /pudər/, with essentially the same meanings.

A small number of fishing and coastal words were also offered, such as *swarbeck* for 'black back gull' and *willie beeb* 'oystercatcher' (both from an older man). An interesting spread of a seaborne word was given by two middle-aged informants: *sail* being used in relation to moving on land in a wheeled vehicle: the example they give is related to childhood home-made carts. At the very least this last example demonstrates the importance of the concepts of sailing to the community as a whole in the recent past.

Informants in Lossiemouth provided an impressive number of words and phrases for this question. These included words about food, such as *biled ham* (offered by two middle-aged women), *chappers* 'mashed potatoes', given by one older and one middle-aged woman, *ham end* 'joint of ham' (from a middle-aged man) and *gulsuc(h)s* (or *gulshachs*) 'sweets', given by two older informants and one middle-aged woman. Clothes, such as *sansheen* 'sandshoes, plimsoles' (from an older man) and *semit* 'vest' (from a middle-aged woman). Many archetypically Scots words were offered, including *mishanter* 'accident (from a middle-aged woman). *Limmer* 'feisty', from an older man, was given by another man for 'woman, but not a complimentary term' (another older man claimed not to know that the word was associated primarily with women). The language of childhood was represented by *juckin* (and variants) 'to play truant', given by an older man. Weather words, like *jilt*, 'frozen, freezing' also turned up, as did the archetypal Moray *gineppin* 'speaking in a "posh" manner', given by two middle-aged women. A number of /f/ for <wh> words were offered, not least phrases such as *fa yacht a hurly?* 'who owns that wheelbarrow'?, given by an older man, apparently said by fishermen when cleaning out docked boats. Rather less colourful, but probably rather more commonplace, is *faw de ye acht ye?*, 'who are you related to?', given by an older man which, as we have seen, was often thought to be among the phrases incomers would learn.[41]

A number of words offered had a relationship with the sea and fishing. This included *fry* for smaller fish, offered by a middle-aged woman, *branquer*, 'what you roasted fish in the fire in' (from an older woman), *partan* 'crab' (from an older man), *rope-a-ree* 'place for making ropes', *sauce* 'fish soup', offered by five middle-aged contributors, and *firkin* 'a smaller barrel of salted herring, which was what, alongside a bag of oatmeal and a sack of potatoes obtained through barter, people survived on in the winter', given, strikingly, by an older woman.

Rather fewer examples were given in Anstruther, although the actual diversity of forms was striking, running from *lows* 'flames in the fire', given by a middle-aged woman, through *hallecht* 'clumsy', given by an older man and *fairfurfuchen* for 'stressed out', from the same informant. Indeed it would have to be recognised that well over three-quarters of the material offered under this category in Anstruther were offered by this one authority, whose knowledge of even unusual Scots vocabulary – *manting* meaning 'stuttering', for instance – is impressive. Whether this means that he has a particularly impressive memory for lexis or that he is merely able to retrieve lexis of this type more readily than his contemporaries is, of course, impossible to say with the evidence we have. What is striking, however, is that, with one exception, *smeekit* 'smoked', no fishing vocabulary at all was offered at this port. But this is highly fecund in comparison with the Eyemouth response to this question. All five of the lexical items offered – *cundy* 'drain', *ben* 'in', *poke* 'bag', *duddys* 'slippers' and *seamit* 'vest' – were provided by one middle-aged woman. None has a fishing or seaborne connection.

4.3 A preliminary thought, in place of a conclusion

In this chapter a considerable wealth of lexical material derived both from print and online resources as well as new fieldwork has been compare and analysed. In the next chapter we will consider some of the central features of this analysis; there will be no attempt to pre-empt this in this section. One observation might be made, however: while age appears to affect your knowledge of local vocabulary, it is noteworthy that some people appear to have better memory of use (and possibly active use) than others who would be perceived as their peers. Why should this be the case?

5 Conclusions

While largely cataloguing the loss of local lexis in these fishing communities, so much material has been assembled, often very rich in nature, that it makes sense to step back and discuss some of the usage (and non-usage) patterns found before attempting a conclusion.

5.1 Geographical variation

From a very early point in the analysis it became apparent that location was a central feature in establishing both the quality and quantity of material collected. In general, inhabitants of the northern communities – Wick, Lossiemouth and Peterhead – produced a great many more words and phrases across the board and particularly in relation to fishing and fish. The least productive community was Eyemouth; indeed occasional pockets of productivity in that settlement often turned out to be a small group or even an individual with a long and broad memory of past usage (it should be noted that such knowledgeable individuals can be found in any of our communities). Anstruther people fall somewhere in between: often their knowledge not only of their own usage but also that of their neighbours is considerable; on the other hand, there are occasions where we might expect Anstruther informants to produce particular words – in relation to herring, not so long ago the staple of the community, for instance – and knowledge (never mind use) is at best patchy.

A number of explanations might be put forward for these differences. In the first instance, Peterhead is still very much a working fishing port. Men and women are employed in fishing and ancillary trades on a permanent basis. This is not, of course, carried out at anything like the level it was a hundred years ago; fishing is still a major part of the economic make-up of the town and its environs. Neither Wick nor Lossiemouth can claim this reinforcement, however; nevertheless, many of their inhabitants appear to have considerable knowledge (if not use) of local vocabulary (including fishery lexicon). Anstruther informants do not have quite this level of knowledge (although this can involve counter-tendencies, such as knowledge of the word for porpoise or dolphin); all but hobby fishing has disappeared from this port. Eyemouth, however, where very limited knowledge of traditional fishing vocabulary was found, has a somewhat healthier fishing trade than many of the other ports (although its importance to the town's economy is probably relatively small; this cannot, of course, be immediately compared to the symbolic cultural importance continuing the industry might have). It is likely therefore that while the maintenance of commercial fishing may help to perpetuate local lexical use, primarily because of the necessity for a fully functioning lexis for an economically central set of semantic fields, it is not of itself a primary spur towards maintenance.

Is the differentiation therefore a matter of distance from the main population centre of Scotland, the Central Belt? Again, to some extent this is the case: Wick is about as far as it is possible to go from Glasgow or Edinburgh and remain on the Scottish mainland; both Anstruther and Eyemouth are on the edge of the heavily populated industrial and post-industrial heartland of Scotland. Although communication between both Lossiemouth and Peterhead and the south is more straightforward than is the case for Wick, they are still not exactly near neighbours. On all three occasions, moreover, the surrounding agricultural dialects are still in relatively good health. Obviously there is something in this view, but it does not explain why Peterhead has the 'healthiest' knowledge of traditional lexis. Nor does it explain why Anstruther, relatively close to the industrial areas of Fife, should be quite traditional in its usage. It is worth noting that while living in Eyemouth now represents a rela-tively straightforward commute up the A1 to Edinburgh, the road from Anstruther to the Forth Road Bridge is not, at least to begin with, of the same standard. Commuting to Edinburgh is therefore not always as easy from the East Neuk as might be expected, even if the city is readily visible across the Forth.

Finally, is there any reason to suspect that close connections to other fishing centres, nearby and relatively distant, might encourage reten-tion of lexis? It is noteworthy that all three of the northern ports have a strong sense of neighbours and rivals, including those sundered from the home port by a considerable distance, demonstrated by the names they give them and often at least some of the vocabulary for central items (such as their words for 'seagull' for instance). There are, of course, dif-ferences between these settlements. Both Peterhead and Lossiemouth have many near neighbours along a highly populated coast. Wick has a number of neighbours along the east coast of Caithness; these are normally small even by the standards of Wick. Wick also has, of course, a long-standing rivalry with Thurso, a settlement on the north coast of Caithness of around the same size. Beyond these, however, local settlements and their inhabitants are few and far between. This may explain why Wick people often take a broad view of which ports are within their 'immediate neighbourhood'. Eyemouth is also isolated in a similar way; an unexpected situation, given how many people live in the immediate neighbourhood. The fishing villages around are small and have had little professional fishing in living memory. In fieldwork, some awareness of their neighbours was demonstrated, with Dunbar, historically the town's biggest rival to the north, being given one mention (although strikingly the town's neighbour to the south, Berwick-upon-Tweed, was never mentioned). Anstruther, on the other hand, is part of a conglomeration of relatively small-scale communities at the East Neuk of Fife; while generally friendly rivalries exist in the immediate neighbourhood, the promontory's position far out into the North Sea (in comparison to Eyemouth's position at the head of a long inlet) perhaps explains why knowledge of communities at a considerable remove – most notably, Peterhead – should be present. Geographical position can therefore be said to be an issue in the survival and use of traditional vocabulary; it cannot be said, however, that it is anything like the *only* variable influencing this retention or loss.

5.2 Gender variation

Until very recently fishing was by tradition a solely male profession. But women were central to the trade, mending and *barkin* nets, gutting and dressing fish and, historically, selling the fish to the surrounding countryside or urban settlements. It was assumed, therefore, that a division of vocabulary knowledge would exist, with terms for fish being better known by male participants while vocabulary associated with occupations ancillary to the trade might be better known (or at least as well known) by female participants. As the material above demonstrates, this is indeed partly the case: knowledge of fish terminology was to a considerable extent male-oriented, as was, surprisingly, knowledge of the names for birds and other marine wildlife. The primary exception to this tendency, however, is the words offered for different sizes of fish, almost all of which (with the exception of 'salmon') did not always relate to the maturational cycle of fish, but rather to their size and eventual purpose on the slab. Both men and women gave these terms in considerable numbers, with women at least at times appearing more successful than their male counterparts. Interestingly, however, *barkin*, referring to the treatment of nets, and *faurlan*, referring to the central trough where gutted fish were placed in the mass-production herring trade, were both shown to be the subject of considerable knowledge and interest by male informants. With the former it has to be recognised that men did take part in the process – in particular retired fisherman, but also younger men who, for whatever reason, were not permanently fishing. Work at the *faurlan* was wholly female, however, except for male contractors and overseers. As will be suggested later in this chapter, examples of this type may be taken at least partly to imply a mediated knowledge of culture and language, rather than knowledge as a direct result of personal involvement. Leading on from this, it is striking that, largely in Peterhead, but to an extent elsewhere, a small number of younger women appear to have a fair knowledge of traditional vocabulary, despite having connections with the heritage industry rather than directly with fishing and its ancillary trades.

5.3 Variation according to age

In theory the most straightforward variable to analyse is age. In these communities most older people know (and use) a great many more fishing-related lexical items than do younger. This is unsurprising, of course. In those settlements where commercial fishing (or, indeed, fishing of any type) has ceased, most words will be remembered only by those who can remember the reason why they were used. But even in Peterhead, where commercial fishing is still a going concern, a considerable 'knowledge gradient' appears to be in place, with younger people not truly appearing to know more about the traditional vocabulary of the trade than is the case elsewhere on the coast. To some extent this is because the technology and techniques of the trade have become globalised to the extent that the local manufacture of local solutions to global problems has essentially disappeared. While it is quite possible that a centrally produced machine to be found in every port in the world might have a local name, this is less likely than when local goods produced for a local market filled a gap (an early version of this can be seen in this research in the near-universality of *sou'wester* in comparison to the many names given to types of protective clothing prior to the spread of that waterproofing technology's products).

There are some unexpected counter-currents which can be observed, however. In the first instance, it was striking that, in a number of ports, many of those best equipped to discuss the meaning and use of various words and phrases were not among the older group (although there were certainly examples of this type of knowledge there as well);

instead, middle-aged informants (in particular, but not exclusively, men) were often able to remember a great deal of information related to fishing and the coastal life. One of the most striking examples of this was to be found in Eyemouth, which otherwise did not offer a great deal of evidence for lexical survival. Why should these members of the middle grouping be apparently dedicated to the continuing use and understanding of these words?

Without further fieldwork it is impossible to give a categorical answer (even then it might prove elusive). But one possibility which might be worth examining is whether at least some of these who witness change in early life (particularly, perhaps, at the beginning of their working lives) are inclined to remember both the names for new ways of doing things and those which are past; to some it may become a sacred cause, but there can be little doubt that an interest in the past is still strong in those who witnessed the transformation. Many of those who have largely known only the older ways of doing things may, on the other hand, never have had much need to analyse how things were done: things were just the way they were. Some support for this is given by the sole younger male informant in Lossiemouth, who, while not a fisherman, worked in an occupation intrinsically connected to the sea. His knowledge of fishing-related words and phrases was considerable, particularly since many of the words he knew represented beings and things he cannot have known in a work capacity (it is worth noting also that the change away from fishing in Lossiemouth to 'leisure sailing' had apparently embittered him; in some ways he must have seen himself as the last of a line; the last who cared, perhaps). There is a powerfully conscious element to these informants' knowledge which would have been far less common when the communities and their dominant occupation were stable, working with the material for which they had vocabulary in an everyday, unmarked, setting.

This conscious aspect to memory and use has a further, somewhat unexpected, set of results. In the first instance, in most of the settlements younger people appeared to know a considerable amount about local traditions; in particular in relation to taboo-avoidance words and phrases, perhaps (Eyemouth did not demonstrate this to the same extent, perhaps predictably; even there, however, some knowledge was present). This was unexpected, in much the same way as the relatively unimpressive knowledge of weather terminology was unexpected. To some extent this knowledge was based on continuing use of these traditions by older members of the communities; a sense of local colour cannot be ruled out, however.

These views cannot explain one feature which turned up with *faurlan* and a range of similar words: the 'hazy' knowledge of what a word relates to, rather than what it actually meant to those who took part in the work and communal culture of the time. It might, in fact, be suggested that this 'haziness' represents a secondary order of relationship where the informant has perhaps had the process expressed to her or him or has seen a photograph, diagram, diorama or other display which included the work. Knowledge therefore falls, perhaps, into the category of heritage rather than direct experience. A number of younger women in Peterhead, moreover, had a knowledge set impressive for their age; all had some connection to the heritage industry.

5.4 Discussion and analysis of these categories

In the first chapter of this book much was made of the idea of 'dialect death', the replacement of one dialect by another to the extent that the original dialect ceases to be used by anyone within the community. The question therefore presents itself: can these processes to some extent be found in the material discussed in this book?

We could begin with what might be defined as a simplistic 'yes': with occupational and cultural change comes much loss of originally important but now marginal lexical material. This is such a commonplace presentation of traditional dialect change that it would be surprising *and* disappointing if this were not the case in the communities discussed in this book, in particular when the trade which so defined most inhabitants and their lives has at the very least ceased to have such a pivotal role within the community and on a number of occasions has ceased outright to have any bearing on the contemporary economic existence of the community. It could be argued, in fact, that this tendency towards loss of this type, of attrition due to societal change, is the central feature of this research. It must be recognised, however, that local lexical features *not* entirely, if at all, connected directly to the fishing trade – local plants and animals, weather conditions, and so on – should also apparently suffer from intergenerational attrition. It is still worth noting, however, that with both categories, survival does take place among younger informants in what at least at first is a random way, while some older speakers are not always as knowledgeable of their 'native' lexis as might have been expected. We have not, of course, attempted to assess new word formation in the communities in anything like a systematic manner. Experience and anecdotal evidence – as well as evidence assembled for names for work clothes – appear to demonstrate that largely material borrowed from outside the community is preferred.

The question could also be answered with a simplistic 'no': while there is a winnowing out of no longer current lexis, it is striking how much intergenerational transfer there is. Therefore it is possible to argue simplistically that our material does not demonstrate linguistic attrition. As has been noted on a number of occasions, transfer of traditional local lexis into the younger generations of these communities is often more widespread than would have been predicted. Indeed, some younger people often have a more impressive knowledge of the vocabulary associated with local heritage and past occupations than some middle-aged people do. Moreover, other middle-aged people were among the most informed informants in our survey, in particular, perhaps, in the southern communities.

But as discussed above, much of the lexical knowledge found with younger people appears to be culturally conditioned through some degree of connection to the heritage industry and its products. Knowledge of this type should not be downplayed, but it has to be recognised that its acquisition is likely to be later in life than the lexis gained through first language acquisition. As we have also noted, particularly knowledgeable middle-aged speakers may represent lone users of the dialect who take a particular interest in the vocabulary of fishing and the seaborne life as a heritage item, probably because the trade was changing (and contracting) at a considerable speed in the communities during their early lives. It should also be noted that all communities, as far as we can tell, possess members whose knowledge of traditional local vocabulary is considerable alongside people with very limited knowledge of the same lexical items. In Wick in particular this appeared almost dysfunctional, perhaps because of the tension between the historical importance of the town (and its centrality to the fishing and whaling trades) and its present condition.

In other words, therefore, what evidence we have for counter-currents to lexical attrition are largely confined to individuals and can be viewed as having an origin discrete from 'normal' lexical acquisition, making the words and phrases involved receive a place much closer to full consciousness than would be the case with most other vocabulary.

But if, as seems apparent, lexical attrition is taking place in these communities, changes to their occupational and cultural natures cannot be the sole reason for the changes involved, not least because similar changes can be found in communities where a single occupational background did not embrace a large part of a community, Macafee (1994), focusing on lexical use in working-class communities in Glasgow, being a particularly good example of this broader phenomenon within Scotland.

All Scots-speaking communities appear to respond to similar stand-ardising forces in similar ways. Near universal literacy in Scottish Standard English, backed up by the hegemonic force of that variety in school, bureaucracy and church (each of these having different levels of importance, depending on the nature of the community), has made that variety central to the experience of all Scots speakers. On occasion, the external variety may assume greater centrality in the community. It is likely, therefore, that many people with ambitions beyond their immediate surroundings have focused on the standard code as a marker of ambition. To a lesser extent, however, similar phenomena are present in all speakers in these communities. While it is often difficult to gauge the extent to which the mass broadcast media influence local vocabu-lary use, it would seem unlikely that the colloquial and non-standard English varieties used in, for instance, television dramas, viewed by many members of the communities, did not have some influence upon the lexical use of younger members of the community in particular. But these undermining forces cannot be the only tendencies affecting the local nature of traditional dialect features.

As has been shown regularly over the last thirty years, moves away from traditional dialects in highly literate communities rarely imply an immediate shift towards the prestige standard. Instead regional koines, expressing regional identity across a wide geographical expanse, develop as a replacement for more localised expressions of identity, with phonological rather than lexical features at the heart of the expres-sion of difference and distance. While the materials assembled for this research were not intended to provide evidence of this sort, it would be very surprising if such developments were not present along the Scottish coast. Indeed the questions intended to encourage informants to produce lexis particularly native to the area did not produce any-thing like the amount of fishing and sea and coastal centred vocabulary expected. Instead, most of the vocabulary offered was shared with the general neighbourhood (although the levels of knowledge may have been different).

It could therefore be argued that, as was initially posited in Chapter 1, what the evidence contained in this books represents is *lexical vari-ation and change*. The lexical make-up of no variety remains the same: changes in lifestyle, community way of life, technology, along with the need by younger generations to express their youth, inevitably means that a considerable turnover of lexis is likely in all varieties (perhaps particularly with varieties which have limited or no literate expression, and therefore do not suffer from the innate conservatism of literate varieties). Most of what was discussed in Chapter 4 represents just such sets of changes.

There is a major issue, however. The sources for the new vocabulary tend to be entirely external – Standard and colloquial English, primarily. This appears even to be the case with fishing-specific lexis, which we would expect to survive well. Even in Peterhead, where fishing remains a major employer, vocabulary has become strikingly non-local, in particular (although not exclusively) for younger informants. It may be that being asked about local life and employment by outsiders would have encouraged this apparent innovation, but this can only be a partial explanation. What we must be seeing in these communities is genuine and irreversible lexical attrition. Some communities are further along the cline than are others, for whatever sociolinguistic reasons, but all are heading inexorably in the same direction. When we find younger or middle-aged people with impressive vocabulary knowledge, this represents not survival for a cohort but instead for an individual who has had personal sociocultural reasons for learning vocabulary otherwise confined to older people. Each of these features lies very close to the *linguistic attrition* put forward by Schmid, mentioned in the first chapter, with the caveat that the variety which is being abandoned and the variety which is drastically affecting the lexis of that variety are very close relatives (sharing most of their morphosyntactic structures, for instance), with the dominant variety acting as lingua franca through use in education and government, for all members of the local community. In ways which cannot be the case between discrete varieties, linguistic attrition may not be as conscious with such interwoven varieties.

The same is true for Sasse's theory of language death. We are at almost the end of the process he outlines. In a sense, it could be argued that the retention of vocabulary in these communities represents the need to express cultural and social distinctiveness in relation to a not-so-distant past. But the changeover to the new varieties found in these communities cannot have been as traumatic as the competition and changeover between wholly discrete varieties. Instead, it is likely that the non-use of certain vocabulary items has gone largely unmarked by many members of these communities on a day-to-day basis.

This observation brings our evidence close to the *dialect attrition* discussed in Chapter 1. It has to be recognised, however, that the socially distinctive nature of these communities (which led to their linguistic separateness) in many ways makes for a greater leap than would be the case for most dialects dissolving into a greater *koine*. On the other hand, the level of knowledge and concordance across considerable distance between different fishing dialects could be seen as a partial koine in the making which economic forces eventually rendered moribund.

5.5 Dialect Death?

It seems, therefore, that what has been catalogued and analysed in this book is the ongoing death of the traditional dialects of the Scottish fishing communities. Unsurprisingly, dialect death is not normally as dramatic or as easily observable as language death. When two essentially discrete varieties – discrete at all linguistic levels but particularly in morpho-syntax and phonology – exist side by side, it is normally straightforward to decide when one variety is being replaced by another. With two dialects derived from the same source, it is much more difficult to map where one stops and the other starts. Indeed it could be argued that *shift*, generally preferred by some scholars instead of *death*, might actually be better applied to dialect death, since the process involved is generally a cline of use rather than a sudden transition; it is often difficult to observe the place where one dialect ceases to be used, with some of its material being incorporated into another language. 'Island' dialects, such as those associated with the Scottish fishing communities, make observing the shift much more straightforward. The evidence for the process is inevitably contradictory and inchoate, however, particularly when we consider it synchronically.

Notes

Chapter 1

1. Strikingly, Milroy and Gordon's advanced textbook (2003: 185–90) barely touches on lexical attrition. It is, in a sense, the variation which 'dare not speak its name'.
2. This present discussion does not immediately concern itself with *semantic* variation and change (although occasionally discussion of how the two sets of variation inter-relate in the material collected for this research will be presented). Recent, often admirable, discussions of semantic variation and change in English can be found in Robinson (2010), Beal and Burbano-Elizado (2012) and Durkin (2012).
3. It should be noted that one major figure in the field has cast doubt on some of the findings of *attrition* studies mentioned here (Myers-Scotton 2002: ch. 5). While some of Myers-Scotton's views are undoubtedly insightful, they are concerned almost wholly with contact between absolutely discrete languages and therefore do not have much immediate effect upon the material discussed in this book.
4. See Dixon (1972) for a description of the original state of the language's grammatical gender system. Mylne (1995) discusses the changes through which the system has now passed.
5. Of course none of these changes need necessarily mean that a language is dying out. English encountered similar sociolinguistic and linguistic influences and changes in the late Old English and early Middle English periods without disappearing. It could nonetheless be argued that the language went through 'traumatic' circumstances not dissimilar to language death in a transition which – at least in morphosyntax – involved rapid change and the 'beheading' of the native lexis through the importation of many high status French words (for a discussion of many of these issues, see Millar forthcoming).

6. Awareness of this observation runs through the history of sociolinguistic analysis of dialect use, as shown in a work as early as Wright
   (1966); for the Scottish context, see Macafee (1994).
7. In a sense the theme represents the 'dark brother' of the other prevailing interest on the boundary between sociolinguistics and historical linguistics – new dialect formation, as discussed, for instance,
   in Kerswill and Williams (2000) and Trudgill (2004).
8. Indeed Wolfram and Schilling-Estes (1995: 715) make a strong
   case for the processes ongoing in threatened traditional dialects
   being very similar to the forces inherent in language shift: 'Further,
   some middle-aged and younger speakers now use the traditional
   Ocracoke dialect chiefly for performance, whether for telling
   humorous stories about fishermen or for displaying the oddities
   of the language itself. The traditional Ocracoke dialect has almost
   become too 'quaint,' too much of an object of curiosity – or an
   OBJECT LANGUAGE (Tsitsipis 1989: 121) – to be used in many
   situations in which the focus is not on language itself. The sociolinguistic situation in Ocracoke, along with the sociohistorical background and the linguistic change observed within the Ocracoke
   community, clearly support our contention that the Ocracoke
   brogue in its traditional form is receding rapidly and therefore it
   should be classified as an endangered language variety.'
9. In the following sections we will deal primarily with examples of
   these phenomena in Scotland. Observation of these processes can
   be found in the work of scholars dealing with dialects of English
   spoken elsewhere. Dialects in England have been analysed regularly, often in a dialectological rather than sociolinguistic manner,
   primarily as a result of the fieldwork of the *Survey of English Dialects*,
   Upton and Widdowson (1999) being a particularly salient example.
10. The following analysis is informed by Macafee (1997) and (2002) as
    well as Millar (2010a) and (2012).
11. Inevitably similar concerns of a dialectological type are present in
    England, as Sanderson and Widdowson (1985: 43–4) point out, the
    most apposite studies being, perhaps, Wright and Smith (1967) and
    Wright (1968).

Chapter 2

1. A dramatised version of this interplay and transfer is remembered
   in Rosehearty, a small fishing community on the Moray Firth.
   According to Taylor (1988: 38), 'A party of Danes were ship-
   wrecked in the early fourteenth century on the shore near to the

site of the present town. They befriended the local community of crofters and unfolded to them their knowledge of fishing.'

2. This phenomenon still holds in folk-memory, even where fishing has essentially stopped (although of course, this 'folk knowledge' is mediated through the heritage museums in Wick, Lossiemouth and Anstruther).

3. Smith (1985: 35) notes that, in Fife, some split their time between winter work in coal mines and the summer herring fishery.

4. Although, at least for a time, local railway networks allowed fish-wives to penetrate rather further into their hinterland and identify new markets.

5. As a number of authorities (for instance Sutherland 1983: 62) point out, an awareness of the potential threat of trawling to a sustainable fishery was present from an early period, with tension, and sometimes violence, developing between line and trawl fishermen.

6. That evangelical beliefs were not the only Christian tradition can be seen in the discussion of Episcopalianism in the East Neuk of Fife in Hall (2004).

7. In an interesting memoir (Patrick 2003), Belle Patrick describes growing up in the East Neuk of Fife in the period before, during and after the Great War, in an environment saturated by evangelicalism, self-help, temperance and political conservatism (not always the political tradition of choice among evangelicals, as she readily admits). A number of revivals are described in the book. Strikingly, she makes the case (Patrick 2003: 29) for fishers being 'middle class', their tenement houses distinguished from the 'cottar houses' of the agricultural poor.

8. He goes on (Sutherland 1983: 31) to note that '[a]t one time, from the 1840's to the 1860's, Wick had the largest Gaelic speaking congregation of any church in the world. Over 1500 people would attend the services and prayer meetings which required 3 ministers to officiate over them.' Gaelic-speaking 'fisher lassies' continued to come to Wick until the immediate post-war period (Sutherland 1983: 80).

9. Why the Doggers are thus named is a matter of considerable debate. Stewart (1999: 4) relates it to the use of dog skins in the production of buoys in the nineteenth century; the fishing community would hunt and skin the animals for that purpose. That these hunts did take place is corroborated in Sutherland (no date: 121).

10. Smith (1985: 8) reports that the railways were essential to the development of the winter herring fishery, since fish caught at that time were 'lacking in fat and would not cure properly'.

Chapter 3

1. This critique does not include a particularly worrying feature of much purely dialectological research: the assumption that any individual is intrinsically connected to only one 'real' community – in particular, perhaps, the NORMs ('Non-Mobile, Older, Rural, Males') within that community. The complexity of association and identification which individuals within any community hold in the modern age (and which was probably always present) is not given much in the way of recognition in this model. Having said that, many of the communities associated with this book possess a more egalitarian social structure than many others in the British Isles, so that a more horizontal than vertical model might apply.
2. A fuller discussion of the pilot study results can be found at http://fisherspeak.net.

Chapter 4

1. It should be noted that, according to the corpus, practically all of these fish have other names not connected to *fluke*; these are often highly localised.
2. For a discussion of diminutives and their 'expressive use', including some discussion of Scots phenomena, see Bratus (1969).
3. These stairs and the use of Scots terms on them were somewhat controversial among our informants, at least one younger informant going so far as to suggest that some of them had been made up. A middle-aged female informant pointed out, however, that the words were actually collected from local schoolchildren.
4. One older female informant offered *saithe* as the equivalent to dab. This is likely to be a mistake, however, with *saithe* being a local word for the very different coalfish.
5. This may explain why this particular type of *fleuk* was not considered good for eating, although other forms of seafood which are sometimes not considered 'good' are often said to be found around the sewage outlet, thus explaining their great size.
6. Interestingly, the corpus gives this as a word for younger *coalfish*, suggesting, perhaps that *podlie* has replaced *coalfish* as the generic term for the fish or that regional variation of attribution of species was always present.
7. Cod, for which a range of terms relating to maturity and size were collected in the corpus, was not given the same foregrounding, largely because only some of the communities covered had had

much experience of a large-scale cod fishery. It is also not much consumed in Scotland, even when it is landed here.

8. It is worth noting that the project and its questionnaire essentially imposed the framework of fish stages in the way the questions were constructed; the informants' own conception of the different sizes of fish was not necessarily the same.

9. This usage is interesting in relation to *fleuk* above, with one of the premodified forms being present in the community; it should be noted, however, that the original focus – *fleuk* – has obviously been abandoned, making the connection opaque.

10. Interestingly, no reference to the protection offered by *barkin* is mentioned in this definition. This is likely to be an oversight, however.

11. One older woman added the phrase *farra ganjey*, referring to a 'thicker oiled ganjey of white and black speckled wool'. It is somehow appropriate that the group which made the jumpers remember the different types. This particular type of jumper appears to be that described in the *Lossie Glossie* as a *lousy ganzie*. See the discussion below of the use of *faira ganzey* in Lossiemouth.

12. Indeed one older woman produced *Guernsey troosers*, obviously an extension of the field to include knitted trousers. *Corsy troosers* will be discussed shortly.

13. The *Oxford English Dictionary* defines *fearnought* as 'A stout kind of woollen cloth, used chiefly onboard ship in the form of outside clothing in the most inclement weather, also as a protective covering or lining for the outside door of a powder magazine, the portholes'; all of the examples cited fall between 1772 and 1883. The Lossiemouth evidence suggests that the usage continued for at least two further generations, however.

14. An example of this can be seen, perhaps, in a discussion inspired by this question. It generated the phrase 'redd the line' from one participant, signifying 'baiting the lines'; however in the *Fisherspeak* corpus, *redd* means to disentangle lines, a slightly different meaning. This confusion is particularly interesting, because *redd* 'to clean, to tidy' is a common word in most Scots-speaking communities.

15. It is noteworthy that ideas constructed from seeing old photographs did not appear present in Wick in the way they were (perhaps) in Anstruther: both ports have large museums and Wick has a considerable archive of nineteenth-century photos, but perhaps the Wick museum just does not have the same levels of funding or impact that the Anstruther museum does.

16. One middle-aged informant connected the word to *furlong*, an

archaic distance measurement perpetuated by the practices of horse racing; he also made the herring connection, however.

17. The word choice here is most interesting. *Quine* would not be the natural word for 'young woman' or 'girl' in the East Neuk of Fife; instead it represents north-eastern usage and is further evidence for a close relationship between that area (in particular its larger ports) and fisher communities in Fife.

18. It is striking that this distinction is particularly strong in Lossiemouth. The Dog Wall tradition makes this division part of the (historic) environment and in many ways absolute, perhaps in a different way from the other towns in the survey.

19. For a broad treatment, see Allan and Burridge (2006) and, in relation to the use of taboo avoidance, Merlan (1997); for an example of maritime ritual avoidance elsewhere in the world, see Poggie and Pollnac (1988) and Seixas and Begossi (2001). Perhaps the most apposite (and universal) discussion of fishing taboos is van Ginkel (1990).

20. One pilot study informant knew it was a taboo-avoidance term, but thought that it referred to sole.

21. Interestingly, one older man claimed that he had never heard *cauld iron*, but likened it to 'touch wood', used when fishers want to avoid using a word.

22. In the pilot study an older woman, resident of Peterhead for a long period but brought up in St Combs, made exactly the same observation.

23. The American dialectologist Frederick Cassidy has observed that 'People are annoyingly casual about the application of names [for beings or things]' (Cassidy 1988: 327). Closer to home, Jackson (2013: 1) notes that 'One feature of the list [of bird names in Scots] which is likely to annoy the serious ornithologist is that one name can refer to quite different birds (e.g., huidie craw = hooded crow, carrion crow and black headed gull; chackart = stonechat, whinchat and ring ouzel).'

24. 'Yer ain cod guts for yer ain hill maws' is a Wick proverb offered by an older male informant with considerable pride.

25. It is, of course, important to remember that *scurry* does not mean 'seagull' in this area (although knowledge of the word in that sense elsewhere along the coast *is* present).

26. One older woman went into considerable detail over why she would only use English *downpour* because as a child she was discouraged or even prohibited from using dialect at home and at school.

27. One younger woman did recognise the meaning 'shallow water' as

something she has heard. Three middle-aged men also recognised it as referring to a sheltered sea or lea.

28. The DSL provides the verb *marl* with the meaning 'to mottle or streak, to cause to become variegated in colour', which probably included the meaning given here, although no 'sea' citations are found.

29. Given, as we saw, that Wick people associate themselves strongly with the local word for 'seagull' – *scorrie* – it is surprising that this name is never mentioned in these contexts.

30. One middle-aged male informant gave *Thurso crowd* as an epithet. *Crowd* here may have the meaning 'mob'; the informant recalled (with some relish) teenage gang-fights between Wick and Thurso.

31. It is worth noting, however, that people from John o'Groats were termed either *Groaters* or *Groaties* by a small number of younger speakers. This does not sound derogatory, although *groaties* in particular refers to a particular type of quite pretty shell (and the animal inside), as we saw in 4.2.4.1.

32. It is worth noting that the first leap forward in nineteenth-century boat technology was associated with the name *Zulu*, in the news at the time because of the Zulu war. Whether any connection exists between the two uses of South African terms is impossible to say.

33. Unusually, the /fu/ pronunciation is found in Shetland, although all other <wh> words have either retained their original pronunciation or altered to /kw/ (in northern Shetland) (Millar 2007).

34. Discussion of *why* these words were used by incomers was limited, with informants putting forward the views that the words were mentioned were among the commonest (one young woman makes the perceptive point that <wh> words are regularly used in directions and descriptions). The sociolinguistic explanation that outsiders wished to 'fit in' was also put forward.

35. The diminutive -*ie* (but not -*ock*/*ag*) was offered by a middle-aged man and an older woman as a specific feature which outsiders would pick up.

36. While there is no doubt that *til* is used throughout the Scots-speaking world, its use in Caithness, Orkney and Shetland dialect is, from experience, greater (in relation to *tae*) than anywhere else, with the exception of some speakers of Ulster Scots. That all these regions are, with the exception of the last, heavily influenced by direct contact with Norse is noteworthy.

37. The English lexical items *all* and *today* may be explained as being due to the example being written for someone who is not a native speaker of Scots. The use of <w> may be merely a spelling mistake.

In the material assembled by the fieldwork for this book, however, <w> for <wh>, occasionally with the explanation that local people do not use /ʍ/, does sporadically occur in the northern ports. It is possible that older inhabitants of these regions may never have learned /ʍ/ in an entirely natural way. It is certainly possible to hear elderly people from around Aberdeen who say /xwɔt/ instead of /ʍɔt/ when obliged for whatever reason to speak their 'best' (Scottish) Standard English.

38. There are a number of exceptions to this. One older woman offered *glyte* (as in *glyte ee*) 'squint'. The same woman gave *queets* 'ankles'; and, along with one middle-aged woman, *shackle beens* 'wrists'. It may be that these examples demonstrate greater concentration on smaller-scale features; there is only so far that we can go with arguments of this type.

39. This same informant offers *perk* as the Cairnbulg equivalent to *park* 'field' and *shaav* 'sew' for the same locale, suggesting both considerable awareness and strong connections to that area.

40. The participant goes on to suggest a Norse origin for the word. According to the *Oxford English Dictionary* the Scottish and northern English distribution of the word is genuine enough. The word itself is a variant of *quilt*, however, a word of Anglo-Norman origin.

41. That some people may see decline in different ways from others can be demonstrated by one older man saying that *mingin* 'foul smelling, unpleasant, ugly' is less common than it was in the past, when it has actually spread into colloquial registers of the English of England.

References

Agutter, Alexandra and Leslie N. Cowan. 1981. 'Changes in the vocabulary of Lowland Scots dialects'. *Scottish Literary Journal*, Supplement 14: 49–62.

Aitchison, Jean and Stella Dextre Clarke. 2004. 'A historical viewpoint, with a look at the future'. In Roe and Thomas (2004): 5–22.

Aitchison, Peter. 2001. *Children of the Sea: The Story of the Eyemouth Disaster*. East Linton: Tuckwell Press.

Aitchison, Peter and Andrew Cassell. 2012. *The Lowland Clearances: Scotland's Silent Revolution, 1760–1830*. Edinburgh: Birlinn.

Aitken, A. J. 1979. 'Scottish speech: a historical view with special reference to the standard English of Scotland'. In Aitken and McArthur (1979): 85–118.

— 1992. 'Scottish English'. In McArthur (1992): 903–5.

Aitken, A. J. and Tom McArthur (eds). 1979. *Languages of Scotland*. Edinburgh: Chambers.

Allan, Keith and Kate Burridge. 2006. *Forbidden Words: Taboo and the Censoring of Language*. Cambridge: Cambridge University Press.

Anderson, Raymond. 2007. *Trawling: Celebrating the Industry that Transformed Aberdeen and North-East Scotland*. Edinburgh: Black and White.

Anderson, Richard C. and Peter Freebody. 1981. 'Vocabulary knowledge'. In Guthrie (1981): 77–117.

Anonymous. 1928. *Glossary of Names Used in Scotland for Fishes Taken in Scottish Waters*. Edinburgh: Fishery Board for Scotland.

Anson, Peter F. 1932. *Fishermen and Fishing Ways*. London: Harrap.

— 1950. *Scots Fisherfolk*. Banff: Saltire Society.

Beal, Joan and Lourdes Burbano-Elizado. 2012. 'All the lads and lasses': lexical variation in Tyne and Wear – A discussion of how the traditional dialect terms *lad* and *lass* are still used in the modern urban dialects of Newcastle-upon-Tyne and Sunderland'. *English Today* 4: 10–22.

Bealey, Frank and John Sewel. 1981. *The Politics of Independence: A Study of a Scottish Town*. Aberdeen: Aberdeen University Press.

Bergs, Alexander and Laurel Brinton (eds). 2012. *Historical Linguistics of English*. Berlin and New York: Mouton de Gruyter.

Blair, Anna (ed.). 1987. *Croft and Creel: A Century of Coastal Memories*. London: Shepheard-Walwyn.

Bochel, Margaret. 2008. '"Dear Gremista": the story of Nairn fisher girls in Lerwick'. In Coull, Fenton and Veitch (2008): 294–9.

Bratus, Boris Vasil'evich. 1969. *The Formation and Expressive Use of Diminutives.* Cambridge: Cambridge University Press.

Brenzinger, Matthias (ed.). 1992. *Language Death: Factual and Theoretical Explorations with Special Reference to East Africa.* Berlin: Mouton de Gruyter.

Britain, David. 2009. 'One foot in the grave? Dialect death, dialect contact, and dialect birth in England'. *International Journal of the Sociology of Language* 196/197: 121–55.

Buchan, Alex R. 1986. *Fishing out of Peterhead.* Aberdeen: Aberdeen & North-East Scotland Family History Society.

Buchan, Peter and David Toulmin. 1989. *Buchan Claik: The Saut an the Glaur o't: A Compendium of Words and Phrases from the North-East of Scotland.* Edinburgh: Gordon Wright.

Bugge, Edit. 2007. 'En studie av kjennskap til og oppfatninger om det shetlandske dialektforrådet' [A study of relationship with and understandings of the Shetland dialect]. Unpublished Masters dissertation, University of Bergen.

Campbell, Lyle and Martha C. Muntzel. 1989. 'The structural consequences of language death'. In Dorian (1989): 181–96.

Cassidy, Frederic. 1988. 'Focus on change in American folk speech'. In Thomas (1988): 326–32.

Chambers, J. K. and Peter Trudgill. 1998. *Dialectology.* 2nd edn. Cambridge: Cambridge University Press.

Coull, James R. 1993. *World Fisheries Resources.* London: Routledge.

— 1996. *The Sea Fisheries of Scotland: A Historical Geography.* Edinburgh: Donald.

— 2000. 'The fisheries of Fife'. In Omand (2000): 170–80.

— 2008a. 'Landing places and harbours used in fishing'. In Coull, Fenton and Veitch (2008): 186–207.

— 2008b. 'The herring fishery'. In Coull, Fenton and Veitch (2008): 208–35.

— 2008c. 'White fishing'. In Coull, Fenton and Veitch (2008): 253–76.

— 2008d. 'Women in fishing communities'. In Coull, Fenton and Veitch (2008): 277–93.

Coull, James R., Alexander Fenton and Kenneth Veitch (eds). 2008. *Boats, Fishing and the Sea.* A Compendium of Scottish Ethnology 4. Edinburgh: Donald.

Dickson, Neil T. R. 2002. *Brethren in Scotland 1838–2000: A Social Study of an Evangelical Movement.* Bletchley: Paternoster.

Dixon, R. M. W. 1972. *The Dyirbal Language of North Queensland.* Cambridge: Cambridge University Press.

— 1997. *The Rise and Fall of Languages.* Cambridge: Cambridge University Press.

Dobson, David. 1992. *The Mariners of St Andrews and the East Neuk of Fife, 1600–1700.* St Andrews: David Dobson.

— 2008. *The Shipping of Anstruther and the East Neuk of Fife, 1742–1771: Ships, Shipmasters and Voyages.* St Andrews: David Dobson.

Dorian, Nancy. 1981. *Language Death: The Life Cycle of a Scottish Dialect.* Philadelphia: University of Pennsylvania Press.

— (ed.). 1989. *Investigating Obsolescence: Studies in Language Contraction and Obsolescence*. Cambridge: Cambridge University Press.

Dossena, Marina. 2005. *Scotticisms in Grammar and Vocabulary: 'Like Runes upon a Standin' Stane'?* Edinburgh: Donald.

Dossena, Marina and Charles Jones (eds). 2003. *Insights into Late Modern English*. Bern: Lang.

Dossena, Marina and Roger Lass (eds). 2009. *Studies in English and European Historical Dialectology*. Bern: Lang.

Downie, Anne. 1983. 'The survival of the fishing dialects on the Moray Firth'. *Scottish Language* 2: 42–8.

Durkin, Philip. 2012. 'Variation in the lexicon: the "Cinderella" of sociolinguistics? Why does variation in word forms and word meanings present such challenges for empirical research?'. *English Today* 4: 3–9.

Elmer, Willy. 1973. *The Terminology of Fishing: A Survey of English and Welsh Inshore Fishing. Things and Words*. Bern: Francke.

Fenton, Alexander. 2008a. 'Craig fishing'. In Coull, Fenton and Veitch (2008): 85–9.

— 2008b. 'Shellfish as bait'. In Coull, Fenton and Veitch (2008): 90–102.

Ferrari-Bridgers, Franca. 2010 'The Ripano dialect: towards the end of a mysterious linguistic island in the heart of Italy'. In Millar (2010c): 131–49.

Foden, Frank 1996. *Wick of the North: The Story of a Scottish Royal Burgh*. Wick: North of Scotland Newspapers.

Freeman, F. W. 1981. 'The intellectual background of the vernacular revival before Burns'. *Studies in Scottish Literature* 16: 160–87.

Goeman, Ton and Willy Jongenburger. 2009. 'Dimensions and determinants of dialect use in the Netherlands at the individual and regional levels at the end of the twentieth century'. *International Journal of the Sociology of Language* 196/197: 31–72.

Gunn, Neil M. 1999 [1941]. *The Silver Darlings*. London: Faber.

Guthrie, John T. (ed.). 1981. *Comprehension and Teaching: Research Reviews*. Newark, DE: International Reading Association,

Hall, Stuart George. 2004. *Heritage and Hope: The Episcopalian Churches in the East Neuk of Fife, 1805–2005*. Elie: Stuart George Hall.

Hendry, Ian D. 1997. 'Doric: an investigation into its use amongst primary school children in the North East of Scotland'. Unpublished MLitt dissertation, University of Aberdeen.

Hinskens, Frans. 1996. *Dialect Levelling in Limburg: Structural and Sociolinguistic Aspects*. Tübingen: Niemeyer.

Hughes, Jim. 1985. *Airfield Focus 11: Lossiemouth*. Peterborough: GMS Enterprises.

Hutchinson, Mark and John Wolffe. 2012. *A Short History of Global Evangelicalism*. Cambridge: Cambridge University Press.

Jackson, Robin. 2013. *A Guide to Scots Bird Names*. 2nd edn. Banchory: Ptarmigan Press.

Jones, Charles (ed.). 1997. *The Edinburgh History of the Scots Language*. Edinburgh: Edinburgh University Press.

Kastovsky, Dieter and Arthur Mettinger (eds). 2000. *The History of English in a Social Context: A Contribution to Historical Sociolinguistics*. Berlin: Mouton de Gruyter.

Kay, Christian J., Carole Hough and Irené Wotherspoon (eds). 2004. *New Perspectives on English Historical Linguistics*, vol. II: *Lexis and Transmission*. Amsterdam: Benjamins.

Kennington, Fred. 2006. *As Spoken in Berwick: The Unique Dialect. A Dialect Dictionary*. Stockport: F. L. Kennington.

Kerswill, Paul, Carmen Llamas and Clive Upton. 1999. 'The first SuRE moves: early steps towards a large dialect project'. *Leeds Studies in English* 30: 257–69.

Kerswill, Paul and Ann Williams. 2000. 'Creating a new town koiné: children and language change in Milton Keynes'. *Language in Society* 29: 65–115.

Kirk, John M., Stewart Sanderson and J. D. A. Widdowson (eds). 1985. *Studies in Linguistic Geography: The Dialects of English in Britain and Ireland*. London: Croom Helm.

Kynoch, Douglas. 2004. *A Doric Dictionary*. 2nd edn. Dalkeith: Scottish Cultural Press.

Llamas, Carmen. 1999. 'A new methodology: data elicitation for social and regional language variation studies'. *Leeds Working Papers in Linguistics* 7: 95–118.

Llamas, Carmen and Dominic Watt (eds). 2010. *Language and Identities*. Edinburgh: Edinburgh University Press.

Lawrie, Susan M. 1991. 'A linguistic survey of the use and familiarity of Scottish dialect items in NE Fife'. *Scottish Language* 10: 18–29.

Lockart, G. W. 1997. *The Scots and their Fish*. Edinburgh: Birlinn.

Lossie Glossie = Anonymous. No date. *Lossie Glossie*. Lossiemouth: Lossiemouth Library.

Macafee, Caroline. 1994. *Traditional Dialect in the Modern World: A Glasgow Case Study*. Frankfurt: Lang.

— 1997. 'Ongoing change in Modern Scots'. In Jones (1997): 514–48.

— 2002. 'A history of Scots to 1700'. In *A Dictionary of the Older Scottish Tongue* 12. Oxford: Oxford University Press: xxi–clvi.

McArthur, Tom (ed.). 1992. *The Oxford Companion to the English Language*. Oxford: Oxford University Press.

Macaulay, Ronald K. S. 1977. *Language, Social Class and Education: A Glasgow Study*. Edinburgh: Edinburgh University Press.

— 1991. *Locating Dialect in Discourse: The Language of Honest Men and Bonnie Lasses in Ayr*. Oxford: Oxford University Press.

McClure, J. Derrick 1985. 'The Pinkerton Syndrome'. *Chapman* 41: 2–8.

McGarrity, Briege. 1998. 'A sociolinguistic study of attitudes towards and proficiency in the Doric dialect in Aberdeen'. Unpublished MPhil dissertation, University of Aberdeen.

MacLeod, Iseabail, with Pauline Cairns, Caroline Macafee and Ruth Martin. 1990. *Scots Thesaurus*. Aberdeen: Aberdeen University Press.

Malaws, Brian and Miriam McDonald. 2009. 'The last mill on the Eden: Guardbridge Paper Mill, Fife.' *Industrial Archaeology Review* 31: 116–33.

Mather, J. Y. 1965. 'Aspects of the linguistic geography of Scotland I'. *Scottish Studies* 9: 129–44.

— 1966. 'Aspects of the linguistic geography of Scotland II: east coast fishing'. *Scottish Studies* 10: 129–53.

— 1969. 'Aspects of the linguistic geography of Scotland III: fishing communities of the east coast (Part I)'. *Scottish Studies* 13: 1–16.

— 1972. 'Linguistic geography and the traditional drift-net fishery of the Scottish east coast'. In Wakelin (1972): 7–31.

Merlan, Francesca. 1997. 'The mother-in-law taboo avoidance and obligation in Aboriginal Australian society'. In Merlan, Morton and Rumsey (1997): 95–122.

Merlan, Francesca, John Morton and Alan Rumsey (eds). 1997. *Scholar and Sceptic: Australian Aboriginal Studies in Honour of L. R. Hiatt.* Canberra: Aboriginal Studies Press.

Meurman-Solin, Anneli. 1993. *Variation and Change in Early Scottish Prose: Studies Based on the Helsinki Corpus of Older Scots.* Helsinki: Suomalainen Tiedeakatemia.

Middleton, Sheena Booth. 2001. 'A study into the knowledge and use of Scots amongst primary pupils on Upper Deeside'. Unpublished MLitt dissertation, University of Aberdeen.

Millar, Robert McColl. 1994. 'A possible etymology for Scots *smirr* "traces of rain in the wind"'. *Notes and Queries* 239: 312–14.

— 1999. 'Some geographic and cultural patterns in the lexical/semantic structure of Scots'. *Northern Scotland* 18: 55–65.

— 2000. (with the assistance of Dauvit Horsbroch) 'Covert and overt language attitudes to the Scots tongue expressed in the *Statistical Accounts of Scotland*'. In Kastovsky and Mettinger (2000): 169–98.

— 2003. '"Blind attachment to inveterate custom": language use, language attitude and the rhetoric of improvement in the first *Statistical Account*.' In Dossena and Jones (2003): 311–30.

— 2004. 'Kailyard, conservatism and Scots in the *Statistical Accounts of Scotland*'. In Kay, Hough and Wotherspoon (2004): 163–76.

— 2005. *Language, Nation and Power.* Basingstoke: Palgrave Macmillan.

— 2007. *Northern and Insular Scots.* Edinburgh: Edinburgh University Press.

— 2009. 'The origins of the northern Scots dialects'. In Dossena and Lass (2009): 191–208.

— 2010a. 'An historical national identity? The case of Scots'. In Llamas and Watt (2010): 247–56.

— 2010b. *Authority and Identity: A Sociolinguistic History of Europe before the Modern Age.* Basingstoke: Palgrave Macmillan.

— (ed.). 2010c. *Marginal Dialects: Scotland, Ireland and Beyond.* Aberdeen: Forum for Research on the Languages of Scotland and Ulster.

— 2012. 'Varieties of English: Scots'. In Bergs and Brinton (2012): 1951–60.

— forthcoming. 'At the forefront of linguistic change: the morphology of late Northumbrian texts and the history of the English language, with particular reference to the English gloss to the Lindisfarne Gospels'.

Miller, James. 1999. *Salt in the Blood: Scotland's Fishing Communities Past and Present*. Edinburgh: Canongate.

— 2001. *A Caithness Wordbook*. Wick: North of Scotland Newspapers.

Milne, William P. 1955. *Eppie Elrick (an Aberdeenshire Tale of the '15)*. Peterhead: Scrogie.

Milroy, Lesley and Matthew Gordon. 2003. *Sociolinguistics: Method and Interpretation*. Oxford: Blackwell.

Moore, Robert. 1982. *The Social Impact of Oil: The Case of Peterhead*. London: Routledge & Kegan Paul.

Murray, Mary. 1982. *'In My Ain Words': An East Neuk Vocabulary*. Anstruther: Scottish Fisheries Museum.

Myers-Scotton, Carol. 2002. *Contact Linguistics: Bilingual Encounters and Grammatical Outcomes*. Oxford: Oxford University Press.

Mylne, Tom. 1995. 'Grammatical category and world view: Western colonization of the Dyirbal language'. *Cognitive Linguistics* 6: 379–404.

Nadel-Klein, Jane. 2003. *Fishing for Heritage: Modernity and Loss Along the Scottish Coast*. Oxford and New York: Berg.

Nässén, Greger. 1989. *Norn Weather Words: 323 Meteorological Terms in Jakobsen's Dictionary and their Extent in Present-Day Shetland Dialect*, Norn: The Scandinavian Element in Shetland Dialect Report no. 3. Stockholm: Department of English, Stockholm University.

Omand, Donald. 1989. *The New Caithness Book*. Wick: North of Scotland Newspapers

Omand, Donald (ed.). 2000. *The Fife Book*. Edinburgh: Birlinn.

Ong, Walter J. 2002. *Orality and Literacy*. 2nd edn. London: Routledge.

Patrick, Belle. 2003. *Recollections of East Fife Fisher Folk*. Edinburgh: Birlinn.

Poggie, John J., Jr., and Richard B. Pollnac. 1988. 'Danger and rituals of avoidance among New England Fishermen'. *MAST Maritime Anthropological Studies* 1: 66–78.

Pollner, Clausdirk 1985. *Englisch in Livingston: Ausgewählte Erscheinungen in einer schottischen new town* [English in Livingston: well-chosen examples from a Scottish New Town]. Frankfurt: Lang.

Riach, W. A. D. 1979. 'A dialect study of comparative areas in Galloway'. *Scottish Literary Journal Supplement* 9: 1–16.

— 1980. 'A dialect study of comparative areas in Galloway (2nd report)'. *Scottish Literary Journal Supplement* 12: 43–60.

— 1982. 'A dialect study of comparative areas in Galloway (3rd and last report)'. *Scottish Language* 1: 13–22.

Richard, Jan Lauren. 2003. 'Investigating lexical change in Caithness'. Unpublished MA dissertation, University of Aberdeen.

Roberts, Callum. 2007. *The Unnatural History of the Sea: The Past and Future of Humanity and Fishing*. London: Gaia.

Robinson, Justyna Anna. 2010. 'Semantic variation and change in present-day English'. Unpublished PhD dissertation, University of Sheffield.

Robinson, Mairi. 1999. *Concise Scots Dictionary*. Edinburgh: Polygon.

Roe, Sandra K. and Alan R. Thomas (eds). 2004. *The Thesaurus: Review, Renaissance, and Revision*. New York: Haworth Press.

Røyneland, Unn. 2009. 'Dialects in Norway: catching up with the rest of Europe?' *International Journal of the Sociology of Language* 196/197: 7–30.

Rush, Christopher. 2007. *Hellfire and Herring: A Childhood Remembered*. London: Profile.

Sanderson, Stewart and J. D. A. Widdowson. 1985. 'Linguistic geography in England: progress and prospect'. In Kirk, Sanderson and Widdowson (1985): 34–50.

Sasse, Hans-Jürgen. 1992. 'Theory of language death'. In Brenzinger (1992): 7–30.

Schlötterer, Rainer. 1996. 'Fishermen's dialect on the south-east coast of Scotland: lexical aspects'. Unpublished Masters dissertation, University of Bamberg.

Schmid, Monika S. 2011. *Language Attrition*. Cambridge: Cambridge University Press.

Seixas, Cristiana Simão and Alpina Begossi. 2001. 'Ethnozoology of fishing communities from Ilha Grande (Atlantic Forest Coast, Brazil)'. *Journal of Ethnobiology* 21: 107–35.

Smith, Peter. 1985. *The Lammas Drave and the Winter Herrin': A History of the Herring Fishery from East Fife*. Edinburgh: Donald.

Smylie, Mike. 2004. *Herring: A History of the Silver Darlings*. Stroud: Tempus.

Soukup, Barbara. 2007. 'Dialect death by concentration: glide-fronted /aw/ in Smith Island adolescent speech.' *eVox* 1: 1–15.

Stewart, Donald. 1999. *Old Lossiemouth*. Ochiltree: Stenlake Publishing.

Stewart, William. no date. *Fishing in Scotland from the 16th Century to the Present Day*. Lossiemouth: no publisher given.

Sutherland, Iain. 1983. *Wick Harbour and the Herring Fishery*. Wick: Camps Bookshop and The Wick Society.

— 1992. *The Caithness Dictionary*. Wick: Iain Sutherland.

— 2005. *The Fishing Industry of Caithness*. Wick: Iain Sutherland.

— no date. *From Herring to Seine Net Fishing*. Wick: Camps Bookshop.

Taylor, James. 1988. *From Whinnyfold to Whitehills: Fishing the North East*. Gartocharn: Northern Books.

Thomas, Alan R. (ed.). 1988. *Methods in Dialectology*. Clevedon: Multilingual Matters.

Thompson, Paul, with Tony Wailey and Trevor Lummis. 1983. *Living the Fishing*. London: Routledge & Kegan Paul.

Trudgill, Peter. 2004. *New-Dialect Formation: The Inevitability of Colonial Englishes*. Edinburgh: Edinburgh University Press.

Tsitsipis, Lukas D. 1989. 'Skewed performance in language obsolescence: the case of an Albanian variety'. In Dorian (1989): 139–48.

Turner, W. H. K. 1957. 'The textile industries of Dunfermline and Kirkcaldy 1700–1900'. *Scottish Geographical Magazine* 73: 129–45.

Upton, Clive and J. D. A. Widdowson. 1999. *Lexical Erosion in English Regional Dialects*. Sheffield: National Centre for English Cultural Tradition.

Vandekerckhove, Reinhild. 2009. 'Dialect loss and dialect vitality in Flanders'. *International Journal of the Sociology of Language* 196/197: 73–97.

van Ginkel, Rob. 1990. 'Fishermen, taboos, and ominous animals'. *Anthrozoos: A Multidisciplinary Journal of the Interactions of People and Animals* 4: 73–81.

Wakelin, Martyn F. (ed.). 1972. *Patterns in the Folk Speech of the British Isles*. London: Athlone Press.

Walker, Robert. 1985. 'An introduction to applied qualitative research'. In Robert Walker (ed.), *Applied Qualitative Research*. Aldershot: Gower: 3–36.

Watt, Dominic. 2002. '"I don't speak with a Geordie accent, I speak, like, the Northern accent": contact-induced levelling in the Tyneside vowel system'. *Journal of Sociolinguistics* 6: 44–63.

Watt, Robert A. 1989. *A Glossary of Scottish Dialect Fish and Trade Names*. Scottish fisheries information pamphlet 17. Aberdeen: Department of Agriculture and Fisheries for Scotland.

Wilson, Gloria. 2009. *Kindly Folk and Bonny Boats: Fishing in Scotland and the North-East from the 1950s to the Present Day*. Stroud: History Press.

Wolfram, Walt and Natalie Schilling-Estes. 1995. 'Moribund dialects and the endangerment canon: the case of the Ocracoke brogue'. *Language* 71: 696–721.

Wood, Lawson. 1998. *The Berwickshire Coast*. Ochiltree: Stenlake Publishing.

Wright, John T. 1966. 'Urban dialects: a consideration of method'. *Zeitschrift für Mundartforschung* 33: 232–47.

Wright, Peter 1968. 'Fishing language around England and Wales'. *Journal of the Lancashire Dialect Society* 17: 2–14.

Wright, Peter and G. B. Smith. 1967. 'A Lancashire fishing survey'. *Journal of the Lancashire Dialect Society* 16: 2–8.

Index

A1, 165
Aberdeen, 17, 29, 181
  Peterhead names for, 146–7
  'seagull', 115
Aberdeenshire, 67, 81, 82, 86
age, variation according to, 167–9
Agutter, Alexandra and Leslie N. Cowan,
  14, 47
Aitken, A.J., 'Jack', 13
angler fish *see* 'monkfish'
Anglo-Norman, 181
Angus, 72, 87, 107
Anstruther, 26, 112, 164, 165,
  176
  arles, 102
  barkin, 95–6
  buckie, 109–10
  'clothing', 92–3
  cold iron, 105
  'cormorant', 120
  flukes/fleuks, 69–70
  history, 29–31
  incomer borrowings, 159
  lexis, perceived loss, 163
  'marine mammals', 123
  maturity cycle, 78–9
  'monkfish', 83–4
  names for local community and its
    inhabitants, 144
  names for other communities and their
    inhabitants, 151–2, 153
  scull, 98
  'seagull', 120
  seaweed, 113, 114
  weather and sea conditions, 125–6, 129,
    130–1, 133, 134, 138, 140
Aramaic, 6
Arbuthnot Museum, 58
arles, 57–8, 102
As Spoken in Berwick, 29, 37
attery, 56
attrition, dialect, 9–11
attrition, first language, 4–5, 173
attrition, lexical, 1–2, 10–14

Auckengill, Wick names for, 148
Avoch, origin traditions, 20

Baltic Sea, medieval fishing technology, 17
Banff, 112
Banffshire, 71
Baptist tradition, 25
barkin, 62, 92–3, 93, 94–6, 100, 102, 166–7
Basque, 6
Berwick-upon-Tweed, 3, 37, 81, 152, 166
Berwickshire, 159
Black Isle, 1
Boddam, 97
'Borneo kutch', 95; *see also barkin*
Britain, David, 10–11
The Broch *see* Fraserburgh
Buchan, 126
Buchan, Peter, 37; *see also Buchan Claik*
Buchan Claik (BC), 37, 43, 44, 45, 81, 111, 112
Buckfast Tonic Wine, 59, 108
Buckhaven, 29
Buckie (Moray town), 24, 28, 59, 82, 108,
  118, 121, 157
  Lossiemouth names for, 150
  'seagull', 116
  Wick names for, 149
buckie (seafood), 59–60, 107–10
Burghead (Moray), 143
  Lossiemouth names for, 149–50
Burnmouth, 31, 38
  Eyemouth names for, 152
Burns, Robert, 12

'cagoule', 86
Cairnbulg, 161, 181
  Peterhead names for, 146
Caithness, 20, 27–8, 38, 74–5, 77, 78, 82–3,
  86, 102, 111, 113, 128, 134–5, 137, 148,
  150, 156–7, 165–6, 180
Caithness Dictionary (CD), 38, 43, 86, 111,
  119, 137
Caithness Wordbook (CW), 38, 42, 72, 111,
  112, 137
Caledonian Canal, 151

Campbelltown, Lossiemouth names for, 151
Canada, Peterhead involvement in inter-war
    fishery, 75
Canis Bay, 113
Cellardyke, 29, 30
    Anstruther names for, 151
    oilskin factories, 92
    'seagull', 120
Central Belt of Scotland, 165
Church of Scotland, 23, 31
clearances, highland, 6–8
clearances, lowland, 31
Clyde, Firth of, 151
'coalfish', 76, 80
    maturity cycle, 77–8, 79
'cod', 16, 17, 21, 113
    East Neuk of Fife, 30
    maturity cycle, 61
cold iron, 103–6; see also 'salmon'; taboo
    avoidance
Coldingham, Eyemouth names for, 152
The Collach, Lossiemouth names for, 149
Common Fisheries Policy, 23
Concise Scots Dictionary (CSD), 35, 36
congregationalism, 25
'cormorant', 58, 116–21
Corpus, 34–45
Crail, 29, 30, 112, 138
Cromarty, 1
Crown Fishery Agents (Lossiemouth), 105
Cummingston, Lossiemouth names for, 149

Dictionary of the Older Scottish Tongue
    (DOST), 35, 127
Dictionary of the Scots Language (DSL), 34, 35,
    42, 43, 82, 86, 87, 89, 91, 93, 111, 117,
    120, 121, 122, 126, 127, 128, 129, 132–3,
    137, 149–50, 159, 180
Dixon, R. M. W., 6
'dolphin' see 'marine mammals'
Dorian, Nancy, 6–8
Doric, 85
Doric Dictionary (DD), 37, 42, 81, 85, 107,
    112, 118
Dossena, Marina, 12, 13
Downie, Anne, 14, 38–9, 85, 90, 115, 118, 121
drave (herring), 30, 31
Dunbar, 166
    Eyemouth names for, 152
Dundee, 148
Duns, Eyemouth names for, 152
Dutch, 37, 72
Dyirbal, 9, 174

East Anglia, 24
East Neuk of Fife, 14, 26, 29–31, 92, 96, 123,
    138, 144, 151, 176
East Neuk Vocabulary (ENV, In My Ain
    Words), 38, 45, 85, 86, 96
Edinburgh, 12, 165

Elgin, 102
    Lossiemouth names for, 150
Elie, Anstruther names for, 151
England, Wick names for, 149
English
    Highland, 20
    (Scottish) Standard, 3–4, 7, 11–14, 57, 83,
        97, 111, 122, 155–7, 158, 171, 181
Episcopalianism, 25, 176
European Economic Community, 23; see also
    European Union
European Union, 23, 26, 32
Evangelicalism, 176
    views on superstitions, 106
'Extravaganzey', 93
Eyemouth, 26, 31–2, 96, 107, 165, 166, 168
    arles, 102
    barkin, 95
    buckie, 109, 110
    'clothing', 93
    cold iron, 103
    faurlan, 101
    fish maturity cycles, 79–80
    flukes/fleuks, 69–70
    incomer borrowings, 159
    lexis, perceived loss, 163
    'marine mammals', 123
    'monkfish', 84
    names for local community and its
        inhabitants, 144
    names for other communities and their
        inhabitants, 152, 153
    scull, 98
    'seabirds', 116
    'seaweed', 113, 114
    weather and sea conditions, 126, 129–30,
        130–1, 133, 135, 138, 140

Faeroe Islands, 22–3, 55
Fair Isle, 90
farlan/faurlan/foreland, 52, 58–9, 99–101,
    167
    connection to Lerwick, 59
    'The Farland and the Creel', 101
Ferrari-Bridgers, Franca, 10
feudalism and the fishing community, 17,
    18, 31
Fife, 45, 72, 77, 81, 86, 107, 112, 165, 176; see
    also East Neuk of Fife
First World War (Great War), 22, 256
fish curers, 18–19
fish maturity cycles, 70–81
fisher culture, 19, 20, 23–4, 24–5, 25–6
fisher lasses/quines, 21; see also gutter lasses;
    'herring': herring lasses
fishertoun, 19, 32
fishing trade lexis, 84–103
    'clothing', 84–96
    female-specific lexis, 99–103
    scull, 96–8

fishwife, 21
Fleetwood, 143
flora and fauna, not related to fishing, 106–23
flukes/fleuks, 60–1, 66–9, 177
Forth, River, 165
Fraserburgh, 17, 28, 54, 113
   Lossiemouth, 149–50
   Peterhead names for, 145–7
   'seagull', 115, 116, 119
   Wick names for, 149
Free Church of Scotland, 25
Free Presbyterian Church of Scotland, 25

Gaelic, 19, 20, 72
   East Sutherland, 6–8
   Wick, 176
Gamrie, 17
   Peterhead names for, 146–7
   'seagull', 115, 116
ganzie, 85–6, 87–8, 89, 93, 178
   barkin, 62
   'Extravaganzey', 93
Gardenstown *see* Gamrie
Gateshead, 148
gender, variation by, 166–7
geography, variation by, 164–6
German, 4–5
Germanic, North, 74; *see also* Norse (Old)
Germany, 22
Glasgow, 118
   Wick names for, 149
A Glossary of Scottish Dialect Fish and Trade Names (Glossary), 38, 67, 71, 75, 77, 81, 85, 107
goshens, 53
Greek, 9
   koine glossa, 9
Greenland, 17
Gunn, Neil M., 72
gutter lasses/gutter quines, 57; *see also fisher lasses*; 'herring': herring lasses

'haddock', 21, 31
   maturity cycle, 71
halfalesmen, 53–4
'halibut', 55, 66, 69
Hebrew, 6
Helmsdale, Wick names for, 148
Hendry, Ian D., 14, 47
heritage, 100, 101, 167, 169, 176, 178
'herring', 16, 27
   fishery, 20–1, 30–1, 37, 59, 176
   gutting, 19
   herring lasses/herring quines, 101, 102; *see also fisher lasses*; *gutter lasses*
   maturity cycle, 61, 71, 72–4
Hopeman, 80, 119
   Lossiemouth names for, 149
Hornsby, Michael, 49–50

Iceland, 17, 55
   'Cod Wars', 22–3
International Journal of the Sociology of Language, 10
Inverness, 1
   Wick names for, 148–9
Ireland, 151
   Potato Famine, 6
Irish, 6
Italian, 10

Jacobitism, 12
Jehovah's Witnesses, 25
John o'Groats, 107, 180

Keiss, 143
Keith, Lossiemouth names for, 150
Kincardineshire, 67, 111
Kintyre, 151
Kirkcaldy, 92–3
koineisation, 9, 172–3
Kynoch, Douglas, 37; *see also Doric Dictionary*

language death/shift, 6–9
Larbert, 47
Latin, 6
Lawrie, Susan M., 14, 47
Lerwick, 59
lexis, cultural, 103–6
lexis, female-specific, 99–102
lexis, perceived loss, 160–3
line fishery, 18, 21
   great lines (*gartlins*), 18, 21, 52
   smaw lines, 21, 55–6
Linguist List, 47
Linguistic Survey of Scotland, 39, 49
Llamas, Carmen, 49
London, 12
Lossie, River, 105
Lossie Glossie (LG), 34, 38, 69, 85, 112, 119, 120, 121
Lossiemouth, 26, 28, 86, 164, 165, 168, 176
   arles, 102
   buckie, 108, 109
   'clothing', 90–2
   cold iron, 104–5
   farlan, 100–1
   fish maturity cycle, 80–1
   flukes/fleuks, 69
   incomer borrowings, 157–9
   lexis, perceived loss, 162
   'marine mammals', 122
   names for local community and its inhabitants, 143
   names for other communities and their inhabitants, 149–51, 153
   'monkfish', 83
   scull, 98

'seabirds', 115, 118
'seaweed', 113, 114
weather and sea conditions, 123, 128, 130–1, 132, 134, 136–7, 139
Lossiemouth Museum, 98

Maastricht, 10
Macafee, Caroline, 13–14, 47, 48–9, 170, 175
McClure, J. Derrick, 12
McGarrity, Briege, 14, 39, 47–8
Mallaig, 20
'marine mammals', 121–3, 163
Mather, J. Y., 38–9
meagrim, 69
Mediterranean, 17
Methodism, 25
Meurman-Solin, Anneli, 11
Middleton, Sheena, 14
mind-mapping, 49–50
'Mini Ice Age', 17
Mintlaw, 52
'monkfish', 52, 81–4
Montrose, 18
Moray, 112, 128, 159
Moray Firth, 14, 20, 39, 67, 71, 72, 77, 81, 82, 112, 113, 114, 121, 122, 123, 149, 150, 175
Mull, Sound of, 134
Myers-Scotton, Carol, 9, 174

Nadel-Klein, Jane, 19, 23–4, 31
Nairn, Lossiemouth names for, 150
Nässén, Greger, 47
nets
  barkin, 95
  cleaning and mending, 21, 95–6
  superstitions, 25
New Caithness Book, 6, 77, 121
new dialect formation, 173
Newcastle-upon-Tyne, 148, 161
Newfoundland, 17
Norn, 74
Norse (Old), 112, 180; see also Norn
North America, 82
North Atlantic, 27
North Berwick, 31
North-East of England
  dialects, 10, 130
North-East of Scotland, 18, 72, 77, 87, 96, 103, 111, 112, 123
North Sea, 16, 22, 23, 107, 114, 152
North Sea Oil, 29
Northern Isles, 17, 111; see also Orkney; Shetland
Norwegian, 11
Norwegian Sea, 16

Ocracoke, 175
oilskins, 86, 89–93
Orkney, 72, 77, 86, 111, 129, 149, 180

Oxford English Dictionary (OED), 35, 68, 89, 122, 127, 128, 159, 178, 181
oystercatcher, 56–7, 162

Pennan, seagull, 116
Pentecostalism, 25
Pentland Firth, 107, 118, 151
Peterhead, 18, 23, 26, 28–9, 37, 74, 75, 81, 82, 84, 96, 101, 164, 165, 166, 167, 169, 179
  arles, 102, 103
  barkin, 94–5
  buckie, 108, 109–10
  'clothing', 86–9
  cold iron, 103–4
  faurlan, 100, 102
  flukes/fleuks, 66–8, 78, 80
  incomer borrowings, 153–6, 157
  lexis, perceived loss, 160–1
  'marine mammals', 121–2
  maturity cycle, 78–9
  'monkfish', 83–4
  names for local community and its inhabitants, 140–2, 144–5
  names for other communities and their inhabitants, 145–7, 153–4
  Pilot Study, 52–62
  scull, 97, 98
  'seabirds', 115–17, 119
  'seaweed', 112–13, 113–14
  weather and sea conditions, 124–5, 126–8, 130–1, 133–4, 135–6, 137, 139
  Wick names for, 149
Pilot Study, 52–62, 73–4, 82
Pinkerton Syndrome, 12
Pittenweem, 29, 30, 138
  Anstruther names for, 151
  'seagull', 120
Pollner, Clausdirk, 14
porpoise see 'marine mammals'
Portsoy, 113
Presbyterianism, 25
Pultney(town), 157
  Wick name for, 148

questionnaire, 62–4

RAF Lossiemouth, 159
red fish, 104, 105; see also cold iron; taboo avoidance
Reformation, Protestant, 11, 17
Richard, Jan Lauren, 14
Roget's Thesaurus, 40
Rosehearty, 116, 175
Ross-shire, 72

St Abbs, 138
  Eyemouth names for, 152–3
St Abbs Head, 101
St Andrews, 144

St Combs, 115, 179
    Peterhead names for, 146, 147
St Monans, 29, 30
    Anstruther names for, 151
'salmon', 16, 73, 122
    maturity cycle, 61, 71, 75–6
    taboo, 103–6
    see also cold iron; red fish; taboo avoidance
Salvation Army, 25
Sasse, Jans-Jürgen, 8–9, 172
Scandinavia, 17
scaup/scaap, 53
Schlötterer, Rainer, 14, 39, 48, 50, 96, 107, 109, 112, 138–9
Schmid, Monika S., 9, 172
School of Scottish Studies Archives (SSSA), 39, 96
Scots, 3–4, 7, 11–14
    Central, 129
    East Central, 111
    Northern, 112
    Shetland, 1–2
    Ulster, 180
    West Central, 111
Scots Thesaurus (ST), 35–6, 40, 42, 45, 67, 69, 71, 77, 79, 81, 86, 96, 107, 111, 112, 118, 119, 121, 123, 131, 135
'Scotticisms', 12–13
Scottish Fisheries Museum, 30–1, 178
    'Extravaganzey', 92
Scottish National Dictionary (SND), 35, 39, 49, 82, 107, 126
Scrabster, 28
scull, 96–8
sea and wind conditions, 131–40
'seabirds', 115–21, 162, 180
'seagull' *see* 'seabirds'
'seaweed', 59–60, 110–14
Second World War, 22
semi-speakers, 7–8
Seventh Day Adventists, 25
Shetland, 47, 72, 82, 86, 96, 111, 112, 149, 159, 180
    name given to Peterhead people, 142
Silver Darlings, 20, 72, 74
skate, 69
snood/snuid/sneed, 54–5
sociolinguistics, 2–4; *see also* variation and change
sole, 66, 69
Soviet Union, 22
Spey, River, 105, 150
Staxigoe, Wick names for, 148
stylistic shrinkage, 8–9
superstitions, 24–5, 85, 106; *see also* taboo avoidance
Survey of English Dialects, 46, 175
Sutherland, 21

taboo avoidance, 24–5, 79, 103–6, 179; *see also cold iron; red fish*; superstitions
Tay, River, 23
Thurso, 28, 142, 166, 180
    'seagull', 118
    Wick names for, 147–8
Torry, 14, 39
Trainspotting, 149
Tweed, River, 37
Tyne and War, 148

Ulster Scots, 180
United States of America, 122

variation and change
    lexical, 1–4, 169–73
    morphological, 2
    phonological, 2
    semantic, 174
    syntactic, 2

ware/waar/waur see 'seaweed'
Watt, Dominic, 10
Western Isles, 19
whaling, 16, 26, 68
Whitehills, 'seagull', 119
Wick, 25, 26, 27–8, 81, 82–3, 96, 107, 164, 165, 166, 176, 179, 180
    arles, 102, 103
    barkin, 95
    buckie, 108, 109–10
    'clothing', 89–90
    cold iron, 104
    faurlan, 100
    fish maturity cycle, 74–6, 77, 78–9
    flukes/fleuks, 71–2
    incomer borrowings, 156–7
    lexis, perceived loss, 161–2
    Lossiemouth names for, 150–1
    'marine mammals', 122
    museum, 178
    names for local community and its inhabitants, 142–3
    names for other communities and their inhabitants, 144–5, 153–4
    scull, 98
    'seabirds', 118
    'seaweed', 113, 114
    weather and sea conditions, 123–40
Wick, River, 148
witch (fish), 69
Wolfram, Walt and Natalie Schilling-Estes, 10, 175

Yarmouth (Great), 101
Yorkshire, 158